REVOLUTION AND THE NAPIER BROTHERS

1820-1840

Also by Priscilla Napier

A LATE BEGINNER

THE SWORD DANCE

A DIFFICULT COUNTRY

From a miniature—Colonel Charles Napier in his early forties; "so knavish a looking son of a gun", he was considered. The artist was James Holmes, 1777–1860

REVOLUTION AND THE NAPIER BROTHERS

1820-1840

Priscilla Napier

London

MICHAEL JOSEPH

First published in Great Britain by Michael Joseph Ltd
52 Bedford Square, London, W.C.1
1973

ISBN 0 7181 1186 9

Printed in Great Britain by
Ebenezer Baylis and Son Ltd.
The Trinity Press, Worcester, and London
Bound by James Burn at Esher, Surrey

To my daughter
Anne

Contents

Foreword

This tale of what happened to Donny and Sarah Napier's children continues where *The Sword Dance* left off, and is the third volume in a leisurely history of some of the Napier family. Volume four, *Raven Castle*, which is about Charles in India, is due next year.

My thanks are due to the late Mr Harold Kurtz, of Pedantry Limited, Oxford, for his scholarly help and corrections; to Mr Nigel Nicolson and Messrs Constable for permission to quote from the late Sir Harold Nicolson's *Byron, the Last Journey*, to Lady Longford and Messrs Weidenfeld and Nicolson for permission to quote from her *Wellington, Pillar of State*, and to Macmillan and Co. for permission to quote from C. F. Mather in *Chartist Studies*, edited by Asa Briggs.

And once again, to all those cousins and kinsmen who have lent me letters and unpublished memoranda for this and other volumes, my most grateful thanks. Particularly in this volume I wish to thank Mr Greville Napier, for letting me reproduce as frontispiece his fine miniature of Sir Charles Napier. The late Miss Lilias Napier most kindly lent me the unpublished journal kept by her great-grandfather, Captain Henry Napier, Royal Navy. And lastly I am deeply grateful to the late Miss Freda Doughty, great-granddaughter of Sir Charles Napier. Although she never mentioned the subject, a day spent in her company even in her extreme old age convinced me that Charles's legendary charm and humour were no legend but fact.

Part I

Greece

And glory long has made the sages smile;
'Tis something, nothing, words, illusion, wind—

Byron, *Don Juan*

CHAPTER I

Ionia

The market-place at Argostoli on the island of Cephalonia was newly built in fine white stone, and here, one summer morning of the 1820s, an argument was raging with all the fire and expertise that the Greeks devote to this activity. An old fisherman had brought in a huge fish, and had barely concluded his bargaining with the fishmonger when the agent of one of the island's many feudal chieftains put in an appearance and claimed the great fish as part of his master's feudal due, owing to its unusual size. Voices rose, bystanders joined in, partisan small boys scuffled in the dust, elderly gentlemen arose from under trees and slippered across to have their say. The seller protested, the fisherman despaired, rough hands were laid on his beautiful fish, and the agent's voice rose high in triumph. Suddenly a figure on a white horse was seen to be approaching, elbows working, determined chin thrusting between furry side-whiskers, spectacles gleaming in the bright sun. No further words were needed. The old fisherman pocketed his cash, the fishmonger laid hold of the fish, the feudal agent faded instantly into the landscape. For this was the despot of Cephalonia, the ruthless upholder of justice and of an odd kind of mercy always exercised in the interest of the oppressed, ὁ Νεπιος, the British Resident; the omnipresence on a white horse, known to family and friends as Charles and Blanco.

Colonel Charles James Napier, now in his late thirties, had led an adventurous life of near misses and miraculous survivals. Eldest surviving of the seven sons of Colonel George Napier, Charles had been commissioned into the 33rd Regiment at the age of eleven, had joined it at fourteen, and fought with distinction in the Peninsular War as a major in the 50th. This had brought him fame, recurrent fevers and headaches, and life-long pain from many wounds; but secured him no regular job, no regular income. In 1821, after five years on half pay, he crossed war-torn Europe and took ship at Otranto for a post in the Ionian Islands under Sir Thomas Maitland, their High Commissioner, from whence in due course he was sent as Resident to Cephalonia.

Brought up in Ireland, Charles had cut his teeth on the problems of government, and had his infant spirit seared by the fires and carnage of revolution. A murdered eighty-year-old woman—the mother of an alleged Irish informer—lying in her own blood in the village gutter of Celbridge as he made his way to school one morning in the 1790s had vividly and horribly taught him the meaning of civil war and revolution, and from whom its bitterest tolls are exacted. His father Donny Napier, a sympathizer with the cause of Catholic emancipation and with Irish grievances in general, had yet, as a professional soldier, been obliged to oppose the rebel cause in arms. But he had kept order with as much mercy as the times allowed, and at the height of the troubles had twice prevented the authorities from burning Celbridge village to the ground.

Donny, Colonel the Honourable George Napier, sixth out of the ten sons of Scottish Francis, sixth Lord Napier, exerted a lifelong influence upon his five surviving sons and perhaps most powerfully in this question of behaviour in civil strife. Men, he taught them, rarely rebel unless their plight is desperate: men in revolution should be understood, reasoned with, and yet opposed in all force until they laid down their arms. In an age of revolutions and near-revolutions, his five sons stuck to his principles. Donny himself had three times been in arms against revolution: most unwillingly against the American Revolution; willingly against the French Revolution as soon as, but not until, it struck out at its neighbours; with bitter sadness against the Irish Rebellion of 1798 when the rebels threatened to link up with France and so menace the country in whose defence he had signed on—Britain.

Physically, as well as in every other way, Charles had looked up to his father. Donny was very tall for his epoch—six-foot-two—highly educated and observant, determined and independent-minded, and reputedly one of the handsomest, as well as the physically strongest, men in the British army. The Lennox family, into whom he married, found him rather stiff and intransigent until he got to know one very well; too proud, too aloof, a bit of a rugged Scot, with a harsh voice and blue eyes that felt too penetrating. He would laugh at solemn things, such as Whigs and Tories; and socially had far too little give and compliance. His wife (who had been Lady Sarah Lennox, daughter of the second Duke of Richmond, nearly marrying King George III when she was fifteen, setting up in unsuccessful matrimony with a smart Suffolk squire called Sir Charles Bunbury, and leaving him to elope with Lord William Gordon to Scotland) had been left by Gordon with a little daughter with whom she spent eleven years of virtuous solitude in a house in Sussex provided by her kindly brother. She had eventually been married, to their mutual and permanent content, by Donny Napier, a penniless soldier. Sarah delighted in him physically, and thought him simply the best character she had ever known. "Till I was past thirty-six," she told her great friend, Susan Fox-Strangways, "I find I never knew what *real happiness* was, which from my marriage with Mr Napier till now is much greater than I had any idea of as existing in human life." In this ambience their five sons, and their five assorted daughters, had grown up; mainly in Ireland.

As a husband Donny had had, as they say, nothing but himself to recommend him; but it had been enough. Very few things, except his blissful second marriage and his flourishing second family, ever went right with him. His education had been admirable; he and his nine brothers had been taught their lessons by the famous philosopher and historian David Hume, sitting at work in the war-battered red limestone Merchiston Castle, which a fifteenth-century forbear, Sir Alexander Napier, had built on his lands to the south-west of Edinburgh. Provided with a wide-ranging general education and bought a commission, Donny had been launched on the world in the wake of successful naval and military brothers: his looks and intelligence immediately attracted attention and seemed equally immediately to attract ill-luck. His parents had taught him to tell the truth and shame the devil, to be true and just in all his dealings; and David Hume had taught him always to observe and question, never to accept that what had always been must continue to be, whether right or wrong. No-one had taught him how to get himself on.

An infusion of worldly ambition was supplied by Sarah, his lively and fascinating wife. She had found him in poor shape. He had won some *réclame* fighting the French in Corsica, but had there met and married a soldier's daughter called Elizabeth Pollock, "as poor as himself", and had further complicated his life by having four children in as many years. In 1775 he met Sarah for the first time, having dinner with her aunt, Lady Albemarle, a splendid kindly creature who was one of the few to brush aside her social disgrace and entertain her. Donny's reputation had preceded him: here for once, Sarah thought, was someone as handsome and as intelligent as he was cracked up to be. Donny for his part was enchanted; and quite unable to imagine why someone hadn't married Sarah the moment her divorce was through. After this he left for the American War of Independence, and for terrible trouble.

While he was away from them, besieging Charlestown in the south, his wife Elizabeth, his two baby sons and one of his little daughters had all died in New York of yellow fever. He himself became so desperately ill soon afterwards with the same nauseous disease that any recovery seemed out of the question; and General Clinton, as a friendly act, sold his commission while he was *in extremis*, so that there should be something for his one surviving little girl, Louisa, to live on. Donny, unconscious and near death, was put on to a homebound transport, where he flew in the face of all responsible medical opinion by recovering. He landed in England with one small pale daughter, no money, no commission, no job. The promising young Colonel Napier was now plain Mr Napier, with a blighted career and permanently impaired health.

He was in Ireland, four years later, trying to recover his lost commission by recruiting a company, when he met Sarah again, staying with her sister Lady Louisa Conolly at Castletown in County Kildare. On the strength of a job which brought him in £300 a year, he and Sarah were married amid a universal shaking of heads. He was a poor match for Sarah, and she, as she pointed out, "was undoubtedly a very poor match for him . . . but he laughs at every objection that is raised". They instantly proceeded to add eight children to the two Louisas they had severally already: married in 1781, they had by 1794 produced Charles, Emily, George, William, Richard, Henry, Caroline and Cecilia. The outbreak of war took Donny in due course to the campaign in the Netherlands against the invading armies of revolutionary France—"he writes in astonishment at the strange confusion that pervades in everything there"—which ended in retreat but also in teaching one young officer, Arthur Wellesley, how not to make war. Donny had worked through to being a major again, aided by the flashes from Sarah's bright eyes, and was now made colonel of the Derry Regiment just in time to be involved in waylaying the Irish Rebellion of 1798. He died six years later, of consumption brought on by overwork in a stuffy little office in Dublin, where Lord Cornwallis, out of the kindness of his heart and the admiration he felt for Donny's unusual intelligence and integrity, had installed him to sort out army pay—"The only comfort of this place is that we can treat all *Dirty Ministers* with the most sovereign contempt", Sarah commented. The previous incumbents had collected a steady twenty-thousand pounds a year from bribes and other ruses: obstinate Donny had refused to take more than the six hundred pounds a year that was the job's official rate. His three eldest sons had meanwhile all gone into the army, and Henry, his youngest, into the navy: clever Richard, fourth son, who had got a first in mathematics at Oxford, had been distracted from his original intention of going into the Church by a tutoring parson (who had tried to indoctrinate him, although he was already eighteen, with violently anti-revolutionary principles), and had become a barrister. At twenty-five Charles had found himself head of a family, with no money, no prospects, and a great deal of *esprit*, coupled with a steady determination to win itself fame.

The Napiers had been lucky to survive. Driven out of all possessions in Northumbria in the eleventh century by William the Conqueror, on account of their stubborn loyalty to the rightful Saxon heir to the English throne, they had landed on their feet amongst the ravishing scenery around Loch Lomond, from whence they had taken their original patronymic of Lennox, from the Gaelic Levenax—the field of the quiet stream. A younger son was awarded the name of Napier for his peerlessness in battle ("Thou hast nae peer", the King had said) in the twelfth or perhaps the thirteenth century. But from this small green kingdom they were driven forth again by loyalty to King James III of Scotland against his rebel son, who won, and awarded their land to his cousins. From Merchiston, their lands and fortress acquired near Edinburgh, they were driven out by the Covenanters and by Cromwell for their loyalty to Charles I and Charles II. Loyalty, or intransigence? "Yet, loving brother, never embrayce dishonorabill agreyment", a sixteenth-century Alexander Napier had urged his elder brother John, busy inventing logarithms and the decimal point and analysing the Revelation of St John the Divine in the teeth of plague and civil strife.

They were against extremism. "Aim not at absoluteness, the people of the western parts of the world could never endure it any long time, and they of Scotland less than any", Archibald, first Lord

Napier, had vainly urged King Charles I. "Practise, Sir, the temperate government. It fitteth the humour and disposition of the nation best." Be sensible, in a word. Archie Napier had married Montrose's sister; he and his son both fought in Montrose's campaigns for the King; the son died in loyal exile, and the sixteen-year-old grandson was imprisoned in Stirling Castle for refusing to swear allegiance to Cromwell and his republic. Restoration of the monarchy restored young Napier to freedom but only minimally to fortune. Much of what was left disappeared in the eighteenth century in financing plans for the Forth-Clyde canal, which contributed greatly to Scots prosperity. "He *will* prefer the publick business to his own", Sarah Napier had complained of her husband Donny; and there was the family failing.

Fortunate to have survived in the world of the educated, by the early nineteenth century the Napiers were certainly not in the world of the rich. Aware of the need for change in government since the industrial upheaval, they preferred sense to revolution. Civil slashing and firing harmed the innocent and rarely advanced a good cause. On the whole their root characteristics seemed to be honesty and resilience.

To this tale of narrow survival Donny's life of wars and fevers had been no exception; and his sons had recently scraped through the Peninsular War by the skin of their teeth and with much fame, but very little chance of future employment, since the British government to date continued a process of wholesale rejection of the combatants the minute the danger was past. Charles had had sabre wounds and an appalling crack on the head at Corunna, followed by a shattered jaw at Busaco, a battle where George also was badly wounded. George (second son) recovered in time to be wounded in the spring advance through Portugal in 1811, and to lose his right arm storming the breech at Ciudad Rodrigo next year. William (third son) had caught pleurisy in the Corunna retreat, been wounded in the hip at the Coa action, and condemned at twenty-five years old to a life of grinding pain by a shot near his spine in an unnecessary scrap—brought on by a foolish general—at Casal Noval. In the Far East during these same years on board H.M.S. *Good Hope*, Henry (youngest son) a midshipman, had endured a shattering form of cholera which had all but killed him, jaundiced his liver for life, and permanently depleted his fine frame. Richard (fourth son) was, like his mother, now suffering a gradual loss of sight.

Battered, penniless, unemployed for most of the time, how would they make out in an unsympathetic post-Napoleonic-War world? They were sensible by nature, and (in the miserable circumstances of England caught in the toils of industrial change) revolutionary in ideas. The balance could swing either way.

Charles was a practical man. Though visited by occasional forebodings he lived his life on common-sense lines and left the fates to get on with it. But he had been brought up on Froissart, on Malory's *Morte d'Arthur*, and on the heroes of classical Greece and Rome; a part of him remained in the realm of romance and dream. As a boy on those long slow journeys, wind-dependent and horse-drawn, between Dublin and London, he had passed often through Llangollen and seen, high above this Welsh border town on the Dee, the steep and narrow hill on which a ruined castle stood. Above the shine and tremor of the river, guarding the green valley between its mountain ranges that was one of the great gateways into Wales, the broken walls soared up, black against the sunset or clear in the morning sun as the horses drew the gazing boy slowly up the valley—the towering frontier fortress of Dinas Bran. "A high and lonely place", he called it; and had dreamed boy's dreams of reigning there in solitude and splendour, in this place somehow holy, above the howl and dissonance of the world. Dinas Bran was not only a feudal and princely stronghold, it was a sacred place. Old people in Llangollen believed it was that same mysterious Raven Castle to which the bravest few of King Arthur's knights had won; it was the shrine, the sanctuary, of Western Europe's most reverberant myth; Dinas Bran was the fortress that guarded the Holy Grail.

By 1820 seven years of bitter war and five of frustrating unemployment had tended to sear the dreams out of Charles. But as the ship beat up through the fresh morning, or lolled in the windless calm of a Mediterranean evening, and the high mountains of Cephalonia loomed ahead, it could have seemed to him, at some wordless level, that he was come indeed to Dinas Bran. Would he make of it Raven Castle? Or a place "of so great marvels that no tongue may tell, and more than any heart can think"? Or, more humbly, a place of justice and happiness, and a viable economic unit? He intended to be king; and king he was.

The Greek Ionian islands, of which Corfu was the principal, and Cephalonia one of the larger, had been taken during the Napoleonic

Wars by the British Fleet from the Austrians who held them, because they were about to fall into Napoleon's hands and be used as a base for the French Fleet from which to protect his eastward lunge. After six hundred years of Venetian sovereignty, and brief occupation by French, Russians and Turks, they were created, under the Treaty of Paris in 1815, "a free and independent state" under British protection, a euphemism which deceived few but which made the more sensitive Britons feel better. The Septinsular Union thus came for fifty years under British rule: in the 1860s it was handed back to Greece without appreciable fuss; possibly the first instance of an imperial people at the height of its power doing any such thing.

When Charles arrived in 1819 the overall command of this scattering of earthquake-ridden islands—one of the most beautiful places in the world—was in the hands of an eccentric but genial authoritarian known through his domain as Old Tom, King Tom, and other less polite names. Sir Thomas Maitland, ruling in Corfu in sultanic state and "with talent, but not of the first order", was, thought Charles, "narrow-minded, seeing many things under false lights, constantly drunk, and surrounded by sycophants who imagined him a god because he had more intelligence than themselves". He liked Maitland all the same. Peculiar he might be, but after three years he had been sagacious enough to pluck Charles out of the unrewarding task of inspecting field-officer to which the Horse Guards had appointed him, and to make him Resident of Cephalonia, in effect Governor.

First visiting Jannina on the Turkish-dominated mainland privately in 1819, Charles was sent in the following year by Maitland on a confidential mission to Ali Pasha of Jannina, a potent but unappealing best hope for the cause of Greek independence, the Greek ruler of a Turkish province. Carelessly out alone without his pistols in Jannina, Charles had been all but assassinated by two fierce Albanians—"I was in a hell of a funk." He visited much of Albania, besides Jannina, the course of the Thamis river, Suli, Arta and Prevesa: on later excursions he was at Patras, Corinth, Megara, Argos, Nauplion, and at Athens, Plataea, Thebes, Livadia, Cheronea, and Thermopylae; thence up Mount Oeta and to Amphissa, Delphi and Lepanto.

Riding through the mountains of this romantic enslaved country, Charles resolved "to gain an exact knowledge of the Greek people" —a baffling enterprise. All mainland Greece was still part of the huge Ottoman Turkish Empire, but the Turks were crumbling and the Greek people were astir. If her liberty were won by Russian arms, as seemed likely, Greece would, Charles advised the home government after three visits to the mainland, simply exchange Turkish for Russian rule; which would allow the Czar to dominate the Eastern Mediterranean, Egypt, and places east—a thought which continually hamstrung the British desire to promote Greek freedom. The Greek people were shrewd enough to foresee this outcome for themselves. Sharers though they were in the Orthodox version of the Christian faith, for them the Russian government was the epitome of tyranny, far more than that of the indolent Turks. "The Greeks look to England for their emancipation", Charles reported home when he landed back in Corfu in July of 1820.

Ali Pasha of Jannina, shrewd, unpopular, and grindingly avaricious, seemed an unlikely starter as inspiring liberator of Greece. Nor were his forces impressive, Charles's report went on—"The Greeks and Turks in his army detest each other and have nothing in common but dislike of him." His demands were enormous; while the Greeks in general wanted "no more than common security for their persons and property" (the Turks made free of both). "What the Greeks want", Charles went on, "is a hope of freeing themselves from suffering under the Turkish yoke"; and here was our great chance.

"England may now create a new kingdom, enthusiastic, vigorous, united in opinion," he announced optimistically, "with every requisite for strength, and in form suited for the aid of our maritime power." There must of course be no interference in Greek politics, but oh those incomparable deep-water harbours with British three-deckers riding at ease! If that didn't tickle them up at home, nothing would: those Britons that did not care strongly about liberty did care strongly about safe anchorages. As against this many of Charles's countrymen were besotted by the Levant trade with Turkey, and held (like Byron's valet Fletcher who had spent two years with the poet in Greece and regarded the Greeks with unwavering insularity) that "the Turks are the only respectable people in the country; if they go Greece will be like Bedlam broke loose; it's a land of flies, and lice, and fleas, and thieves; there is very little *country*, it's all rocks and robbers; they live like dogs, on goats' flesh and rice, sitting on the floor in a hovel, all eating out of one dirty round dish . . ."

Privately Charles noted that it was difficult to make out *what* actually went on—"Every Greek likes to be a leader, they all strive to keep a stranger in the dark, and tell him that all other Greeks who he may seem to favour are the very rogues of God's earth. This is a natural result of their superior talent and abject slavery." Life for Greeks in their conquered country, where "everyone knows that a Turk stabs any man who looks at his women even by accident", was not a bower of bliss: he had reliance on their readiness to rise and fight. His only doubt was whether they would hang together long enough to win.

They desperately needed help, encouragement, and above all money and arms. "The isles of Greece, the isles of Greece", sang Byron; to his contemporaries it sounded like a clarion call. Ruined in reputation at home, that superb proselytizer was winning converts to the Greek cause all over Europe, painting a vague outline of pro-Hellenic goodwill with the indelible colours of his genius, and drawing men's hearts eastward. *Childe Harold*'s cantos rolled forth into an astonished and receptive world. "The Giaour" sold 14,000 copies in a morning. Money to assist the Greeks must eventually flow in. Meanwhile matters hung fire. Vigorous spirits such as Charles feared that they might hang fire for ever.

Back in Corfu Charles met an atmosphere of apathy and caution. He felt depressed and idle, and caught fever. "My head is shaved, my beard is enormous, as big as Ali Pasha's and very black, which with my dark eyebrows gives me a patriarchal look." King Tom's court was dull. "Amongst them were however some good men, and one, Lord Sydney Osborne, had no fault save that he thought the sun rose and set in Sir Thomas Maitland's hinder disk . . . Lord Guilford is here, a queer fish, but very pleasant." This son of Lord North was about to found an Ionian university out of his own pocket; a project which Charles reported upon with undue levity. He was far too mocking in a solemn age; the philhellenes in their extremer manifestations caused him a sardonic mirth which made them in their turn consider him arrogant and blood-thirsty.

"Lord Guilford dined with Sir Thomas, and entered the room at the head of twelve little men, professors in black, with powdered heads, bandy legs, cocked hats under their short arms, and snuff-boxes in hand. They 'louted low', flinging and scraping their crooked little legs about with great formality; then waddling each to a chair, snuffed, coughed, hawked, blowed noses all fiery red, gave loud umphs, stuffed their dirty coloured handkerchiefs into their pockets, and sat silent, though brimful of snuff and Greek, and hoping to be full of dinner and claret. Ogling the door, they remained till grub was announced"; upon which everyone was too polite to leave the room first. "At last a fat Scotchman, yearning for dinner, said to himself with a strong voice 'Uts very silly aw this at sax o' the clock.' And then two Frenchmen went out backwards, hitting their disks against half a dozen doors and against each other, and so reached the dining-room . . . Lord Guilford was very pleasant, addressing every person in a different language, and always in that which the person addressed did not understand." Guilford was dressed startlingly in the academic robes he had designed for himself, a kind of purple toga with touches of gold.

From this flimflam Charles endeavoured to escape into the world of action. Ali Pasha had asked his advice about fortification, recruitment, and training, but entirely declined to take it; he was now in open rebellion against the Turkish Sultan Mahmoud and would shortly be assassinated. "Seeing how fit and unfit such a people were for war, I longed to lead them", thought Charles, "and resolved to do so. I saw Greece about to arise in strength and glory and my resolve was to join her if it could be done with advantage to her just cause and honour to myself." But he was still in British service, and not free to act on his own initiative. To take service under a foreign government had recently been made an offence for British officers punishable by law, besides all loss of pay and pension.

He thought the Greeks very like the Irish, and "as I could not do good to Ireland the next pleasure was to serve men groaning under similar tyranny . . . From that period," he wrote later, "my efforts were directed to acquire gradually the confidence of the Greeks, foreseeing it would be a work of years, but might with hope and patience succeed. Feeling myself as belonging to them, I defended their cause on all occasions."

He had fallen in love with Greece, but not blindly. "My task was to wait long and patiently, ere mixing with a people too vain to admit foreigners until misfortune should show their ignorance." The war against Napoleon in Spain had taught him this much. "Every Greek robber thought himself a perfect general . . . My conviction was that Greece must finally be victorious, but that her hour of glory could not be tolled unless foreigners taught her how to war, and defeats made her hearken to the stranger . . . To be a Resident then became an object."

"The next thing of importance to note is the Maid of Athens!" he told his mother, in March of 1821. In February he had finally been allowed, after endless refusals, to travel in southern Greece. "Left Corfu yesterday, and at night bivouacked on the rocks of Morto. Nothing more agreeable or exhilarating than a bivouac; it is a state of nature with the comforts of civilization as to food and the means of eating it; it combines novelty with exercise, and generally with fine scenery: fatigue makes up for want of a bed." He found the Turkish rule everywhere hated, and Turkish power tottering: one good long push and the Greeks would break free from four hundred years of alien rule, endured since even before the conquest of Byzantium by the Turks in 1453. He visited the Peloponnese and Boetia, closely examining all that he saw, as far as was possible while the Turkish authorities were (rather naturally) breathing down his neck. To cut through the isthmus of Corinth would, in conjunction with other works, make the Morea defensible: the Greeks should make the Peloponnese their bridgehead. "A man who knows how to animate an army would make them work with enthusiasm, and they would cut the isthmus like magic!" There was little doubt in his mind as to who that man should be.

Charles halted for a long close look at Athens, at this time a small walled town in an empty plain. From here Lord Elgin, at great personal expense and with considerable public spirit, had recently removed the frieze from the Parthenon, which the Turks had at one time employed as an ammunition dump; causing its partial destruction in an explosion; and were at this point using as a quarry, grinding down its marbles to make mortar. The French removed other interesting pieces, and the Italians a lot more, but as the French ship subsequently sank with its marbles on board and the Italians dropped theirs down the Acropolis and broke them in a thousand pieces, they have acquired far less odium than poor efficient Elgin.

Wandering about the city, thirty-eight-year-old Charles decided that Byron had not overrated the Maid of Athens, but that if no-one had drawn his attention he would have thought the girls of Athens just pretty girls and no more. He admired their eyes and teeth and "tolerably brown skin: very like a Jewess". The Maid of Athens had "gentle pleasing manners, with that natural civility which is to me more admirable than the highest artificial breeding". Above all she was not affected, nor did she scream "as many of the Greek and Italian ladies do, which is to me insufferable". But he thought all the publicity had done the Maid of Athens no good. Englishmen behaved badly to her—"They should either marry or be off. These poor girls have too many admirers among our travellers ever to get married to their own countrymen. Though I think we do as much, or more than other men, when we see a woman in distress, or ill-used, we are very justly complained of by women of all nations. We seldom marry those whose rank and conduct admit of no other thoughts; and those who being married use the liberty their customs admit of, we betray, by boasting of their favours; we seem to forget the proverb: Never kiss and tell. Now without saying it is right to kiss, I am quite sure it is infamous to tell."

From love he switched to war. "From Cleone to the plain of Argos the road is full of passes, every one disputable; and if the enemy had inferior cavalry he would find the plain of Argos dangerous. A Greek army should try one general action at Cleone after losing the isthmus, because able if beaten, to escape; and if victorious, sure of destroying the enemy." On he went, measuring distances, heights, slopes, missing very little. There never was such a country for defence as Greece, he thought. "My time is too limited to be sure, but my notion is that if a general action were to be fought to save Livadia and Attica it should be where the battle of Cheronea was gained by Philip (of Macedon). Pindus and Parnassus secure the left flank; a branch river and Lake Copais the right; all the plain is clayey, intersected by a branch of the Melona and innumerable rivulets, and therefore very difficult for guns to pass in wet." He thought Thermopylae, although the sea had receded, could still be defended by three thousand instead of three hundred.

"Went to Delphi to visit Apollo . . . The priests might well say the god would defend himself: they could defend or hide their treasures with ease." Riding through the red-earthed valleys and up "delightful mountains" he thought that Greece was militarily a prize of a place, "furnished with strong positions in abundance". Gun-hauling would be difficult, but where a goat would go a six-pound gun could also travel. The Greeks were such admirable marksmen that in this they would need no training; stick a few of them over every valley and "the country was impenetrable for an enemy".

He found the beauty of it all beyond description—"What a country to be destroyed by tyranny." The Greeks were ripe for revolt, but "will give themselves up to the first power that will send a regiment to Constantinople". England had better be that one! His charmed life caused him to leave Patras a day or two before the too precipitate revolt of that town burst forth—"to my regret. The Greeks may be barbarous and base; what else can they be under the treatment they get? But my opinion is that they will succeed, yet never having been sure of my own courage I cannot be sure of other people's. If they don't fight hard the Turks will chop them into kebabs."

He had leave, and was on his way home, carrying dispatches, and seeing his mother for what he feared might be the last time. Back in London he published an anonymous pamphlet called *War in Greece*, describing the country and pleading the Greek cause. It had a wide circulation: he hoped it might stir things up. The flame of Greek revolution burned steadily in his heart. Equally strongly, a cool stream of common sense, a firm notion of the practically possible, flowed through his mind.

Early in 1822 Charles was offered Cephalonia on Maitland's recommendation, though he heard on the grapevine that Old Tom's high opinion of him had been qualified—" 'The impetuosity and violence of my character and politics made him fear mischief.' Guy Fawkes! This is the first time I ever heard of my violence in politics except from Tories who call everybody violent that don't agree with them." Yet he was violent; he admitted it to himself. The word had gone round to watch it. Keep a careful eye on Napier, or he may go impetuously and violently liberating Greece.

All the same he was delighted. Cephalonia was a charming domain. About the size of Yorkshire but far more sparsely inhabited, the island was bathed in unimaginably clear light; its rocks and coves lapped by delectable blue water. For most of the year the bright sun shone, the pines murmured, the bees hummed in the aromatic shrubs; and on its high mountains the snow lay all the year round. In spring the hills were a great blush of anemones, the valleys full of almond-blossom and asphodel. Cephalonia was also rife with murder, child-rape, robbery with violence, and well-entrenched feudal lords, one of whom had recently decapitated twenty tribal prisoners in cold blood. And nobody dared live anywhere near the delectable blue sea, for if they did they were liable to wake up any morning and find their throats cut and their wives and children reived away, and not always by Turks.

It was a task perfectly suited to Charles's character and talents: authority over a kind of Ulysses island left decaying and lawless after centuries of oppression and neglect by Venetian, Turkish, and Austrian rule. "My kingdom is of sixty thousand people and martial law exists. This is a fearful power in the hands of one man; but feeling no inclination to be unjust or cruel (except over their horrible trick of maiming animals out of spite to their owners) it does not annoy me. I even like it. My predecessor is going home half dead from the labour; but to me it is health, spirit, everything. I live for some use now."

Government House on the water's edge seemed to Charles magnificent, and had "a bathing room". This was pleasurable, but of course there were drawbacks—"I have a horrible deal of state to endure . . . it wears out my embroidered coat", and people would bow and scrape to him all the time in the most irritating manner.

In a month's time he was building a lazaretto and a quay, a new prison (the old one was "a disgrace to civilization", containing men who had been in chains for twenty years: he unchained them and "liberated five prisoners whose crimes were not great"), and better barracks away from the feverish marshes, which he hoped might save the lives of many soldiers of the little garrison. By June he had got rid of martial law and was planning to build a road over the Black Mountains, the 5,380-foot range dividing Cephalonia in half. "One road has been already carried by me over a precipice to unite two fruitful districts: it was a short but laborious job, and the people were very angry at the work, but now it is done are delighted."

"You must know that the Greeks have, from bad government, come to that strange state, that the instant they are treated justly they conclude it is humbug and try to be beforehand. Such tricks are played", he told his mother, "as would kill you with laughter, but my despotism grows stronger, mixed with good humour . . . The people here are very much to my liking, but the greatest liars in the world." Still dazzled by the British as defeaters of Napoleon, still haunted by the ravages of the Turks, the islanders in the 1820s were not so ready to shout *Enosis* as in time they became.

"Health besets me", Charles declared delightedly on June 10th. "Up early and writing till eight; then feed and work in office till twelve, sometimes till three o'clock, swim, dine, and then on horseback visiting the road-making. I take no rest myself, and give nobody else any: all were getting too fat. I have begun to dry up a portion of a large marsh near the town; this gives great satisfaction as the summer sickness comes from the marsh. Expect no letters from me save about roads . . ." There was nothing, he told his mother, "so good for everybody as having something to do; it diverts the mind and preserves health: therefore, read, and amuse yourself dearest mother, amusement is even better than busyness for old people. Read novels, laugh, cry, scold, eat, drink, and even get Crib to give you a few lessons in the fancy way.

"I am called despotis or tyrant. Well, there are sixty thousand people here, and not a dog or a cat have a quarrel but they come to the tyrant to settle the matter." Active and truly happy at last, he was out on the new roads at every available moment with John Kennedy, Royal Engineers, who became a lifelong friend. Together they designed and pioneered, taking the lead at the dangerous places; more than once owing their safety to accidental shrubs which they caught hold of when slipping from rocky ledges. In September Charles was suddenly called upon, at twenty-four hours notice "to accommodate the Suliot nation", exiled by the Turks, who had broken their surrender treaty and killed many of their women. There turned out to be only fourteen hundred of them left; not a very considerable nation.

"They came starving and dying of seasickness, of want, of fatigue, having been crowded in little boats under a broiling sun: my first step was to get the women and children ashore, and at last all landed and were fed. Cephalonia wants people, and the Suliots are the best of the Greeks. [Charles, with his mind on the war of independence, was unconsciously apt to judge people primarily by their fighting qualities.] They are to be placed in a fortress, which is so large that they will have fields and vineyards within, and be four hundred feet above the sea on a steep rock. No warrior deigned to carry baggage, their poor wives had to do that . . . many of the women carried the arms of dead husbands and brothers . . . Their arms are magnificent, and great presents they have offered to conciliate my good will, which they have however got on cheaper terms. Eight or ten of them have died of fatigue" before they could be got into the shelter of Charles's hastily-built wooden huts. "They have given me three thousand dollars to pay for their expenses, and as it has been done for one thousand they will be agreeably surprised."

The surprise was less agreeable when Charles demanded the surrender to justice of one of their men who celebrated his arrival on the island by killing his wife. The shores of Cephalonia in previous days had often been raided by men who swept off women and children and raped them and left them to die on some desolate rock. Charles's carry-on about one wife seemed incomprehensible: the Suliot leaders protested volubly, and Charles made a bargain with them, feeling perhaps that he was at once meeting them half-way and providing a useful exercise for his troops. If the man could escape in three days from the fortress he could go free. At night his soldiers lay hidden to guard the escape route; and after a midnight chase the wife-murderer was caught on the cliff and sent back for his remaining two days. It had been cleverly done. "In the British army", Charles exulted, in spite of his conviction that courage existed everywhere, "are to be found men who will overmatch those of any country, in force, courage, intelligence and dexterity." The Suliots duly gave up the man when the three days ran out, not objecting to his death but to its reason—to take the life of a brave man only for killing a woman! Charles was to get into trouble in Sind later on for this pedantic habit.

What with conciliating a rebel chieftain by being diplomatic with his wife, and beginning a new market-place, Charles's hands were full, and—"I am building a bridge, which excites the people's curiosity, they never saw one before, having but one river, fordable except in floods." Most of these things were paid for by cutting down on administrative expenses, but the roads were built by making every able-bodied man in the island lay off gambling or fighting and do a day's work a week on them: nobles and priests had also to work, or pay for a day's work instead. As Charles himself shovelled away, and so did the British soldiers, the Cephalonians were obliged to overcome their scorn for manual labour and shovel too: they were even seen working in the fields which Charles made them terrace out of the hillsides. Their delighted wives (to whom in general all field work had been left, while their husbands sat in the shade and talked politics and war) could now sometimes stay at home and spin and weave through the heat of the day. This interference with a pattern of life many centuries old made Charles a great many friends and some powerful enemies; but the *corvée* road-making was on a general order from Corfu.

On the mainland all went exceedingly ill. Two European unofficial expeditions in aid of Greece had faltered and failed. Early Greek successes, though brave and skilful, had been accompanied by such savage butchery of Turkish prisoners, men, women, and children, that Turkish vengeance on a like scale was assured. As a revolution it had gone off at half-cock; as a war it was stalemate. Enough success had been won to alert the Turks; not nearly enough to ensure Greek liberty. The situation was one of exceeding danger, of which the Greeks, though not their observant well-wishers, were blithely unaware.

By the autum of 1822 Charles had the quays, the market-place, the new prison, and the roads so well under way that he felt they could not now be stopped even if he left the island; and "The incessant activity here is heart's ease to me." The part of government he hated was punishing delinquents; but even here it was "pleasing to protect the innocent". A great project was stirring in his mind. King Tom was with him in November and Charles asked him for leave on half pay. The shrewd Maitland probably suspected where this would lead —to adventures on the mainland in the Greek cause—" No, Napier, I will not accept your resignation."

"Why I am such a favourite now I neither know or care, but think it an odd sort of affection to hinder me from doing what I so earnestly wish to do: at forty one is not a child to be taken care of", Charles grumbled to his brother William. By January of 1823 the Turkish assault on Missolonghi had been repulsed, and "Odisseus one of the ablest Greek chiefs is on the march with 5,000 men to aid the besieged." Mavrocordato, an educated Greek leader, defending this western port, was "the only gentleman amongst the chiefs, except Ypsilanti, who is a goose. The Greeks have taken Napoli di Romano [Nauplion] . . . At the battle of Petra, near Arta, they abandoned the foreign corps, who alone fought and were cut to pieces by the Albanian Turks, not more than twenty escaped . . . Colocotronis is a ruffian acquiring riches, but decidedly the chief in the Morea: he is without talent, yet bold and bloody, ridiculing all discipline." The Greeks would listen only to their own chiefs, "who all fight with musquets, the great merit of the famous Marco Boszaris is the being a good shot. Mavrocordato is different, but dares not offend a chief, for the followers would then quit him, perhaps deliver him to the Turks. However the cause gets on step by step . . .

"The Greeks will tire the Turks, who might finish the affair in a month, but their brutality prevents submission, their ignorance gives license to Greek faults." The Jews, as ever, had fallen between both; the Turks took their money and the Greeks roasted them alive on a report that Jews had been to blame for the hanging of the Greek Patriarch at Constantinople.

In the Septarchy the official line had altered. "Our politics here are all changed as to the Greeks, why is not explained, but we are quite conciliatory." (Castlereagh, wedded to the Holy Alliance and the *status quo*, had been replaced by Canning.) "My people go on well, and are surprised to find an Englishman can be a gentleman"; recent occupants had given another impression. By March "the Greeks are so full of triumph and constitutions that Mavrocordato is ungeneralled". Missolonghi was freed from Turkish threat, and Mavrocordato applied to Charles for his advice on the next step. Charles told him to move at once on Lepanto and Prevesa before the Turks had gathered force to return.

But this vital step Mavrocordato was unable to take as his year of power was ending—a Greek leader was elected for a year—and his Greek troops had all gone home for Easter.

In a long memorandum Charles advised Mavrocordato to concentrate on Greek establishment in the Peloponnese; to fortify the easily defended Corinth isthmus; to reduce the Turkish-held fortress of Roumelia and the Morea, leaving the minor ones of Modon and Coron to the efforts of the unsubdued Petro Bey and his Maniotes on their rugged peninsula, and to go on across the isthmus when this was accomplished, holding a secure base in case of retreat. In case of success, he outlined a further advance to secure the rich plain of Thessaly, pointing out the ease with which the mountain passes could be held by such marksmen as the Greeks.

Above all, they should keep one *supremo* while the war continued, and not play politics. But politics was the Greek national sport: they could no more stop playing them than the English could stop playing football. Mavrocordato had been whipped away from his scene of triumph—"When his courage and talent thus saved the Greek cause, and all his activity was required to follow up his victory, he found himself a simple citizen, and compelled to abandon military affairs to attend to those of the senate." Civil and military powers in Greece became increasingly at odds and were soon fighting each other, while in Constantinople Sultan Mahmoud laid his plans. Philhellene groups arriving to help received little welcome, and their advice on how to fight the war no credence at all. No-one without ample funds behind him would, Charles was certain, achieve Greek co-operation.

"Go I will, with or without leave", Charles wrote on March 3rd, 1823. (But like other philhellenes, he had official hurdles to jump, as well as emotional entanglements to unravel.) "My liver torments me and my leave has been stopped", he reported crossly in June.

This spring a committee was formed in London by a bunch of assorted liberals, some admirable and some the reverse, to collect money and arouse support for the cause of Greek independence. To this Charles sent a memorandum on the military possibilities of the situation in Greece, and a plan of operations, roughly that which he later gave Byron. But Cephalonia for the meanwhile was his pride and joy. He was happier than ever before or after, and how much was due to his Greek love, Anastasia, and how much to her native island, it is now impossible to disentangle.

Charles was now thirty-nine and, through sad happenings, single, but a natural and vigorous man. Up every narrow lane, in every stony village, moved the brown-faced Cephalonian girls, with the bright eyes and white teeth that had caught his fancy in Athens; with perhaps something of the same "pleasing gentle manner". There was a wildness and freedom about them, something warm, laughing, and defiant that reminded him of the Irish girls who had charmed his youth, some quality that blossomed above poverty and conquest. "Cephalonia is never out of my mind and heart" he wrote; and a daughter of the island had lodged there likewise. "They say first love is the truest, and Cephalonia is mine", and here he certainly did not speak of Anastasia, far from being his first love.

He was not a boy; and would have had no time for a pleasing dalliance, or a palpitating chase amongst the rocks and olive trees of this magic place. For all we know Charles may simply have bought Anastasia, a willing purchase, from her father, for the going price of about £11-17-6d. He had always had charm, and an attraction that rose above the scars and nervous twitchings of his wounds, his ripe oaths, his spectacles and his limp. Anastasia, it seems, loved him. Like Englishmen he had blamed in Athens, he did not either marry or be off. But surely he also loved her.

*

Across a narrow strait eastwards from Cephalonia was the island of Ithaca, shaggy with stone pines and myrtle scrub, and breathing, despite its absence of drains, an everlasting romance. High on the slopes an eternal Penelope spun her web, and through the dusty arbutus an immortal Odysseus rolled up the steep cliff path on legs still staggering from the sea. From the Black Mountain above Argostoli on his own island Charles could look further east to where, three-humped, an ashen mountain guarded the plain of Missolonghi, a green and yellow tongue of land licking out of the surrounding hills into the deep blue of the Ionian Sea.

In this direction, in the early days of 1824, Charles's gaze was directed with great hopes and a certain apprehension. Could genius and passion of themselves unite Greece and sweep her faltering revolution into triumph? How was the struggle opening, and were the wrong people getting hold of his gold? For there, just across the strait at Missolonghi, at once enhancing and complicating life as such characters always do, was Byron.

CHAPTER II

Byron

In August 1823 the brig *Hercules*, chartered by the poet for his voyage to Greece, had sailed into the harbour at Argostoli. Her destination had originally been Zante, but Hamilton Browne, a young man who had joined Byron at Leghorn, pointed out that Cephalonia was the only one of the islands whose Resident, Colonel Napier, was sympathetic to the Greek cause. Famed all over Europe for his poetry and his rebellious politics, Byron was still in disgrace at home. In an age when marriages between first cousins were a commonplace, and papal dispensations granted to uncles who wished for dynastic reasons to marry their nieces, Byron's alleged romp with the fond sympathetic half-sister he had never known in childhood caused a disproportionate row, for which his own indiscretions were in part to blame. There were times when Byron seemed to go out of his way to be thought a cad; playing for ostracism like a naughty boy rampaging over Tom Tiddler's ground. To the process of his self-destruction a great element of the show-off had entered in. Too much fame had blazed round London, too much scandal; too many coaches bearing invitations to Byron had blocked St James's Street. In the end that fierce and shallow world had exiled him by its coldness. The poet had now a nervous expectation of being cold-shouldered by the British garrison on Cephalonia, whose bugles sounded from Argostoli fort over the water to where lay, with its varied crew, the anchored *Hercules*.

"The Greeks get on from Turkish folly, not their own wisdom", Charles reported on August 10th; "Lord Byron is here, and I like him very much." Charles was unlikely in any case to have joined the hue and cry against the poet, and was in no position to be censorious, with Anastasia under his wing. He went on board *Hercules* the day after she anchored, told Byron how things were at the moment in Greece, assured him of his belief in the Greek cause, and added that if the poet conducted his business discreetly (as he felt sure Byron would), he would turn a benign blind eye on the purpose of his mission and soothe the susceptibilities of Maitland at Corfu.

Next day he sent Byron a letter asking him to say when he wanted a change, and offering assistance on the island in any way he could—"I have not called on you because I am afraid of boring you." Thus encouraged, the officers of the garrison, far from being stand-offish, asked Byron to dinner, drank his health, applauded his slightly nervous and showing-off speech of thanks, and assured him how much they had enjoyed "The Corsair" and the Assyrian coming down like a wolf on the fold. Honest in his bleak self-knowledge—"I am not famous for decision"—shaken by the demands about to be made on him in his role of doughty hero and man of action, alternately gloomy and elated amid his motley crew of followers, the poet was in need of a friend and supporter of the calibre of Charles.

"When Byron arrived, diffident and irresolute, at Cephalonia," wrote Harold Nicolson, "he found in Napier a person of remarkable originality and decision; a soldier who, while discounting, even as Byron did himself, the faults of the Greeks, never wavered for an instant in his affection for them or in his conviction of their ultimate triumph; a man of action who, while expert in the science of warfare, was also skilful in the arts of civil administration; and finally a man of infinite humour, of infinite energy, and above all, of infinite resolution. For it was Napier who inspired the despondent Byron with that self-confidence which vitalized him during those last months at Cephalonia, and which carried him finally, gay but determined, across to Missolonghi."

To Charles, Byron was a breath of fresh air, generous-hearted to the Greeks, stirring company, and sharing his own sardonic brand of humour. Both men suffered from spasms of presentiment: to both laughter was an essential ingredient of life. "I have a quantum of nonsense in me beyond the ordinary run," Charles felt; "if it had no vent my death would ensue from undelivered jokes": and Lady Blessington had thought that Byron's worst fault was his flippancy. "The laughing devils will return", Byron complained, "and make a mock of everything." He and Charles mocked together; and the fact that Charles was the grandson of a duke did him no disservice with Byron, one of those republicans with a nice sense of who is who.

In the weeks while Byron waited for good news from the Greek committee, and sent money to pay the Hydriot fleet to break the

Turkish blockade of western Greece, the poet was full of jokes and teases, many of them launched at old Scott, captain of the *Hercules*, who rarely failed to rise. Scott himself came to put down his employer's eccentricities entirely to the Suliot bodyguard whom Byron enlisted; referring to them as "they damned Zodiacs"; and telling the poet he would have none of his heathenish tricks, such as landing horses on a Sunday. Byron's dubious friend Trelawney had found the poet "not romantic enough" and departed for the Morea: he presently became hand in glove with the capable but treacherous chieftain Odysseus. In October Browne and Trelawney reported from the Morea that only a great deal of money in the hands of the central government of Greece could diminish the authority of the chieftains who had usurped power, or deflect their followers from incessant private warfare. This echoed Charles's view, and he thought the poet sensible to wait till the loan was forthcoming, and to forward the departure of the Greek deputies for London.

Apart from the pleasure of his company—and Shelley had called Byron's serious conversation "a sort of intoxication"—Charles felt for him the admiration evoked in a man of action by an artist who actually makes money. Byron had been unable to resist boasting of what his next publication would bring in. "He is going to Greece," Charles wrote home to Lady Sarah, now almost eighty but as keenly interested in life and affairs as ever, "but it is hard to get there and harder to get back; and if the Turks catch him off goes his poetical nob! He lives in his ship but comes ashore to my house . . . he tells me he has touched up the Duke of Wellington in Don Juan. He means to write one hundred and fifty cantos, and he gets £2,000 a canto! Good trade a poet's!"

On his ceaseless rounds of the island that were both duty and pleasure, Charles would ride through the olive woods and down among the orange and lemon groves to visit Byron in his cottage at Metataxa, get off Blanco, and stride in, limping and *affairé*, to tell the poet the latest news from London and from Greece. He found him besieged by demands for money and help from a score of Greek leaders, ranging from the piratical Odysseus to the abbots of Mount Athos—"The worst of them is that they are such damned liars", Byron admitted. Charles rejoiced at his realism. His own task was not easy; he must combine sympathy with Greek aspirations with the neutrality enjoined by his post. But Byron neither questioned Charles's sincerity nor underrated the difficulties of the official

British position. The least outward sign of sympathy and the Greeks in a flash would be using the Ionian islands as refuge and even base, which would immediately involve England in war with Turkey, last barrier between the Czar and Mediterranean domination. King Tom of Corfu had thus acquired great odium in Greece and among the London Philhellenes, but "there is a great deal of fine stuff about that old Maitland", Byron said.

His disreputable friend Trelawney, inaccurate but shrewd, afterwards recorded that the only two British officers who understood the Greek situation were Colonel Napier and Commodore Rowan Hamilton. Still less did any of the Greek leaders understand it, or see the dire necessity for sinking their differences. "It must be the Cause, and not individuals or parties, that I endeavour to benefit", Byron insisted. But where exactly, in the tangle of Greek politics, was the Cause?

Waiting for news from the mainland, sitting with Charles and his company beside the lapping waters at Argostoli, Byron would be relaxed and eager: conversation ranged over Greece's struggle, over Charles's cherished subject, the roads of Cephalonia—"every priest is made to work or pay which delights the poor people"—over blood sports. "We are all a hot violent crew," Charles told Byron, speaking of his brothers, "but with the milk of human kindness. We were all fond of hunting, shooting, and fishing; yet all gave them up when young men because we had no pleasure in killing little animals. George and I were bold riders . . . we however found it pain, not pleasure, to worry animals . . . As to cat-hunting and dog-fighting, feeling and principle unite to condemn; a domestic animal confides in you and is at your mercy; a wild animal has some fair play. Cat-hunters and dog-fighters are therefore not only cruel but traitors: no polished gentleman does these things."

"I am serious," Byron said, "when I say I don't believe it possible for a fisherman to be a good man."

"Meaning anglers for amusement?" Charles could not follow him here, but "I am sure a cat-hunter and a dog-fighter cannot be a good man: nor a gentleman either", and to this Byron agreed.

James Kennedy the garrison doctor (not to be confused with John Pitt Kennedy the Royal Engineer) had evangelical leanings and endeavoured during the months that Byron spent on Cephalonia to make a convert of this rich plum; but mocking Byron told Augusta that the doctor had made more converts to the beauty of his wife than to the soundness of his theology. "Yet few people", Finlay reported, "were better acquainted with the Scriptures than Byron." Dr Kennedy thought him "a kind-hearted, benevolent and feeling man" but "led by passions and prejudice . . . he excited intense sympathy in my mind". He admired Byron's candour and patience, "though these were damped by an occasional levity"; and it is probable that Byron was entirely candid whilst listening to him, however amusing he might be about it afterwards in a letter. At the first session Kennedy had preached for an hour, and read passages aloud for three more, during which "I observed signs of impatience in some of them, especially Colonel N. and his lordship"; and after which Colonel N. had opted out. Byron called the doctor Kennedy the Saint, and John Kennedy, Kennedy the Sinner; though the latter was, as Sidney Osborne described him, "a very agreeable young man".

In evenings still warm with autumn they would sit out on the balcony of Charles's official house by the sea; the talk ranged widely; there were serious interludes intermingled with the laughter. Moths bumbled into the lamps, the crickets shrieked in the olive trees; had Charles imported wines or did they drink the resinous vintages of Cephalonia? In later years Charles's indifference to comfort amounted to asceticism; his dress could never be called smart, nor were his dinners lavish by the eight-course standards of the day; but he held a certain minimum state as Resident. He lacked pomp, but had a great capacity for convivial enjoyment.

He impressed Byron, as well as making him laugh. "Just the man for a Chief, if it could be managed", Byron sighed to Augusta. "You know he is a famous soldier, one of Sir John Moore's 'Well done, my majors!' left for dead at Corunna, and all alive and martial at this moment. He is besides an excellent fellow, greatly liked, and a thorough Liberal . . . He has been extremely kind and hospitable."

As the autumn days passed Byron became ever happier to stay where he was. He was well, and emotionally recovered from his severance from Teresa Guiccioli, the fair-haired Italian countess who had been his last and best-loved mistress: "It is awful work, this love", he had written, struggling in her charming and reproachful toils. More and more, he would have liked to take Charles with him to the fight on the mainland, where waited an appalling situation he felt himself unable to handle. More and more, Charles wanted to go. And he was no more immune to the magic of Byron's personality than were the rest of his generation. Nor was Byron immune to Charles's resolution and clear-headedness, two qualities at a premium on the mainland. "All the stories of the Greek victories by sea and land are exaggerated or untrue", Byron thought; and the Morea, Schilizzi had written to him, was a chaos of civil war. The confusion, Byron told Charles in a letter, came from "what Mr Braham pronounces Entusy-musy, expecting too much and starting at speed. It is lucky for me so far that, fail or not fail, I can hardly be disappointed, for I believed myself on a fool's errand from the outset. I will at least linger on here or there until I see whether I can be of service in any way; and if I doubt it, it is because I do not feel confidence in my individual capacity for this kind of bear-taming, and not from a disbelief in the powers of a more active or less indifferent character to be of use to them, though I feel persuaded that that person must be a military man."

With this Charles was in complete agreement, but what was the military man to live on? He liked Byron more and more—"a very good fellow, very pleasant, always laughing and joking . . . very compassionate, and kind to everyone in distress". Long before Byron's brig sailed into the harbour Charles had set his mind on fighting for Greece, but to join him without official leave was to break the laws of Britain and to throw his livelihood away. "I would willingly go to Greece, but will only go there if I can live on my income," Charles wrote to Byron, "which ceases if I am struck out of the Army List by the King: therefore I can do nothing till it is ascertained whether this would happen or would not happen." As soon as he could jump old Maitland into giving him some leave, he was going home to find out.

George Finlay, afterwards an admirable historian of the Greek War of Independence, during his two months' stay this autumn on Cephalonia spent nearly every evening in Byron's company, and interestingly observes that it was Charles's ardour for the Greek cause that had sometimes to be doused by Byron's cynicism about the Greek character; and not the other way round. "No stranger estimated the character of the Greeks more correctly than Lord Byron. At Cephalonia he sometimes smiled at the enthusiasm of Sir Charles Napier . . . To nobody did the Greeks ever unmask their selfishness and self-deceit so candidly."

Finlay thought that Byron was two people, a man and a woman. Talking with another man, the poet would show an extraordinary practical sense, a depth and range in his thought, a calm far-sighted grasp of the situation. And then suddenly, when someone else joined the party, he would switch to his exhibitionist side and become all temperament and petulance and performance, like an ageing actress seeing how far she could go. This was a side Charles never saw: his influence on Byron was too strong: Byron perhaps cared too deeply about retaining his good opinion.

But Finlay noted also the sad and pitiless self-knowledge of Byron in bleak moments, his realization of the Greek situation and of his place within it. "I was a fool to come here," he said, early in October, "but having come here, I must see what can be done." Later, on going to Missolonghi, Byron truly saw himself as "one of the many waves that must break and die upon the shore before the tide they help can reach its mark." With Charles, he went in rather less for breaking and dying and rather more for funny stories. Byron needed and liked every kind of friend; but more particularly now he needed the kind like Charles.

Letters arrived for Byron from Colocotronis, from Tricoupi. "You have been so kind to me", Byron told Charles; and he hesitated to trouble Charles further for his advice. "Whenever you come up this way I hope you will look in and see how comfortable we are under your auspices", for Byron and his following were now lodged in a village at Metataxa. Charles answered that he felt guilty of presumption in advising "one of those men who mark the age in which they live", but that if he were Byron he would recruit abroad—"A foreign force is the only thing which can give a speedy and decisive turn to the war—all is chaos." The Turks would be easily disposed of; but the difficulty was to make the Greeks unite. Byron was not to let them regard him as a gold-mine; once they had got his money "they will pay no attention to a word you say: the damnedest idiot amongst them is satisfied that his abilities are far superior to your lordship's."

"To give the government money will be to throw it away; it will go into Colocotronis's pocket, or that of some other chief. Were I in your place I would unite my own funds with those of the committee, and, with all that was collected, pay the two hundred Germans said to be at Napoli [Nauplion] de Romania, and also a body of men from England as numerous as the funds will admit of—reserving some money to pay those Greeks who are fugitive from the northern provinces, and will flock to your standard. With this force seize Napoli and open the gates to all the people of Greece . . . Pay the soldiers yourself, and form a bodyguard of the most trustworthy. A few enlightened men, like Tricoupi and Mavrocordato, will see that you are doing what alone can do good, and they will stick to you and support you; particularly while you hold sword and purse, which secures your power, and the faith of the mass of men. Once established in that impregnable fortress of Napoli, and allied with Hydra etc., use every means in your power to conciliate, short of giving up the purse, which in your case I would not trust to my own brother. You might then send forth troops under the constitutional banners . . . Allow the leader to conduct the war against the Turks as he might, giving him, if you could not accompany him, as much money as would serve to pay his troops for a certain time, but telling them how much he had, and when he was to pay them: they would force him to be honest when pay day came.

"In this way I think you would collect round you all enlightened Greeks, whom your money would conciliate and your bodyguard maintain in obedience . . . Thus you might disarm or destroy the warlike chiefs, the government would gradually consolidate and take a liberal form . . . you or your general would perhaps find your fame and safety both encreased by remaining simply members of a republican government. This scheme may appear at first a wild one, but if your lordship thinks it worth while to give it full consideration you will, I think, see that it is both a humane and a practicable one; and far the best that Greece could in her present confusion desire. One danger however will exist—that of being assassinated by the warlike chiefs the moment they perceived what you were at: but enterprises of this nature have always some point of danger, on which one can only say with Hotspur 'There is danger in everything.' . . .

"If by going on half-pay I can serve the Greeks without further loss, whatever small stock of military knowledge I could offer your lordship in such an enterprise should then be at your disposal."

Officers in this epoch often took service in foreign causes that appealed to them. These were desperate enterprises. If they did so without leave they were struck off the army or the navy list and

2*

naturally lost pay and pension, and might leave their families in penury. One had to be a Cochrane, with £75,000 of naval prize money up one's sleeve, to be a free-lance; or a well-endowed Major Thomas Gordon, or Frank Abney Hastings, who could proceed untrammelled by care or by thoughts of dependents starving in a garret. Many of the philhellenes who came to fight for Greece were desperate men without other objectives or hopes elsewhere, but Charles was in a profession he felt at home with, and in a job he loved.

In October Charles reported that Cephalonia had been "shaken almost out of its skin by a succession of earthquakes: no-one hurt but all frightened"; but in mainland Greece the political earthquake continued to heave rather than to erupt: there had so far been a series of unco-ordinated massacres rather than a war. The two small European expeditions that had ended in failure and starvation had done so through lack of adequate funds or supplies. A sensible observer on the spot could draw his own conclusions: without securing these essentials it was foolhardy to take command.

The Cause wore an unprosperous and divided look. Far from consolidating their earlier successes and fortifying their easily defended passes as Charles had advised, the Greek leaders were increasingly at odds; while in Constantinople the Sultan, who had earlier strung up the Greek Patriarch in full canonicals and exterminated or sold into slavery the 23,000 peaceful Greek dwellers on the island of Chios, was gathering his forces in alliance with Mohammed Ali of Egypt to do likewise in the Morea. A steady trickle of European philhellene helpers arrived, but "expecting", as Charles said, "to find the Peloponesus filled with Plutarch's men, all returned thinking the inhabitants of Newgate more moral". By November 13th the Greek Committee's agent, Colonel Leicester Stanhope, was staying with Charles. "I like him much, and strange to say, he is not a dandy", Charles wrote. Stanhope found Charles "a doing man"—his highest praise.

Under the tall cypresses of Metataxa Byron was collecting some very rum adherents. There were German students; there was George Finlay, who had made Byron jump by looking like the ghost of Shelley; and now came Leicester Stanhope, with his determination to turn Greece into a Benthamite paradise overnight. He had "high-flown notions of the sixth form at Harrow or Eton, Colonel Napier and I set him to rights"; Byron wrote. In identifying with Charles he was gaining reassurance. "Colonel Napier and myself are as decided for the cause as any German student of them all; but like men who have seen the country and human life, there and elsewhere, we must be permitted to view it in its truth." Charles's private thoughts might turn to melancholy or bitterness, but Byron discovered in him the invaluable power to transmit to others his courage and his force. Here was a sensible, active, honest man of repute, who did not think him a laggard or a foolish dreamer. "The future began to glimmer, under the stimulus of Napier", wrote Harold Nicolson, "with the reviving shimmer of hope and of romance."

Was it to Byron—"your atheistship"—that Charles expounded the thoughts he recorded about now in his journal?

"So you believe in God and a future state?" the imaginary Byron enquired.

"Yes! worshipful, or rather nonworshipful sir."

"You soldiers are queer fellows. You ain't afraid of a cannon-ball, yet quiver before a parson."

"Beg pardon, atheistship—I am, and ever was, very much afraid of a cannon-ball, and never feared a parson, except when expecting long sermons in a cold church."

"Then give me proof that your creed is true."

"No friend, I am not able. My faith is made up from feeling, the result of accidents, reflections, dangers, joys, a hotch-potch of many things, many of which I can't remember, but they have produced decided results in my bosom."

The candles guttered in their holders, the talk turned flippant again, and it was time for Byron to ride back to Metataxa. The sea was silent with midnight, the air filled with aromatic scent from shrubs growing thinly through rocks now cooled with the sun's departure. It was the last of summer, the last of the wine, the ending of Byron's thirty-six years of brilliant troubled life.

For the only help that the poet could give Greece was to rouse Europe by risking his life in the Greek cause. By Christmas Mavrocordato and the Greek ships from Hydra were at Missolonghi, the springboard from which to attack Lepanto and Patras, still in Turkish hands. Appeals continued to pour in to Byron at Metataxa—"My Lord, it depends only on yourself to secure the destiny of Greece", Mavrocordato besought him. On the final day of the year, narrowly escaping capture by a Turkish ship, Byron landed at Missolonghi in a gay and gallant mood, velvet-jacketed, bright-eyed, acclaimed like a prince by cheering crowds, to taste in the ensuing months what felt to him the dire failure of a mission and of a life.

But for the moment guns boomed welcome, muskets shouted a *feu de joie*, church bells rang, donkeys brayed, small boys with loud yells summoned each other to the scene. Here at last was mainland Greece; racing clouds revealed bright sun, the waters shone, an air of freedom whistled off the mountains. The poet landed with "the gay and confident assurance which he temporarily absorbed from Napier".* There were tears of joy for Byron's coming, laughter, huggings; loud enthusiastic Greek kisses smacked alternately on either cheek. His heart rose to meet this unequivocal embrace. "Hope and content", reported Count Gamba, the young brother of Byron's final mistress, "were pictured in his countenance . . . I cannot easily describe the emotions which such a scene excited."

Lodged in Missolonghi this January of 1824, Byron found that his immediate task was to capture Lepanto and Patras, fortresses still in Turkish hands. The puzzle was to induce the Greeks to join forces to this end. The English passion for purposeful activity interspersed with intervals for privacy and quiet is incomprehensible to the Greek spirit. Greek leaders of all parties and of none swarmed into Missolonghi, distracting Byron and exhausting him by their noise, their demands for more money, their incessant intrusion upon all his waking or sleeping hours. Why had Napier not accompanied him here, with his easy manner of taking charge, of getting people to shut up and take their turns? On the ground floor of the house Byron's Suliot troops banged about in their *fustanellas*, loudly dropping their muskets, interminably quarrelling about precedence, singing their tribal songs in a piercing monotonous drone. The powerful smells of their cooking seeped up through the doors and walls, mingling with the considerable competition from the open drain that flowed down the middle of the street outside.

It was now, Finlay thought, that Byron finally became acquainted with Greek arrangements, and "abandoned all hope of being able to guide the Greeks, or to assist them in improving their administration". Finlay did not consider that Byron's genius, great though it was, "would have unfolded either political or military talent". Faced

* Harold Nicolson, *Byron, the Last Journey*

with the need for "bear-taming", Byron's heart, as he had known it would, had failed him. He could, and did, suffer: what he could not do was to act effectively. Nor had he the consolation of knowing that suffering is sometimes the most effective act of all. "His abstract enthusiasm for military glory was joined to an innate detestation of the trade of war", Finlay recorded.

Corfu, Paxos, Levkas, Ithaca, Cephalonia, Zante, Cythera—the seven islands of the Septarchy lay in a stormy sea as Charles sailed home this January of 1824: the winds were such that it took him eleven days to arrive at Ancona. In his pocket was a letter to the Greek Committee in London. "Colonel Napier", Byron had written before he left "will present you with this letter. Of his military character it were superfluous to speak; of his personal, I can say from my own knowledge, as well as from all rumour and private report, that it is as excellent as his military—in short, a better or a braver man is not easily to be found. He is our man to lead a regular force or to organize a national one for the Greeks. Ask the army; ask anybody! He is besides, the personal friend of Mavrocordato, Colonel Stanhope, and myself; and in such concord with all three that we should pull together, an indispensable as well as a rare point, especially in Greece at present."

Charles had heard scant good of the London Committee—"a set of ninnicoms who certainly know little of Greece or Greeks". They were already negotiating with Lord Cochrane; and there was General Church on hand, more biddable in nature, and Thomas Gordon, with money of his own, and Stanhope, so unexceptionable a Benthamite. Byron's recommendation could not be disregarded: he was their trump card, and paid at least some of the pipers—but the cut of Charles's jib did not appeal to the Committee. They cared for it still less as the weeks went by and he hammered on at his points—arms for a regiment, ammunition, money to pay them, regular soldiers, the retention of his own commission in the British army. What a difficult, independent, determined man; and so crassly materialist! He did not seem to understand that this was a crusade, a matter not of account books but of knights in shining armour. And the Committee was really busy. Their next public dinner was due, and there was a blood row going on about the menu. Charles found them so closely out of touch with reality that they were sending out a freight of water-colours to a Greek people just now scrambling, firing and starving around the beleaguered rocks of their country.

The Prime Minister, Canning, was now reconciled to the idea of Greek independence, but bent on cautious procedure, for fear of embroiling the ever-rivalrous great powers: a well-known British officer taking the lead in Greece might spark off Russia or Turkey. Besides, Charles's goings on in Ionia were not above suspicion: had he compromised British neutrality by all this advice, however discreet, sent to the Greeks? He had harboured and supported not only Byron and Stanhope, but Finlay, Browne, Trelawney, German students and other odds and bobs. Canning had many spies: one of them reported Charles ashore in Missolonghi in full uniform. This had, in fact, been John Kennedy, sent on business by Maitland: but Canning had a strange addiction to spy information, even if only second-hand hearsay. Charles applied to Robert Bowring, a leading light of the Greek Committee ("that combination for freedom and stock", as William Napier sardonically called it), to urge his cause.

Yes, he told Bowring on February 29th, he clearly understood the vast responsibility of going to Greece as one of the Commissioners for administering the loan, and the commanding position it would give him. After deep thought Charles had decided that he could do the job, and had asked the government to turn a blind eye. "I cannot afford to lose my commission. My military means are a thousand pounds yearly; by going to Greece I lose the whole. If Russia declares war against Turkey, England and Greece become enemies and I fall to the ground [his terms to the Greek government stipulated that he would never fight against England] without a profession or the means of existence after thirty years' hard service in the British army . . . You see I am more calculating than enthusiastic . . . pray let me hear what Mr Canning says."

Bowring wrote next day. He had had "a very pleasant interview" with Canning. "I said all I could about you, but he repeated, *Napier has got his answer*. I could make no further impression: so Lord Bathurst's answer was no doubt one on which there was a previous understanding with the other ministers." This answer had been an emphatic No.

In the cool and detachment of England, Charles had at least listened to advice. "Bowring could not see Canning but is to see him and give me his answer by next Saturday", he wrote to his sister Emily on February 4th of 1824. "I therefore came here to ruminate in quiet. [This was Cookham, the home of Elizabeth Kelly.] As I wanted to have some idea of what the world would say and think I resolved to talk the matter over with a few friends as representatives of London, not so much caring for their advice but to hear what it would be, and what could be urged against the step.

"These friends were Lord William Bentinck, Sir Henry Bunbury, and Alexander Johnstone; the first for the Canning opinions, the second for that of the Horse Guards and the Bathurst party from his personal knowledge of their character, and the third for the general London politics. I find them all *timid*, but the two last saw the game was great. They are both for delay. However I got out of all three what I wanted. I see I have to return; my commission is gone; I have not the least hope from Canning. I like always to look at the worst side, and that is to sacrifice my commission.

"Now I am lost if Russia declares war in less than 5 months against the Turks. I want one month to go to Missolonghi, three to form the army, and one to fortify Corinth, but if I could secure those 5 months England would willingly guarantee the Greeks in what *they held*, on condition that they would not join Russia; and she could help the Turks to defend Constantinople on condition that they made peace with the Greeks. Russia would conquer all between Corinth and Constantinople [if once she began; and in England they seemed certain she would begin].

"This appears to me the only wise plan England could follow, and in that case I could make my own terms; but if Russia comes down before Corinth is fortified the Morea is lost, for the Greeks would in that case have no choice but to join Russia against England and Turkey. Consequently I should be lost.

"In this point of view I think I shall write to Bowring to say that I am ready to go if the Greek deputies will guarantee [besides the money for troops and the equipment for these] a certain income to me should I lose my commission, and this sum I leave to their decision. Without this I should play a more desperate game than any Greek, because a Greek necessarily stakes all upon the issue of the war, whereas I do the same voluntarily . . .

"I think George and Henry will approve of what I think of doing. It is being in some measure like the Condottieri of Italy. But I cannot avoid that—a man must eat."

But no blind eye was to be turned. Charles fighting for Greece would embarrass the government. He was categorically not to go;

and his job as Resident hung in the balance. Why couldn't he stay put, like any other British officer, and not butt in to what was no concern of his? A few months later Bathurst, married to Charles's first cousin Georgina Lennox, sent him a friendly verbal warning through his eldest sister Louisa. Charles thanked him, but responded with characteristic indignation; sending a copy of his letter to George and Emily for their comments.

"The above was drawn forth by a message from Lord Bathurst through Lou saying two of his colleagues told him they heard I had said I intended to assist Greeks on return to Cefalonia, that he was sure it was false but begged me to send him word so that he might have my authority to contradict it. I hope you and George will find my letter what I wish it, respectful, open, but not submissive, or saying I will be good, I will be good. As to the Greek Committee I felt no cause to spare them or to suffer from them. I have reason to think Bowring and Hume tried to show me up because I caught at their goings on; if so they will have *manqué leur coup* . . . The reasons why I was disgusted in the fullest sense of the word were:

1. They sent water-colours, trumpets, fine drapes, to fight the Turks.
2. They tried to make a show of helping the Greeks when good sense pointed to the propriety of doing all they could, without show.
3. They commit their affairs to such men as Bowring and Blanquière, miserable wretches unfit for such work.
4. I could see dirty works going on about the loan. [In this Charles was all too right.]

"These and many more things excite contempt", and if Em was still at Bowood and had "any confab with Lord Lansdowne about the committee", she was at liberty to say all this to him.

Yes, his letter told Bathurst, when in London he had been asked to go as Commissioner for the Greek loan and had refused, as being on full pay; "and to say the truth what I saw of the Greek Committee so disgusted me that from that time I never had more to say to them. Since then I have been offered a high command in the Greek army by the Greek deputies. My answer was—that I could not accept their offer unless they made it worth my while to quit the British army. The Greeks as I expected refused: but that I could ever think of becoming a sort of concealed agent for the Greeks as Resident of Cephalonia, your lordship has done me but justice in believing to be false."

When he left his post early in the year, Charles continued to Bathurst, he had promised Byron and Mavrocordato "to be of what service I could in explaining the real state of Greece to the Committee in London. I saw and heard this famous committee—from any further connection with which the Lord deliver me, though I feel for many individuals comprising it the highest respect and regard. As for the Greek deputies, I have for Orlando a personal friendship, and I mean to continue it." If the government wanted to, they might replace him at Cephalonia and he would not argue, nor recant any of his expressed opinions. "No. With respect to the Greeks as a nation, I admire the people, their courage, and their cause, but no soldier can indulge his opinions at the expense of his duties", and in this case opinion and duty coincided. Whatever help individuals could bring by enlisting for Greece, he believed that official neutrality was best for her as well as for England; since to become the cockpit of great powers still at odds would be worse even than her present state. (Did he remember how in the 1770s the Empress Catherine II of Russia had encouraged a rising in the Morea, sending an expedition under the brothers Orloff and then recalling it as soon as they had set foot ashore, thus leaving the Greeks defenceless before a sustained and terrible burst of Turkish vengeance?) There were no further communications upon this subject from Bathurst.

Here was a blank wall; he was cut off from the only source of supplies, guns, pay for troops. And Charles was no longer the free-lance who had stravagued round Greece in 1820 and 1821, dreaming and planning her victory. He now had Anastasia; he now had their daughters Susan and Emily. And not for all the noble sentiments in London was Charles prepared to lead an army into Greece to be chopped in pieces amongst the stony hills when their bullets ran out. Pay and ammunition for his men must rely on well-organized supplies, on something stronger than Baker Street nostalgia for the ringing plains of windy Troy. Now, before Turkey swung into effective action, would have been the moment to free Greece. Charles could, of course, have snapped his fingers at officialdom and cast his commission to the winds; but he had been turned down by the Greek Committee in London. Byron had lost credit with them; he had served his purpose in drawing attention to their project and in sailing for Greece. Other schemes were in mind.

"There can be little doubt", Harold Nicolson mournfully concludes, "that had Napier's services been accepted by the Greek

Committee the protracted misery of the Greek War of Independence would have been curtailed by several years."

At Missolonghi, increasingly disappointed and unwell, Byron might despair of himself, but he did not despair of Greece. All she needed were a few practical but dedicated men. "He frequently repeated that with Napier to command and form regular troops, with Hastings to arm and command a steamer, and with an able financier, Greece would be sure of victory", Finlay heard from those who had been with him in these last months.

Byron's Greek allies were melting with the deepening of winter. Most of the Greek fleet returned to its base at Hydra: the five Spetsiot ships shortly did likewise. The young philhellenes, the shoals of amiable enthusiasts who had swarmed to Greece in Byron's wake and who floated into Missolonghi from time to time, instantly succumbed to stomach troubles and drifted away to the safety of British Zante again, to dose themselves with calomel and drink restoring cups of tea. After weeks of delay the foreign technicians arrived and were immediately shot—one of them fatally—in quarrels with the Suliots. A Swede called Sass had his arm chopped off and was mortally riddled by bullets; the remaining six, discouraged, left for Zante at the first opportunity. "They are good men enough," Byron commented, in a last gallant piece of flippancy, "but do not quite understand the little discrepancies in these countries, and are not used to see shooting and slashing as a part of housekeeping."

Riding through the olive trees, as he waited for their arrival, Byron had had moments of hope and inspiration—

The Sword, the Banner, and the Field,
Glory and Greece, around me see!

But still the rain fell, with tropical force, the evil smells assaulted his nostrils, the town's garbage nudged disconsolately to and fro in the tideless lagoon.

The land of honourable death
Is here:

he continued prophetically. His ally, Colonel Leicester Stanhope, undeterred by the fact that hardly anyone in Greece could read, was busy editing the *Greek Chronicle*, full to bursting with the pure milk of Benthamism. Stanhope was coming to feel that Byron himself was unsound on this doctrine, and moved further east, where Odysseus, most brigandish of all the Greek leaders, soon claimed his support by his spectacularly warlike aspect and intelligent flattery, and prepared an assault on Byron's gold by summoning the poet to a conference at Salona.

Charles had told Trelawney that he thought no-one should attempt the liberation of Greece without "two European regiments, money in hand to pay them and a portable gallows". As a young soldier in Spain during the terrible retreat to Corunna, Charles had seen Sir John Moore, most humane of men, string up one of his soldiers in front of his assembled army for robbing and killing a Spanish civilian, thereby doubtless saving the lives of many more. With his gallows Charles had hoped to stop or at least discourage the torture and slaughter of prisoners, women and children, by both sides, that horribly accompanied the war in Greece. But at Missolonghi there was only a scattering of trained soldiers, no disciplined army, no gallows; and even Byron's money was running low under the unceasing demands. Under the unceasing quarrels his spirits ran lower still.

By February the Lepanto garrison had been bribed to the necessary pitch and all seemed ripe for the town's fall, when a revolt among the Suliots, engineered from afar by Odysseus, who feared a Mavrocordato success, put paid to this hopeful possibility. Trelawney was away in Athens, collecting a harem and a fourteen-year-old wife, and up to no good in other directions. Surrounded by the dubious or the incompetent, upset by the food and depressed by the climate, Byron became more apprehensive. Debilitated survivors from the German Brigade, the small band of Prussians who had joined from the Morea, held fast and unhelpfully to their military etiquette. Parry, the English artillery expert, when at last he arrived, proved both drunken and inexpert, and there was no coal to engender the necessary heat to fire his rockets; but at least he was practical and friendly and took on Charles's function of making Byron laugh.

When the London Committee's supplies were finally landed, it was a feast day and the Greeks piously refused to handle them: they lay spoiling under the relentless rain till Byron himself started shifting them to cover. A Turkish brig piled up on the shore under their noses, but the forces of liberation failed even to capture this. A miasma of damp and gloom, of friction and failure, rose up from the lagoon and hung over the town. A deputation from the citizens of Missolonghi crowded in on Byron begging him to supply the money to repair their city walls.

By March the gathering hopelessness and failure, the pressure of so many conflicting wills, had brought on a fit which added to Byron's increasing illness. Pale, distraught, but still gallant, he rode out for the last time to reassure the local populace, for the Turkish fleet and some disaffected Suliots were menacing the town. In brightly-coloured liveries, his escort clattered after him; plumes waved, gold-mounted pistols shone; but now Byron's green velvet jacket hung loosely upon his shoulders.

His manservant, the imperturbable and devoted Fletcher, became worried. "My Lord may be very odd," he had said of Byron, "but he has such a good heart." Spasms of nervous irritation and of apprehension shook the poet. He was begged by friends in Cephalonia and Zante to return to their houses and recuperate. "I am extremely obliged but I cannot quit Greece while there is a chance of my being of any (even supposed) utility. There is a stake worth millions such as I am, and while I can stand at all I must stand by the cause."

By mid-April he could no longer stand, and his inexperienced doctors, terrified too late, crowded round his bed insisting upon bleeding him, while the rain lashed along the yellow marshes of Missolonghi and beat on the darkening windowpanes of Byron's upper rooms. No assaults on the Turks had been mounted, and their forces were gathering in preparation for the winter mud to dry off and make attack possible. Letters from Hobhouse in London, cheering and encouraging Byron, telling him that his books were selling in their thousands, that his money troubles were over for ever, that London was ringing with his praises, that support for the Cause was pouring in—letters that might perhaps a fortnight earlier have saved Byron's life, arrived in Missolonghi after he finally lost consciousness. He died late on Easter Sunday, while storm lashed the waters of the Gulf of Patras, and thunder boomed along the hills; and while the kind Greeks restrained themselves from letting off their seasonal *feu de joie*, lest it should disturb his dying moments. "I wish", he had said, shortly before speech failed him, "that Napier and Hobhouse were here: we would soon settle the business."

But Napier was in London, waiting in ante-rooms and being decisively turned away. Byron had done all that he could do, which was to die. And a remarkably efficacious move it turned out to be, in the end.

The Greek loan arrived at Zante a few days after Byron's death. Stanhope, still founding Benthamite schools in the teeth of the odds, and ever more delighted with his jovial cut-throat friend Odysseus —writing home about "his nobleness of soul to pursue the public good"—had even handed over the Greek Committee's guns to Odysseus, who delightedly fortified himself with them in a cave up Mount Parnassus, from whence he was able to harass his fellow-countrymen with impunity. (It was upon Stanhope and *his* commission that the government had agreed to turn a blind eye.) In May his heady course was cut short: he was ordered home by Canning. The Byron brigade and the Greek Committee's attempt had been as little use in securing Greece's freedom as had any other.

Charles was justified; but bitterly sad. So far he had done nothing for Greece but to shelter, encourage, and advise Byron, whose gallant course and whose devotion had been in vain; and had succeeded only in a thorough alienation of his employers at the Horse Guards and at the Colonial Office. He had been too "impetuous and violent" for them; and not impetuous and violent enough for Greece.

Impetuous he might be; but he knew also how to bide his time.

CHAPTER III

Cephalonia

"A too easy chair is the rack for me", Charles had always felt; and his island gave him joy and activity enough; furthermore, "power is never disagreeable". He rose at four, worked till noon after a light breakfast, bathed, rode out to superintend the works in hand all over the island, dined whenever he returned. The new harbour mole was nearing completion, the warehouses were ready, and "my market-place is roofed—one step. My lazaretto almost finished—two steps." Then there was a porticoed court of justice, with police headquarters, treasury, and prison added on—"I found men kennelled like dogs . . . the idea of humanity in imprisonment is an unknown one . . . When you who are an architect in your heart", he told his mother, "recollect my Lennox blood, and how it loves building, you will call me a good fellow for wishing to give up all this for going home to you." He had sent old Marshal Soult a Suliot sword, in gratitude for French chivalry so long ago, after Corunna. The Secretary of War at home, rather less chivalrously, was trying to prove that Charles had received double pay for the year 1806, though of course he had not, and they couldn't even produce the vouchers: he was having the best of three rounds with them.

The roads were over the Black Mountains now, and joining up the isolated valleys whence feudal chiefs had so recently ridden in bands to terrorize the law courts and execute frontier justice. John Kennedy, the sapper, was his right hand; practical, able, forever on the job, and humane to all who worked under him. Gradients were his sole weakness—"John Kennedy, a constant slope for 25 miles will not do. You have but one fault; you would keep a horse on the drag for 25 miles." But on all other counts, "if ever man or woman differ from John Kennedy they are wrong". Charles worked eighteen hours a day, and did his stint of shovelling on the roads, his dark short-sighted eyes blazing with energy; but failed to complete this task. "I would rather", he said twenty-two years later, when he had become a national hero, "have finished the roads of Cephalonia than have fought Austerlitz or Waterloo."

As a ruler he was extremely arbitrary, especially where he considered that bullying was going on. Often enough, it was: even philhellene Byron described the mainland Greeks, if not the islanders, as "an intriguing cunning unquiet generation". Charles admitted that he hated a master: his confidence in his own powers made him rarely afraid of being one. Justice and order, fisheries, plantations, commerce, every aspect of island life engrossed his interest, came under his organizing northern energy. "The only things that bore me are the church and convent affairs, excepting a beautiful nun of sixteen who dislikes being one very much, and I have blowed up her old devil of an aunt, the abbess, for making her one. Nay more! I told the girl's friends that if she would run away with her handsome young Greek, I would, as head of the Church, stand between them and all harm." No coercion of the helpless; "damnable coercion", as he said later in connection with Ireland.

"I have stopped a massacre of the Jews here, all prepared for the love of Jesus! The Greeks have in consequence called me the King of the Jews, and say the latter gave me twelve thousand dollars for protection. Would it were true." The Orthodox Church was a bully sometimes; but all the same he planted a long avenue of trees up to the church and monastery of St Gerasimo, a mile long and sixty feet wide, and joined in the saint's fiesta, and gave money. The Greeks assured him that he would be under the protection of the saint—"I hope he will treat me as a gentleman should."

All this activity perhaps took a toll. It was during these years that Charles felt the first pangs of the liver disease that was to kill him. The Corunna crack on the head gave him pain still, and his Busaco wound in the jaw a nervous facial twitch, occasional pangs, and suffocating feelings from time to time in his nasal passage. A bullet wound in the leg had not improved the lameness he had acquired in a childish accident. With these wounds, though they made him impetuous and irritable, he had come to terms: the liver pains were something new, and aggravated his intractable nature. On his return to Greece through Germany in the spring of 1824 his malaise is reflected in his comments on the Germans, for he was not a man given to racial hatreds. "The scenery exceeds in beauty any I ever saw except in Greece. As to the people of every part of Germany, honour to Caesar for killing so many of them. Stupid, slow, hard animals, they have not even so much tact as to cheat well . . . in Italy we found civilized beings, warm weather, and the human face instead of the German visage." All that could be allowed to them was their good treatment of their horses. Even the Venetians, bar their pleasant women, were "filthy, proud, insolent, and jealous". But Italians in general "suit me better, roguish enough, but merry, saucy, pleasant, laughing fellows, who if they do cheat you serve you at least, and don't sulk: a German is all sulk, and does nothing for you". Venice was too fine an old lady to be devoured by Germans, he thought. "It is sad to see such gorgeous palaces dropping stone by stone into the sea from which they seem to have sprung by magic." Emily had been wrong to think Charles could do any good in a job on the Rhine—"The Germans thwart all measures of improvement as specifically bad in themselves." But he thought the Emperor of Austria was a good and able man, and was against "the people who abuse these august personages, the very knots which tie social order together and save us from every horrible act that wild men would introduce". Change, yes; revolution, no. "Yet how he can see this magnificent city undermined and decaying is incomprehensible."

Best of all was to be back in Corfu among "the merry Greeks who are worth all other nations put together. I like to see, to hear them; I like their fun, their good humour, their Paddy ways, for they are very like Irishmen. As to cleanliness they cannot brag. Yet they are cleaner than the Italians and don't love dirt like the Venetians. They only suffered it out of politeness when the last were their masters, and are now leaving it off out of compliment to us. All their bad habits are Venetian; their wit, their eloquence, their good nature are their own . . . I am enjoying their good company, their fine climate, their pretty scenery, liking them and all belonging to them, and wishing all belonging to me were here. No, not here, in Corfu but in Cephalonia, which is so dear to me that every hour not employed to do her good seems wasted."

For diversion there was, however, Guilford, whom Byron had called that mad Fred North. "He is here again and very pleasant; we go to Cephalonia together. He goes about dressed up like Plato, with a gold band round his mad pate, and flowing drapery of a purple hue." Charles had been home on leave, to have a crack at the London Greek Committee to agree his terms for going to Greece and had once again drawn a blank, and been obliged to occupy himself by writing, and a course of study on the new Poor Law. Now he was reluctantly accepting a pause in Corfu for a commission on the last administration.

"I told you my opinion of Sir F. Adam before I left England, two months in his house confirms it completely. The more I see of Rudsdale the more I like him and think highly of him, and of Lord Sydney Osborne I think the same. You may guess how much I am annoyed at being detained here over this commission, which presents a scene of knavery beyond all I ever witnessed; so much for old Tom's knowledge of government for it is quite disgraceful to him. I do not think he got money himself by it, but the existence of such doings damns him as ruler because he must have known of them." Old Tom had dropped dead of apoplexy in January of 1824, and the Greeks and Ionians, according to Thomas Gordon, "crowded the churches to return thanks to Heaven". But "old Tom was a rock", Charles wrote later, "and Adam like the Goodwin Sands".

"What plagues me most", Charles grumbled on, "is that these two months past and May are just the great working months in these climes and I lose them; for my works don't go on well I hear at Cef. On the contrary, very slow and in a boggling way. The fact is all that Kennedy and I did seems quite easy and plain, but those who perceive its simplicity do not take into their consideration the constant labour we had to keep things at work. Since I left, the courts of Law have been going all wrong, giving Party sentences, martial law has been proclaimed, houses burnt, and the troops sent into the villages at free quarters; and the road making flags, and 40 soldiers have died.

"Now I do not say that all this might not have happened had I been there," he went on to Emily, "I only say it did not . . . The eye of the Chief is everything, and therefore if the Chief don't ride he cannot at any time tell how matters get on", and he knew that Sir Charles Sutton and "poor Wright" never mounted their horses.

"My bottom fairly itches to get on poor Turk's back again. (scusi, signora). My cow is dead: Sir Humphrey Davy's brother attended her tenderly; he is just come from Cef., I like him much. He has found two strong sulphur springs there, so if you get the itch my dear come to your kingdom.

"I work at my Greek here which is my only comfort—pity me when a Greek verb is all my solace." He deplored his badness at languages. "It is a gift, like music. This state of society now produces such great intercourse between nations that two or three modern languages are absolutely necessary . . . Sir F. Adam and I are at issue on the subject of a loan which he is going to raise in England. I think it a most pernicious measure, like drinking it may produce a momentary appearance of strength, which will be immediately succeeded by proportionate weakness of finance." And what the devil did everybody think they were at to promote Lord Forbes, who had never seen a shot fired in anger, to be C.-in-C. in Scotland? As to Focqueville, the French consul at Athens and his writings, "I thought him a namby-pamby antiquarian without genius and full of fiddle-faddle; but I only saw him for half an hour when he was a little god among travellers, but remember I was a traveller and all travellers are liars." The affable Sir Frederick Adam may have felt a certain relief when the commission ended and Charles departed for Cephalonia.

Back in his cherished island he told Emily on June 4th after a brief letter that he was "too full of my new quarry, my new road and my poor people who are in great want of food just now to lose more time in jaw". The poor peasants seemed to him to be too hungry for heavy labour under "the accursed corvée that pains my heart. This *angheria* is very bad. Yet without it the roads could not be made, and the peasants themselves would suffer more than any, they alone live in the country, and each is a small landowner, drawing every necessary of life from Argostoli. Strange as it may appear, the Cephalonians get even their vegetables from the capital. Daily comes the poor man from the most distant parts to buy, when he has garden ground lying waste round his cabin."

At Argostoli he found that Blanco, who had come round by sea, had arrived safely—"my good old beast". Blanco, his white arab horse, intelligent and handsome but a choosey eater, had been with him in the Peninsular War, and now, over twenty years old, was keen as ever. About eight thousand people had been at the quayside to cheer Charles on landing—"How lucky it was not for my execution; these things are all accidental and equally entertaining for the spectators"—and there had been welcoming dinners and dances at Luxuri and Argostoli, where Charles had much enjoyed the Greek way of feeding the poor whenever the gentry feasted, an old and good custom. A new Greek bishop had been appointed, "an excellent pious man who formerly lived by sheep-stealing which he now calls his pastoral life". When the bishop solemnly assured Charles that the

Emperor Justinian wrote the Code Napoleon out of friendship for Buonaparte because they had been at school together, Charles was quite unable to resist telling him that "an ancestor of mine had been sent to Jerusalem to teach logarithms to the architect who built Solomon's temple". There was a remnant of truth in Charles's myth: a sixteenth-century forbear of his, John Napier, had in fact invented logarithms. The bishop was comforted to find he had twice the governor's pay.

A letter from home telling Charles that his cousin Seymour Bathurst—"as good as he looks"—was to be married, turned his mind to his own deteriorating appearance: he wondered, as he looked in the glass of a morning, how such a villainous looking fellow was trusted with a razor. He was, he thought, a moral well-meaning man; but "so thin, so sharp, so black, so Jewish, so rascally, such a knavish looking son of a gun". Dr Wolff, afterwards a famous missionary in the Hindu Kush area, and shipwrecked on Cephalonia on his way east, came, all the same, under Charles's spell. He was amazed by the Resident's first appearance, limping, black-avised, and jerking nervously from his two worst wounds, "with convulsive eyes and shoulders, fire-flashing glances, and a pleasant countenance".

"I shall send you victuals and you can do just what you like", Charles had shouted at him through the bars of the lazaretto where Wolff was quarantined. "We don't wish to catch the plague, though it's all humbug."

"I shall come tomorrow with the Jews and Greeks to whom you may preach", this eccentric figure next informed Wolff. "You may tell them that there is no difference between Jew and Greek, they are both rogues alike. If you cannot convert them they shall get a damned licking." Wolff, amazed, and uncertain whether or not he was being teased by the formidable colonel, reproved him for his oaths. "I deserve it; I swear like a trooper."

When Wolff emerged from quarantine Charles had him to stay, and when the missionary left the island a month or two later he had conceived an extraordinary admiration for his host. Charles had, he thought, "divine mission". "The greatest man whom not only England but all nations have for centuries had", he recorded in his book.

Divine or otherwise, Charles's mission appeared to be taking shape. The Greek cause was not prospering. The disasters, which as Charles had foreseen, alone would unite them, had magnified upon the Greek forces. "Poor Stanhope was not adapted to meet all the deceit and humbug practised upon him"; Hamilton Browne had written to Charles in May of 1824, in answer to a question from him about the best modern Greek dictionary, for Charles was already hard at work trying to master the language. "I never anticipated much from him in Greece", Browne went on; "I begin to sweat about the loan and its appropriation: Lord Byron dead! Stanhope coming home! and only the sapient humbugging and humbugged Mr Blaquiere left in Greece—this is really melancholy; had it been put in proper hands the loan ought to have fitted out an army sufficient to assume the offensive, and consolidated the Civil Government a little"; as it was, he feared the money would be frittered away on promises rather than on performances. He wished the Committee would agree Charles's terms—"I should then look with confidence to some brilliant results."

The Greek Committee had lost hope of these; at least from the Greeks themselves. "With regard to the Deputies I consider it perfect loss of time to have any more to do with them as all our labour for the past two years on behalf of Greece is rendered comparatively useless by their conduct", Hume mourned to Charles on September 15th. "To get them to do anything on our advice proves fruitless and unavailing." Charles wasted no tears over him; he had asked Hume's advice about iron bridges, and been introduced by him to the manufacturer Galloway. He referred to both as sons of bitches and decided he had never met "two men who pleased me less than these two knaves" on short acquaintance. Hume and his colleague Ellice in the end made considerable fortunes out of the Greek loan; while Hamilton Browne, sent as one of the commissioners to negotiate the terms on which the English gold should be handed over to the Greek authorities, found that it had all meanwhile sunk without trace into the fissures of the Greek mainland.

Gold from Britain continued to pour into Nauplion, where its chief effect was to enrich the Hydriot sailors to such a pitch that they no longer felt so keen to go to sea to fight and plunder the Turks, who had recently ravaged Crete and two other Greek islands, murdering or enslaving vast numbers of their populations. Since their resounding defeat of a Turkish army in 1823, the mainland Greeks had been mostly occupied in fighting each other: the villages of the Morea having been more effectively destroyed by fellow-countrymen than by Turks. On shore, Greek warriors spent their share of English gold in dressing up, "in all the splendour of brigand life, fluttering about in rich Albanian habilments, refulgent with brilliant and unused arms", George Finlay recorded. Those higher up the pay scale salted down their share into western banks.

A terrible retribution was on its way. In February of 1825 Ibrahim Pasha of Egypt, allied to Turkey, landed at Modon, one of the fortresses in the Morea which Charles had vainly urged the Maniotes to reduce, and soon won for himself a secure base at Navarino. "The Greeks are going to hell at a hand gallop" Charles miserably reported; and on May 25th he told William how badly things went for them—"Eighteen thousand drilled Egyptians and Turks have taken Navarino"—Navarino, that the squabbling capitani should so long ago have reduced when the Morea was all but in their hands. Ibrahim was backed by a large, well-equipped, and disciplined army, mainly led by French officers, before which, in spite of immense individual gallantry, the Greeks repeatedly broke and fled, until by summer's end Ibrahim was triumphant over almost all the Morea. In June the Greek leaders in their desperation had offered to place themselves under the rule of Great Britain in exchange for protection: the offer was refused. Ibrahim, finding that the Greeks, in spite of his initial mercies, were still exterminating prisoners, began to do likewise with the unmarketable captives; and Turkish ships sailing east groaned under the weight of their thousands of enslaved Greeks. Central Greece, with each chieftain concerned only with hanging on to his own area, stayed neutral; Odysseus opted back into the Turkish fold; descending from the north Albanian and Turkish forces laid siege once more to Missolonghi both by land and sea.

On September 14th, 1825 Charles's long-awaited summons came —"The Greeks have offered to place me at the head of their army." For once, at long last, in their desperation, they had all agreed; Mavrocordato, Colocotronis, Odysseus (soon to be murdered), "the whole of the capitani have joined in the invitation . . . 'Greece expects you and wishes for you.' " Such a call came not simply from Byron's recommendation and from Charles's own deep desire; it fell on his ears like a summons from Greece itself. To be a free-lance on the mainland, with enough money to pay his soldiers, enough bullets to prime their guns, enough organization to free a tortured country from its enslavers! His hour had come. He had now but to seize it.

But the responsibility he felt towards those who fought under him was equalled by a besetting care for those he loved.

As a bachelor, now in his early forties, Charles was in no position to drag his feet on account of family ties. But he was an odd sort of bachelor. All his life Charles had been a lover of women, in the word's most spacious sense. Throughout his first forty years he had adored his mother: throughout his remaining thirty he would adore his daughters. Female company was to him a necessity and a delight. He had met the love of his life when he was twenty-two, and found her unable to marry him. In his long absences the needs of the flesh were met by others; to date he had waited for her for twenty-one years. The epoch demanded great emotional stamina: engagements of fifteen years were not unusual: a five-year engagement was brief. Love was, and had to be, a long-distance runner.

His sisters, his sisters-in-law, and even their sisters, came into the picture. Louisa Bunbury, sister of William's Caroline, wrote him long letters, cheered him, told him how she was bringing up her sons, and how much she wanted them to meet him. With William's Caroline and with Richard's Anne he was on terms of long affection and intimacy. With women no guards were up, no thistly dignity intervened. His half-sister Louisa, sole survivor of the yellow fever that had killed the other three small children of his father's first marriage, was seven years older than he was: with her he was affectionate, concerned, teasing, mocking, and made her feel at least seven years younger. His love for his full sister Emily, his junior by only eleven months, was of a warmth that the cool-hearted 1970s would look on as extremely soppy, if not downright incestuous. But what his many letters did for Emily, lame with rheumatism, living alone in a small house in Dawlish and teaching one of George's little motherless daughters, may be imagined. To Charles at least she was important, charming, interesting, and loved. He took her into his confidence about his adored Elizabeth, "Mrs. K. at Cookham". If Emily was sexually starved she rollicked along on a full diet of emotion and understanding. A few years later she married: probably Charles's lavish affection had stopped her turning into an old maid. "I have no measure for my love of our family", he had written to Emily from Bermuda in great loneliness.

Love had had its short runs in Charles's life as well. He had not inherited his father's handsome looks, but he had his fair share of the charm with which his mother had cut great swathes through the manhood of Dublin, London, and Paris. At fifteen he had been ADC to General Duff at Limerick; seduced by the housemaid, he had thereafter enjoyed a run with the Limerick girls, whom he described delightedly as the prettiest and wickedest in the world. On the virtue side there had been pretty Miss Massey and Miss Vandeleur, saying Pig will you marry me and dressing up at dusk in men's greatcoats to come and visit him in bed with a broken leg; and Lady Duff, whom he adored and who continued to divert him with long amusing letters after he had left to join his regiment. In Sussex had been fascinating and imperious Miss Gage, at Shorncliff finely shaped Miss Robb, and a devastating twenty-two-year-old widow. "I am a determined rake in love with four misses at once" he wrote home. In Guernsey had been the excessively entertaining Miss Carters, and Miss X with the best legs in the island. "My heart is a cinder", Charles would complain; and "I go about all fire, the devil himself is not more flaming." No comments on the Spanish ladies; though he and his brother George had run two planks together and crossed the Lisbon street four storeys high for the company of two twittering Portuguese girls in a house on the other side. In the troop transport on the passage to Bermuda he had had a cabin next to poor pretty Mrs Steele when she spent the night having a baby with the maximum of difficulty: so thin was the partition that, apart from seeing, he might have been present throughout: it opened his mind still wider to the pains and perils of women, and deepened his sympathy; especially when her stupid husband had hoped, rather mincingly, that he hadn't been disturbed? To spare the wife's nineteenth-century blushes Charles swore he had slept throughout, and she had burst into tears with relief.

In Bermuda were radiant Mrs Byng, a darling of an American, clever, agreeable Mrs Horsford, and sweet and pretty Mrs Butler. In Charles's large lustrous eyes (that were his most striking feature) charm and appeal were everywhere; and it is probable that he named but a few. In youth all, or nearly all, was grist that came to his mill, and quite a lot was grist that didn't.

From Bermuda, too, at thirty, Charles had tried to explain to his sister Emily what it was about fast women—"no jaws, miss!"—that gripped him. "You allow she is cute, and she is; a needle. She is dashing which is exactly the reason I like her, because I think dashing women the most agreeable for acquaintance at least for soldiers; as to loving them that is quite out of the question, but then they are beautiful and flirts for that very reason, and have a very pleasant and entertaining turn for their lovers. This lady I really do like because she liked me *first*, and because she and another beloved were most civil and kind to me, and because she is witty and read Tom Moore's book through before she would eat or sleep—she's a good fellow and a good soldier." His greatest wish, he had told Em earlier, was for a wife and a home. Bermuda was claustrophobic and was driving him wild; he couldn't get to grips with either his family or his enemies, "but if I had a wife to torment I should be very well satisfied anywhere".

His will, dated at this time, on June 2nd, 1813, is very characteristic, and made in case the Americans turned out to be better shots than the French had been. His father's weapons of war were for "my beloved brothers": they were what he and they valued most. Otherwise he owned nearly nothing; but there was something for everybody, with a joke and a loving message. It is a document full of flippant asides and oaths, and probably quite illegal, but it is also brimming with a thoughtful tenderness. To his loved aunt, Lady Louisa Conolly of Castletown, who had everything in the world except a child, he left "my bairns if I have any"; for Susan Frost, who had been his nanny, there was a little pension and his dear love and gratitude. The life-interest on every other penny he owned was for "my most beloved friend Elizabeth Kelly", the capital eventually for his sisters Lou and Emm. To the dear family friend Anne Staples, who was a young widow mourning the loss of her only child and who must not be troubled with any redundant emotions, there was a keepsake—"for Anne who I love as much as it is possible to love any woman without being in love with them".

For years now he had longed for the continuous company of a dearly loved woman, but Elizabeth Kelly the deserted wife, the one he irretrievably loved, was placed by law and belief beyond his reach. It was a situation that had no foreseeable end; that might endure for ever. Hence his setting up on Cephalonia in a kind of near-marriage with Anastasia. He knew it was wrong; but that knowledge had not been strong enough to stop him, a fallible human being with long deferred hopes and strong sexual drives.

How did it go with his Greek love, Anastasia? Never kiss and tell: and this ordinarily open man was concerned to cover up the traces from later Victorian scrutiny for the sake of Susan and Emily. One of Susan's daughters, late in life, questioned her mother, with a wish to elucidate the mystery; and was instantly shushed. All that is sure is that Charles loved Anastasia; that she was beautiful after a wild fashion, laughing, and temperamental. She is thought to have loved but refused to marry him; if indeed he asked her, which is unlikely. She is known to have left him, known to have died young. For the rest of his life, and perhaps after it, Charles supported her relations. Where or when she and Charles met, or if he set up house for her, or visited her in her parental one, is unknown. Her rages were excessive, her laughter entranced him: she bequeathed some of both to her innumerable descendants. The charm, the flashing dark eyes, the liveliness, could have come also from Charles: physically they were two of a kind.

Why, if indeed he asked her, did she refuse to marry him? She was, it is said, extremely proud and patriotic, and Charles as British Resident was in her island in the role of occupying power. Maybe she preferred life on her beautiful home ground to an unknown existence at Cheltenham with an incalculable half-pay colonel and an entourage of fogs and heretics—the Greeks are no-one's fools. When he left for England on leave she refused to come with him, refused to let the little girls go, and finally pushed them out to sea alone in a small boat at a headland where she knew his ship must pass; from which perilous position they were rescued by a fisherman and returned safely to Charles.

Anything helpless and female could quickly have Charles in the hollow of its hand: he was quite unable to resist these two little daughters; henceforth his life was directed towards making them happy and secure. Susan-Sarah and Emily-Cephalonia, bright-eyed, curly-haired, delightedly laughing at his jokes and climbing on his knees, were to hamstring Charles from the liberation of Greece and precipitate him to India and thence to the conquest of Sind. He was no longer the free-lance who had come to Greece in 1819.

But until Anastasia finally launched his two daughters right into his life, Charles perhaps felt more concern than love. The two people nearest to his heart in 1825 were "Mrs. K." and his sister Emily. There was a wide world that Anastasia could not share with him and that these two could; Elizabeth Kelly his good angel; and Emily "so pretty and so pleasant", and yet sharing the wild and romantic side to his nature and an equal spirit of adventure. Charles cursed her lameness and longed to show her Cephalonia. Perhaps only Harry, who had been in the Navy, Charles wrote, knew what these long separations from a beloved family were like; to pass years away from the people one loved needed more courage than going into battle. He felt particularly melancholy on fine summer evenings without female company—"Any woman won't do, it must be one I love and who admires this beautiful world, who devours with unsatiated appetite the sea, the rocks, the sky, the trees, the colours in all their brilliance.

"I love a tree very well, but I would never be content without the mountains and sea . . . The heat is not overwhelming [it was June], 80°, and the air so pure, so dry, so transparent that one seems to breathe without the help of one's lungs." Their sister-in-law Anne had written to Emily deploring her age (she was a few years older than Richard). "Anne ought to have married me and we would have had wrinkle for wrinkle; tell her she had better marry me now and we will pass Dick off for our son and give him cake on Sunday."

He was floating in a caïque in Argostoli's beautiful harbour. "The band is playing on the shore, the harbour like a looking-glass, the rocks and mountains all reflected in it. The sun has dropped behind the nearby mountains, its reflection for an instant throwing a red gleam on the broad expanse of water, the whole colouring so soft, yet so brilliant and so warm, while the music seems mixed with the scene and one almost fears to breathe as it floats along, rising and falling on the ears, while the hum of the city gives life to the wild scenery about, without bringing human nature too close . . .

"Is it on a poor devil like me that the good of 50,000 people is to depend?" He felt anxious, ruffled—"I see so much to do, so much that I leave undone . . . both mind and body become fatigued towards evening and it is then I so want a person I love, to join in all my feelings." So much of his life had to be "punish, punish, punish . . . obliged to isolate myself and harden every feeling", that his longing to give rein to loving feelings became unbearably great. It was "bad to indurate the heart, for after all religion, morality, everything, is reduced to kindness of heart, without that the other two cannot exist . . . Whatever portion of it a man may possess he must lose most of it as a ruler; it is impossible to be a judge and not grow hardened—if you were here you would see . . ." and he started talking to Em about Elizabeth.

*

Such was his state when next month came Mavrocordato's letter. Would he accept command of the liberation forces in Greece—"Cette nouvelle carrière digne de votre vertu et de vos talents? Votre conduite admirable par laquelle vous avez su combiner dans le moment très difficile vos devoirs d'employé d'un gouvernment neutre avec les impulsions de votre âme généreuse, les hauts talents militaire qui vous ont placés parmi les officiers les plus distingués de votre nation, ont depuis longtemps attiré sur votre personne l'attention de la nation Grecque, et fait naitre dans la coeur de tous les Hellènes le désir aussi ardent que sincere de se voir guidé par vous á les champs d'honneur . . ."

"Allow me credit for good resolution when I stood firm against this letter", Charles begged Emily; "it cost me a bitter gulp. Am I a fool? Am I coward without enterprise? I know the Greek character and unless I go with money on which to live independent I can do no good to them and great evil to myself. The first is what guides me, I have little care for the second as I can always dig, but I can't do good as an adventurer." He had now seen the failure of too many missions in Greece.

"But I do feel pride, I own it." The Greeks had put their future in his hands, the hands of an obscure soldier. Emily and "another" would join him in his feelings. He had sent the Greeks his essential terms and must wait. "Meanwhile I try to do well where I am placed and where much is to be done. Do not show Mavro's letter except to George and Henry, Dick and Anne. Podge [William] would talk of it which I want to avoid." And would Emily copy it and send to Mrs. K.?

Colocotronis had offered to serve under him—"All I want is that if I do go I may have Feb and March quiet to form troops so that Ibrahim Pasha may not give me a thrust ere I am in the saddle." "All is nearly arranged, Henry will tell you more", he wrote later in the month of July. "I am to be uncontrolled head of everything military." The dream of a lifetime looked, at long last, like turning into reality.

But his task in the island did not, in the meantime, obligingly ease off. "I am in high war with my judges", he reported to Emily in August. He overruled them sometimes, but how not? "Proceedings are carried on in the Italian language, and peasants, speaking only Greek, hear their lives or deaths discussed without comprehending a word. All the wretch knows is that his lawyer turns round at last and tells him he is to be hanged. The horror of this can only fully be estimated by those who know the virulence of faction in these islands . . . Sixty-five peasants perjured themselves in one day to take the life of a prisoner, innocent but belonging to another faction. Perjury flourishes so that the social order is nearly destroyed . . . clans swear their clansmen through any difficulty." He thought an entirely new system was necessary: meanwhile, undoubtedly, he dictated. "There are very few Greeks who would not assassinate the head of his own party for a dollar: they are to be pitied for this demoralization, but it is a fact to be guarded against, though not to be cast in their teeth."

His plans went on. "I have a docks in my head when we get more advanced." But the pull of mainland Greece and her miseries was stronger. "Egyptians cut 700 families' throats in one place", he heard in August. "Mavro has no power. I have been ill with a deal of gripes"; but he had been up in the Black Mountains looking after his plantations of trees there, and seeing that the goats were really being kept out; and the spectacle of the Turkish fleet, viewed from there, sweeping through the seas that once Greek courage had held, made him feel low-spirited. He seized on every crumb of information about Ibrahim Pasha, with whom he hoped soon to be at grips—"Ibrahim is bold, fierce, sensible, obstinate; if he rushes to run his head against a post he does so without calculations as to the comparative resistance of wood and skull."

The gripes were over, and with a good swim every day, he felt very well. And the Greeks now consented to his terms. On September 14th he sent William a copy of the terms he had agreed with the Greek Government; which were the same as he had sought from the Greek Committee in London. He asked a cash payment of £12,000, in return for the £1,000 a year pay and the pension due after thirty years of service in the British army. This would mean £600 a year for Anastasia, Susan, and Emily, in the event of his death. Who else would care? The future of Nelson's natural child had never been guaranteed by a country which had idolized Nelson but preferred to forget his human weakness: if thrice famous Nelson's child meant nothing, what could his be expected to mean? On £600 they could live in reasonable comfort in either England or Greece. He also asked £1,000 each for two young "scientific officers" who were willing to come with him; one of whom was John Kennedy and both of whom were "masters of modern Greek". He must also have £100,000 for the regular payment of troops for six months; and ten thousand muskets, bayonets, pouches, and belts, with sixty rounds for each, to be delivered at Nauplion. The Committee must pay the five hundred British troops whom Charles knew he could raise, and supply them with like equipment. As Admiral Cochrane had demanded £57,000 for himself alone, these demands for a land campaign do not seem excessive.

"For this I bind myself to the Greek service, except in the event of a war with England." He told William that he must have his terms—"I will not run after impossibilities . . . Many gentlemen of these islands are, it is told me, resolved to go under my command . . . The Greek deputies must be made to understand the necessity of my being accompanied by a strong force of foreign bayonets; they are the only arguments that will be heard in a country torn by national dissensions, and oppressed by a cruel enemy." With them, he felt confident of success; without them, certain of failure. Biddable troops, who would stand or advance at command, and not, like the Greeks, dash boldly on, or whistle panic-stricken off the field, at their own individual whim! Nor could he accomplish anything without pay for the Greek irregulars who, he knew, would flock to him at any serious success: moneyless, he would be at the mercy of every arbitrary decision of the Greek leaders. "Their politics I will not mix in, my business shall be the single act of beating the Turks . . . No temptation, no flattery shall draw me into their politics."

Emily, and perhaps also Elizabeth Kelly, must have lodged a protest. Tales had now penetrated, even into London drawing-rooms, of the fate that had befallen the first foreign volunteers who came from Germany to fight for Greece, of their capture after the battle of Peta, when the Turks had impaled them and left them to die a slow and agonizing death in the market-place at Arta, the sick meanwhile being beheaded. "Consider Greece as she is," Charles besought Emily on October 2nd. "Not a house exists in the whole country except a few in each fortress . . . The wretched peasantry are driven from the ravaged plains into the sterile mountains, along whose high summits they flit to escape from the armed bands of their countrymen, no less cruel than the Turks beneath . . . The Egyptians ravage the Morea and the Greek chiefs riot in Napoli [Nauplion] where a loan of half a million has disappeared into the pockets of a few individuals . . . Am I warranted in not making an attempt to save them?

"There is at least a *fair chance* of success." Life was full of risk; it existed everywhere. "I own my ambition favours this doctrine but have I not a right to be ambitious of doing good, and a good so great? . . . I feel all the anxiety I shall give the two people for whom I live", but they must think of how much was at stake. A few weeks later he felt even surer of the rightness of his course—"Would that I could give two people the resolute feels and confidence which so abound in me." He loved Cephalonia, but his mind was now fixed for Greece, though there was now to be a three-month wait till all was fixed. Who on earth had told Emily that Mr Groucher was a favourite of his—a downright lie. "He is an ill-thriven wishy-washy missish whining singing Methodistical son of a Bitch."

By November "Ibrahim has received 12,000 men, his army is now 20,000 strong well-drilled troops—that is anything but funny. However I really think the Greeks are now in a better way than ever, as they are beaten into common sense." He heard that Odysseus had "put 27 Greek priests to death with his own hand, most of them by burning alive hanging by the heels . . . This is Colonel Stanhope's 'Man for Greece'!" In this same month of November the bitter blow fell.

"A proclamation has just come out from the English government forbidding us to take part with the Greeks: this does not alarm me, but if it stops the Greek loan it will stop the money necessary for my ulterior operations . . . if the money is forthcoming I have no fear for the ultimate result. If Napoli falls the Greek game is indeed over, and Missolonghi can hardly last long; but all is well while Napoli holds out, and a loan can be raised; the proclamation will not stop me then; but it has made the Greeks indisposed as they expect England to go further against them. Ibrahim Pasha gave quarter at first to women and children, who were saleable; now he destroys all, and means to put an Arab population into the Morea . . . If they can supply the arms and money for the troops, go I will; not otherwise, for unless what can be done, and what cannot be done, is clearly before me, no stirring for me: I will not run after impossibilities." He thought that if the money and arms did come there was a good chance of saving the Morea, provided they arrived before Napoli fell. William was to tell Orlando to send the money direct to him and not to anyone else, "that it may not be squandered on the Greek fleet, which cannot get Ibrahim out, though it might have prevented his getting in".

But the Committee in London, who held the purse-strings, had other ideas. Two of its members, Hume and Ellice—"men well calculated to mar any military enterprise" William thought them—eventually persuaded the Greeks that the funds should be spent on Admiral Cochrane, that awkward but far-famed naval deliverer of independence to hard beset foreign countries, and upon General Church. The Greek government also hired the services of General Fabvier, an exiled French general who had fought under Napoleon and cherished his image to the point where he had become unacceptable to the French authorities. Charles had fatally alienated the idealists of his homeland. He had made difficulties, dented the crusader image, kept banging on about soldiers' pay and ammunition pouches, guns, equipment, food. Some of the Committee doubted whether he had a soul at all.

The Greeks, undiscouraged, thought Charles was simply holding out for more for himself, and from time to time, sent him bigger and better offers. He told them, at one desperate moment of the struggle, that he would come for half what they had offered, for free—but not, repeat not, without pay, arms, and equipment for his troops. But his lot was to remain on the sidelines and watch the appalling drama unfold. His last years in the Septinsular Protectorate were not cheered by the spectacle of Cochrane, but more particularly Fabvier and Church, making what he felt was a mess of the agonizing Greek struggle; justifying, in their continuous failures, his old insistence upon a body of at least 500 trained and regular troops.

Away up in the Black Mountains, searching for a cave in which to store summer ice for his new hospital, he would gaze across those deep lapis-lazuli seas to the mainland of Greece, his mind convinced that he was right, his heart heavy with compassion. To land on Greek soil armed with nothing but goodwill was to lead many others besides himself to a cruel and useless death.

CHAPTER IV

War and Peace

Across these narrow miles of dark blue sea the war on the mainland continued its dismal course of cruelty and disaster. With the coming of spring 1826 the siege of Missolonghi by the overwhelming Turkish forces tightened; as also did Charles's responsive nerve-strings. Emily, opening his letters in her small house by the red cliffs of Dawlish on the Devon coast, never quite knew what she would find. In February it was, "You are both spiteful and saucy damn your hazel eyes or whatever colour they are." He didn't want his news and views to be "regularly sung out by the Dawlish Bellman": Emily, irrepressibly interested, must have gossiped. "God bless you," he continued, "how your letters delight me. I begin to twaddle, but I have so much to think and do." By March the pains of Greece were sharper and Charles's desire to help her keener,—"I often think I should be better without this concentrated affection for a few people. We jog on here", he added boredly. Adam had visited the island, and had approved his conduct over Colonel Rhys (who had written home to the Horse Guards and complained that Charles was upsetting military regulations because he was trying to give captains a bit more responsibility, though not, as Colonel Rhys supposed, at the expense of field officers). The Horse Guards had sent an official reprimand—"They have bitterly ill-used me." And Charles, no doubt, had banged down a further nail in his career coffin by writing a sharp letter back. "Perhaps I am not very popular but it seems admitted I do good to the island, that is to say that my good measures balance my bad and something over. I hope so at least."

It was a hope he clung to as the news from Greece worsened. He shared a feeling that is but too familiar now—"The mind grows fatigued with hearing of horrors." In April Missolonghi had fallen to the Turks: the surviving Greek forces, desperately fighting their way out, had had to leave their wives and families to the mercies of the

Turks—almost all died. The chiefs at Missolonghi had sent Charles letters telling him their food had run out and begging him to save them and their families, and the letters had arrived too late—"The Greeks think I can do anything."

"My heart is fatigued with its own feelings of execration. Why is Fabvier at Negropont? Why was he not at Missolonghi? Three days they lived on dead bodies before they sacrificed their families. Fifty thousand men are in Greece able to bear arms, all of whom could have been brought on Ibrahim's rear during the siege. Would to God those stupid deputies had closed with me a year ago and I should have saved all this. What has given Ibrahim this vigour? A few French officers. Could not a few English officers have done a like good for the Greeks? Surely yes. Ibrahim will now march for the Morea. Fabvier may yet oppose him but I doubt his doing any good. He went to Euboea! went with his young troops to assault walls, and was defeated."

He was very nearly ill with rage; and no doubt some of it was directed against himself. Why had he not gone, simply gone to Greece, without money, arms, or backing? Chanced his arm, died under Turkish sabres? Because he was, first and foremost, a responsible soldier, refusing to throw away the lives of those he must lead, in a situation where their success was outside the bounds of possibility. "I did feel very much", he told Emily in June, still thinking of Missolonghi's fate. "I felt more strongly this misfortune because I knew that it might have been saved by good sense and a little military conduct." He did not feel he had missed the moment or failed to grasp the great occasions "except those which enthusiasm alone would attempt". Once started, he never lacked enthusiasm, "but it never enters into my decisions in the first instance". All the same—"I went beyond the bounds of prudence, because the game demanded that something should be trusted to fortune", he now felt.

One had to weigh it all up and do what seemed right at the time and with the available facts. He did not feel to blame for being "timid and shilly-shally. I believed a step further than I went would have been rashness, a step short of it would have been timidity. How far I was right in thinking no good could be done by me with less than my demand will soon be clear. Gordon and Fabvier have a better chance than I could have had with less power than I claimed, and you will soon see what they can do—I fear very little, though much could be done if a man had full command. God knows what will happen. My advice to the friends of the Greeks here is give Fabvier the command they offered to me, but they will not I fear: if he and Gordon go to Monemvasia and march northward upon the town of Tripolitza I have hopes of their success; if they encamp, as I hear they intend, on some heights close to Napoli I think they will be beaten. I have nothing to say to all this", he ended wearily, "and give up my whole time to my island . . .

"Every day teaches one how much there is to be done, and to be learnt in *how* to govern. The great point is not to procrastinate: I never leave a letter or a memorandum unanswered a day except such as cannot from their nature be answered immediately . . . but one cannot well be regular in the office and indoor business and ride a great deal", and it was essential to keep the island under one's eye. Kennedy was away on leave, and "I do everything myself which is bad, but as I have no-one to do it for me there is no choice . . . The worry of such a mass of details torments me sadly, and I long for Kennedy to share with me as usual: we both want a regular fellow to keep the papers in trim, for though I do the thing it is horrid work docketing letters and copying and indexing and God knows how ill I do it."

He read all the cases before confirming sentences. "My chief troubles arise from the impossibility of getting at the *truth*: I think I may safely say that in the course of every year, not one witness can be found who has not perjured himself in the tribunal . . . at the moment a poor devil is condemned to imprisonment who I am certain is innocent, and so I think are his judges, but a host of witnesses are perjured against him, and what can be done: this excludes justice . . .

"My dear Em, if you were here to see the things I do you would be horrified, yet there is no help, where lying is carried to such a pitch that it is impossible to hear truth. I rule with a rod of iron and I cannot help it, but I do not like it . . . The gentlemen suborn the peasants to prove perjury against the evidence", and he told her of a case where a peasant had sold fifty sheep to a gentleman, who denied it when he came to collect the money.

"I hope I shall make something of it with a little law and a little despotism . . . Terror is the only way to manage the gentlemen; no *law* can protect the peasant where there is no press; fear of the Resident can alone check them."

*

He cheered the ageing Lady Sarah with a letter of funny stories about Greeks, gardeners, nuns, and animals, before he came to the grim news at the end: she had always liked to hear the facts. "Missolonghi's fall has been a sad affair: glorious but terrible. The fighting men, numbering eighteen hundred, cut their way out; the old, the sick, the women and children were self-destroyed to avoid worse. The Greeks have now but to put all into the hands of Fabvier, a French officer of name, and so far as I trace his conduct a man of talent: he has made mistakes, but apparently not his own, he is not master." It was the fate he had dreaded and avoided for himself: to free Greece "it needs be aut Caesar aut nullus".

"My best has been done here to persuade the Greeks to throw all into his hands." Nauplion would be besieged; but—he changed his mind before writing "I have told them", as all his letters were now opened on their way through Corfu, and substituted "a friend of the Greeks has convinced them of the importance of Monemvasia, and they have at last provisioned it, but only for six months: that will do if they keep the sea, and the Maniotes are staunch, but Colocotroni is now commander in chief which augurs badly."

Throughout the summer letters came from Captain Rowan Hamilton of the Cambrian, from Tre, from Gordon and others, regretting his absence: sometimes urging him to relinquish his insistence on disciplined western European troops and the money to pay them. He remained convinced that Greece could not be freed without such help, and that it would in time be forthcoming. In April he had regretted the departure of Bathurst from the Colonial Office, "a good master, of whom we had nothing to complain, for he took a fair view, and a liberal one, of our small affairs". Charles's reprimand from the Horse Guards had not come into that category: without pausing to hear his side of the story in the Colonel Rhys affair the Duke of York had sent Adam at Corfu "serious animadversions and censure upon Colonel Napier for having taken it upon himself to introduce innovations into the British Army, confounding ranks and degrading authority on which discipline depended." Adam, having officially approved of Charles's action, accepted responsibility; but it cannot have sweetened his goodwill towards Charles, a difficult fellow, involving blameless characters like Sir Frederic Adam in quite unnecessary dispute with his superiors, simply in order to keep army captains busy and lively in their jobs.

*

An unexpected letter reached Emily this July, causing her to open her beautiful eyes, hazel or otherwise, very wide indeed. On June 22nd Charles had heard of the death of Mrs Kelly's husband, that never clearly focused character who had stood between him and happiness for nearly a quarter of a century; "which brings my long pilgrimage to a point. Twenty-three years of great misery has been some trial", Charles admitted, and he told Emily that he was one who could not really do without a home and someone to love; he had really suffered. "I seemed doomed by fate to be a wanderer. Of late years she tried much to persuade me to marry, saying that she could still be my friend and spend part of her time with me and my wife." But he had told Elizabeth "you will always be first in my heart beyond all other things, how can I marry? The only answer she had to make me was, her great age making it ridiculous in me, and that it would be a great happiness to her to see me have children and a home.

"All this was no answer." He did not care a fig for general opinion, and if the nine days' wonder of such a marriage was an eighteen days' wonder, let it be. Elizabeth Kelly had begged Charles to let a year pass before they married, lest he change his mind, and he had agreed. He was not well, he told Emily; mainly, he thought, from overwork and worry, the row with the Horse Guards, and the infuriating petty details when his mind was on the struggle on the mainland. He had jaundice and pains, his legs were swollen and he was so thin that it was pain to sit a horse; but he thought none of these things were organic and would disappear with the journey and his leave.

Now he could "look forward to tranquil life" at home, and his life outside this haven could be as turbulent as it liked. "I am not sixteen and don't expect Elysium"; but he did expect happiness "with one so very dear to me and so suited to me". He had felt harassed for years "in a way my disposition is not suited to bear—there is nothing placid in me". They could manage all right for money, he thought, "and her active charity will do great good here, the sternness of my rule will be softened down through her gentleness without changing my system . . . But for her and your letters bearing me up I could hardly have gone through the last twelve months. God bless you, my precious and most dear Em."

Elizabeth's active charity would also have to be called into action on behalf of Charles's little Susan and Emily; but on this matter his sister Emily was not yet in his confidence. They were all Georgians by birth; and Georgian women tended to accept their husbands' illegitimate children rather as they might now accept their Labrador dogs, something bumbly and time-consuming but essentially lovable and part of them. The age gap was a much greater obstacle. At twenty-two Charles had fallen passionately and irretrievably in love with a married woman of thirty-seven; a situation that is not so uncommon. What is exceedingly uncommon is for a man of forty-four to marry a woman of fifty-nine; but she was simply the dear love of his youth and she suited him.

Her husband, Paymaster Kelly, had deserted her before Charles appeared on the scene; but this was an epoch when divorce was available only by Act of Parliament and therefore only to the very rich. Elizabeth had a son and three small daughters when first they met: their opportunities to be together had been short and snatched. She it was who had been staying opportunely with his friends the Browns near Torquay when he had first arrived home from the battle of Corunna, where he had been posted for dead; and who had betrayed the strength of their relationship when she fainted on seeing him thus miraculously restored to her. What both had endured in terms of separation and loneliness may be imagined; though Elizabeth had her children, and Charles his devoted family and his casual mistresses.

Anastasia had been more than this. Their love had alternated between ecstasy and tempest: Charles's nearest relations, who are most likely to have heard it from Charles himself and therefore to know, maintain that their love had also been deep and their life together a thing of beauty. Charles was one of those many men who can happily and genuinely love two women at once, specially when one is in Cookham and the other in Cephalonia. But Anastasia, like Scotland's Mary Hamilton, had her Medea side, when she pushed the boat with her two small children in it out to sea—"Go sink or swim, ye bonny babe, Ye'll get no mair of me". Had she in fact now deserted him, perhaps flinging furiously out with a compatriot of her own age? No more than Charles, by all accounts, did she have anything placid about her. Maybe that in his passion for this wild and wilful stranger Charles himself had been badly burned; and that during this year when he found it difficult to go on, he was enduring not only the haunting spectacle of Greece's agony and the feeling that he might have shortened it, but also the enraged termination of a love affair between two exceedingly passionate characters?

Elizabeth represented peace and goodness, two qualities he craved: she was gentle, and brought out the gentleness in Charles. His devotion for her had not wavered through the weary years, when, as he told Emily, he hurried between her, his mother, and the family he loved. When in old age he and William were having a discussion about money, he let slip the information that he had, all through his penniless young manhood, been sending money to a person he did not name, but who was almost certainly Elizabeth. His journal a year or two later reveals that he had eight people to keep in England—the average household of four family and four servants—and four in Cephalonia: these he revealed later to Louisa were Anastasia, her parents, and her grandmother. If Anastasia deserted him, he did not desert her.

Elizabeth was someone to share his joy in the beauty and delights of the visible world, someone to whom to rant and gloom, someone who would be unwaveringly kind to his two children, someone from whom to evoke the laughter which he needed as he needed meat and drink. Life is essentially a battle: Charles had decided not to fight a war on two fronts. Marriage to this elderly delicate woman put paid to all thought of a son of his own, to all ambition to excel in his profession; but in this same year he was writing, "When death comes there is perhaps more comfort in love than in glory."

And this August Lady Sarah, his much loved mother, died at the age of eighty-one, perhaps strengthening Charles's need for the affectionate understanding he had always enjoyed at her hand. The increasing serenity he felt from the prospect of his marriage cushioned the pain of the loss; but to Emily he wrote that he thought her religion better value on such occasions than his own fortitude. He wished he could believe in an after-life, but at the time did not. A year later he had come to believe in it: he had had, he said, irrefutable proof, and he could not believe that such proof had not been afforded to many others besides himself. But, he now told Emily, he believed in God, and respected those, like her, who were lucky enough to believe in both. He besought her not to reproach herself for lost opportunities—and to "be assured the dreadful obligation to be busy is of all comforters the best in grief.

"I see that Anne would like to visit me but Dick has no fondness for travel so they won't come. Anne ought clearly to have been my wife. I think I'll take her yet; when both are old the law might allow two", he added flippantly.

*

His heart steadily lightened, for all the agony of Greece; and his health steadily improved. On July 24th he had been "a great deal better—the prospect of being at last married has taken much unsettled despairing feel from my mind, which has hung on it for so many years and required all my spirits and courage to overcome or rather support. I see no black *uncertainty* for the future. I know well that man is born to suffer, and I shall have to suffer, but only fixed evils that all feel and must bear. Before," he told Emily, "my whole nature was rolled back on itself: my life and my character 'shut into each other's mouth'. I absolutely dote on what I love, and I have been separated from all I love." And as all he loved were alive, "even when at home I was obliged to wear out my bottom in stagecoaches to see you all by starts. Now all is changed and my mind feels the relief.

"I have occasional twinges of pain, but not anything to signify and am not so thin. I fear both Caroline and William suffer sadly. [John Moore Napier, their only son, was thought to have consumption.] God bless them and make their other children thrive better . . . God willing I will be with you between January and May of 1827. I have excellent reports of George's health and spirits from Henry." By August he was "grown so well I really am not the same human being I was . . . I am on horseback by four in the morning and in bed by nine at night. I feel well and light. How I long to kiss your old snout", and would Emily send him de Luc's account of Hannibal crossing the Alps?

Emily, well though she understood and sympathized with Charles's love for Elizabeth Kelly, had perhaps never thought ahead to her husband's death, nor visualized that Charles would marry so elderly a woman; and must have sent him a protest (probably a mild one, because his reply is mild) against abandoning all hope of children and all chance of a further career in the army, since he could not be fully mobile with such a delicate wife. He minded, but kept calm. On September the 9th Charles told Emily he felt low-spirited, though there was some hope of marriage before the end of the year. Elizabeth's reasons for wanting to wait, he told Henry, were excellent but not conclusive, an admirable phrase for use in marital dispute. To Emily he argued—"We all of us have our standards of perfection in this world, and Elizabeth is mine . . . Each man must be judge in his own case; and as I have no particular taste for grey hairs in a wife, it is the opinion that she is superior to all other mortals that causes my marriage. No enjoyment in life is perfect to me without her presence, nothing satisfies me that I do until she approves of it.

"Therefore the world may censure and laugh and be damned. I have a mind", he went on, with characteristic defiance, "to be married in France because as it contains 30 millions of people and England only fifteen, there will be twice as many censurers and laughers as at home . . . I do not think you will like Elizabeth much because there is nothing of wit in her style, she is as like William's Caroline in her disposition as can be, without that similarity of habits which Caroline has with you and which affords food for conversation in the absence of wit; but as she is not your wife this don't signify and when we are together I can entertain you!

"However you will like in her a total absence of scandal, a total absence of ill-natured remarks, an absence of all prejudice, an unbounded benevolence and active pursuit of charity both in deed and feeling, and a mind so grateful to the Creator that she never shows a symptom of discontent." Charles thought it took time to appreciate Elizabeth; and he was "not so unreasonable as to expect you to like my wife upon principle and trust". He believed that her goodness and kindness and universal sympathy would do great good in Cephalonia; a locality perhaps short in these particular qualities.

With this off his chest he felt better; and a week later confined himself to politics and family chat. "I hope Hal will get his promotion, but believing as I do that Lord Melville is a scoundrel I shall be surprised if he acts like an honest man when he has no need to do so . . . The Greeks have been defeated at Eleusis . . . they have no general plan and their victories and defeats are equally inconsequential." Ibrahim was laying waste the country between Argos and Sparta, and "Lord Cochrane seems lost! Where can he be? Collecting troops in Sardinia?" So long as he could rustle up a thousand men "all is safe; but I wish it could have been *another person*, but no matter so as *it is done* and the horror stopped . . . on both sides, for I am just as sorry for the poor Turks, poor devils they have as many good points as any people.

"Only I believe the fact is the European governments want to extirpate the Greeks and then divide the country as they did Poland; there is no other key to their conduct." What the hell were they at? His longing to take part was unabated but he would never get his terms, and it would never be. But if only a victorious end could somehow, by someone, be achieved! And the ceaseless, cruel, pointless deaths be brought to an end!

If the Sultan had really killed all the Janissaries, as he was reported to have done "it will have great consequences because it will fill Turkey with a disciplined force and modern wars. It is a great step in the regeneration of a powerful and warlike nation, but Turkey is too full of corruption to become vigorous. A great genius may make a figure for a moment, but downhill the Empire is going."

Bold words, if true ones, with the Turks and their Egyptian satrapy everywhere triumphant in Greece.

A certain nervousness was now manifesting itself in England—was the government allowing itself to be outgunned by the French in gaining influence in Greece? This was as nothing compared with French nervousness that England was ahead here: Fabvier's Napoleonicness was rapidly being forgotten in favour of his Frenchness. A letter to Charles on May 2nd, 1826 from Bowring in London (now fighting for his reputation after the discovery of his many doubtful goings-on with the Greek Funds) shares this apprehension —"Many thanks for your observations on Hastings' paper," Bowring wrote, "they are shrewd, sensible, and full of experience. As you cannot go, we hope Gordon will go, but it is to me a subject of deep sorrow that the Government will not wink at your visiting Greece, as they lose a fine *opportunity* of political influence." Thomas Gordon wrote to Charles from Zante on May 13th; he had heard from the Greek government "if such it could be called") at Napoli. "I fear their resources as well as their finances are nearly exhausted. The imminence of danger has however put an end to faction, (so it seems at least) and they are determined to make a vigorous struggle . . . From what I hear Fabvier seems to behave well: I know not what induced him to go to Negropont but the failure was owing to want of provisions, and (I fear) to some caballing among the officers. It is very difficult to get the Greeks near enough to the enemy. Ibrahim marches upon Tripolizzia to-day . . . I propose to set off for Napoli at the beginning of next week. God knows there is little to be done. Whatever we can do may be esteemed a miracle", Gordon concluded realistically. For a few weeks of February 1827 he was persuaded to take charge of the Greek forces, but resigned in despair at their insubordination and general incalculability; and years later recorded his history of their war with vigour and accuracy. By 1827 he thought that both Greeks and Turks betrayed signs of lassitude, "especially the insurgents, on whose minds the fall of Missolonghi impressed a deep gloom; they could not hide from themselves the painful truth that the struggle was failing". Their only hopes now lay with the allies of Western Europe, he wrote; and they had reached their lowest depths after Fabvier's failure to relieve Athens, and the consequent surrender of the Acropolis. The Turks now declared that Greece was forever theirs until the day of judgment.

Impervious to its miseries but greatly enjoying its excitements, Trelawney was still bustling round the fringes of the Morea, a delighted spectator, still wearing the fancy dress in which he had so nearly been murdered while hand in glove with Odysseus in that cave up Mount Parnassus. He had early parted company with Byron—"He was past hope: he trifled for months at that miserable island", Trelawney wrote of the poet upon whose generosity he had so long sponged—"Could I waste my life in union with such imbecility?" On the mainland Trelawney had rapidly fallen a victim to the personality of Odysseus—"a man of most wonderful mind, a glorious being". It would be difficult, if not impossible, to make out a case for admiring Edward Trelawney; and the manner in which he hurried to Missolonghi after Byron's death, in order to have a look at the poet's crippled foot before his body was coffined, is gravely lacking in charm; but in spite of Tre's lies, boasts, and double-talk it is easy to see why Byron enjoyed his company, with its raffish insouciance and its unscrupulous vitality. By Trelawney's hand Charles had conveyed a letter of suggestions to Gordon in 1826 on what he believed would be the best methods of opposing Ibrahim Pasha.

"I am embarking this instant from Zante", Trelawney told him, with his usual air of being importantly *affairé*. "As to the terms offered the Greek government, what signifies the terms if they get hold of the blunt? Things are as bad as they can well be. Gordon finds he can do little unaided and is laying to for Cochrane who is hourly expected. I am taking a run to Missolonghi and Patras on board the *Zebra* to see how things are going on there. Gordon thinks nothing but an importation of regulars can liberate Greece. I shall return here in a few days," and he hurried off, with a swing of his *fustanella*; but whether Charles's letter ever reached Gordon is doubtful. His plan outlined a mainly fortress-defending war; employment of guerrilla forces "to harass Turkish communications, to starve the Turks out, or to launch attacks as circumstances demanded; always obliging the enemy to attack you in your own position with your back to a fortress, thus uniting offensive war with defensive positions, which is the secret of mountain warfare . . . My plan is but an outline. The great advantage of it is that these young Greek regulars are *not* required to attack, but to defend positions. Every old soldier knows how to estimate this advantage." He still insisted upon "veteran Europeans" as support.

In July of 1827 Trelawney continued in his role of impervious reporter; savouring disaster with sunny unconcern and occasionally getting his facts wrong. The firm of Messrs Ricardo had lost £100,000 in endeavouring to serve Greece, he had heard. "The Turks seem so secure and are so little molested that they have resumed their indolence or Greece would cease to exist." In August he told Charles that only three or four houses in Missolonghi were left standing: the Turks were not even bothering to rebuild the fortifications, as all Western and Eastern Greece except Athens Acropolis had submitted. "Gordon has uselessly dribbled away £14 or £13,000 in Greece . . . All the Pashas in the Ottoman dominions have been ordered to form regular troops and to admit people of all nations. They are recruiting Greeks in Thessaly and Albania—it is curious", he added detachedly, "that the Turks are the first to form the Greeks into regulars . . . Private hatred runs so high no popular government of Greeks can be established", and they were talking of making Cochrane "King or Dictator or something, I remain Dear Colonel your very obliged Edward Trelawney".

Very different was the purposeful and thoughtful George Finlay, he whom Byron had for a moment suspected of being the ghost of Shelley and who afterwards became a historian of the war, writing to Charles a year later, on October 23rd, 1827 from Syra to urge him once again to take charge—"I write to you without reserve as I know you are a sincere friend of the cause." He had heard that Charles had again been invited into the Greek service, and wanted to send him his views. He thought that Church "has not introduced that organization in the army which constitutes the difference between an army and a crowd of armed men, and as he does not husband his means well, his authority is quite as fluctuating as any Capitano of the whole band". Church's attack on Athens had been badly misconceived, and he had gone back on board his schooner "and drank tea and read the bible . . . Personally he is much liked. I fear he has added his name to the list of Europeans who have lost all credit in Greece."

This was sad. Church had been an early philhellene, had fought in Greece in the first decade of the century and gained the affection and admiration of the Greeks. "Our father has at last come", Colocotronis had declared to his men when Church came ashore at Castris in the spring of 1827. Six years earlier Church had declared—"One great and sublime idea occupies me and renders me insensible to everything else . . . Conceive the great glory of my being instrumental towards the Emancipation of Greece!" Now he had failed to relieve the beleaguered Acropolis, exactly as Gordon and others had earlier done; and 700 dead Greeks and allies lay on the battlefield and 250 were prisoners of the Turks. Enthusiasm had once more triumphed over sense, and a thousand new victims bled in vain.

Fabvier, Finlay continued to Charles, openly condemned Church, but he himself would not learn from his own innumerable mistakes. "He still thinks himself a second Napoleon in the field but has disgusted almost everybody . . . For the moment he has command of the expedition to Scio (Chios). I wish it success but fear sadly [and rightly]. The demoralized state of the government, their ignorance and absurd conduct is beyond conception and I cannot write coolly of it." Finlay came to his point. "If you should come here, and the war continue and Fabvier and Church retire, Greece might be saved, and organization established by Capo d'Istria in the civil government. You might easily have 4,000 or 6,000 Greek regulars." He added reassuringly that "Hastings has at length succeeded with his shells and red-hot shot to his heart's content, he has practically introduced a new system in naval warfare." Charles replied with a detailed and admirable plan for the re-conquest of the Morea, later printed by Finlay in an appendix to his history.

Gordon had resigned six months earlier in despair at Greek indiscipline, and Cochrane had failed in his attack on Ibrahim's fleet in Alexandria harbour. The cause of Greek Independence seemed dead as a doornail. But whatever Charles would or would not have done at this point was forestalled. In July of 1827 the great powers had at last arrived at concord: they had signed the Treaty of London; and a combined squadron of British, French, and Russian warships had been sent as supposedly neutral observers while Greek independence was in negotiation with the Sultan of Turkey. But as the Turks were now in complete possession of the mainland they were unlikely to negotiate with much speed or conviction. The neutrality of a squadron of pro-Greek ships at large in these politically tempestous waters seemed unlikely to last.

A letter from HMS *Asia* in Navarin Bay on October 21st reached Charles. The British admiral and his colleagues "have agreed that we should come into this port, in order to induce Ibrahim Pasha to discontinue the brutal war of extermination which he has been carrying on here since his failure in the Gulph of Patras. Edwd. Codrington, Vice Admiral." The inevitable happened. Though the allied fleet had entered the bay to prevent the combined Turco-Egyptian fleet from leaving, and not to attack it, not surprisingly some Allied boats, sent to investigate the suspicious activities of Turkish fire-ships, were fired upon. These boats were then covered by Allied musket fire, an excited Egyptian ship proceeded to let loose with its guns, and the battle had begun. The *Asia* received five shots before the admiral would give the order to fire himself: but the point of no return had been reached. Before darkness fell sixty out of the eighty-nine ships of the Turco-Egyptian fleet were sunk. Without these the Turks could not hope to reinforce or supply their garrisons or subdue the islands: the Greek War of Independence was successfully decided in four hours of blood and thunder over Navarino's sheltered and translucent seas.

Yet on the mainland a sad, desultory, and bloody war continued: the Turks declining to admit defeat. It continued without Charles. He would not be "commander in name not in fact, like Church, who calling himself generalissimo, is yet obliged to beg of his soldiers to do their duty as a personal favour! The Greek government tried to meet my terms but could not bring it about," he mourned in 1827, "save as regarding my personal interest, which was precisely what I least cared for, and would not accept without the others—yet I would have accepted the other terms without that. They were able and willing to advance my share, but had they assured me of the public money and arms I would have gone at all hazards. Kennedy, Muir, Stevens, and six other Englishmen would have gone under me; and twelve Greek gentlemen of weight and property, looked up to in Greece, were prepared to follow, but I would have started with the Englishmen."

"One of my castles in Greece", he told Charles Robertson ten years later (May 14th, 1837), "was to have you at the head of the ordinance. The whole thing was arranged with the Greeks, they had even lodged the £12,000 that I demanded for myself for sacrificing my profession and the government of Cephalonia. But Ellis and the Greek Committee in London settled that Lord Cochrane with a frigate was much more effectual for dislodging a Turkish army in the heart of the country and knew much more of the matter than I did; so they gave him the money I demanded to pay the troops, viz £100,000, and all the world knows the result. He never took a single *boat* from the Turks, he attempted to raise the siege of Athens and got cut to pieces at the Piraeaus, he and that good-natured charlatan Sir Richard Church escaping with difficulty to their boats."

What a shambles—and how needless a shambles! Charles's heart hardened towards officialdom in general. England—so full of goodwill, energy, courage; taking her time to start but subscribing huge sums to the Greek loan with at least as much of generosity as cupidity; and then letting men like Hume and Ellis purloin and squander it, or ignorantly throwing it into the pockets of the *capitani*, while the Greeks died in their thousands and their innocent women and children were torn from their villages to sweat their lives out in hopeless slavery and separation in some dim, dusty corner of the Ottoman domain. England to him was a brave and clever man permanently entangled about the legs by a skein of strong string—its selfish and dull-minded bureaucracy.

Not that England alone was to blame. "The interference of foreigners in the affairs of Greece was generally unfortunate, often injudicious, and sometimes dishonest . . . The careers of Norman, Fabvier, Church, and Cochrane were marked by great disaster", Finlay wrote. He thought Hastings was the man who did most for Greece, through he had a very good word for Captain Rowan Hamilton of HMS *Cambrian* for persuading the Greeks to honour their promise to spare the Turkish people of Nauplion and to send them to Constantinople, and for himself risking typhus by evacuating five hundred of them in the *Cambrian*.

"But it was by those who called themselves Philhellenes in England and America that Greece was most injured . . . The manner in which the Greeks wasted the money of the English loans in Greece has been already recorded. It is now necessary to mention how the Greek deputies, and their English and American friends, appropriated large sums at London and New York. It will be seen that waste and peculation were no monopolies in the hands of Greek statesmen,

Albanian ship-owners, and captains of armatoli and klephts. English politicians and American merchants had also their share", Finlay concluded.

These years, of comfortable fiddle-faddle in London offices while Greece bled, strengthened every fibre of anti-officialdom in Charles's being, pushing him slowly back into the clan loyalties of his Scottish forbears, into a deepening conviction that only one's own family is to be loved and trusted. This feeling was not decreased by a long visit from his youngest brother, Henry.

CHAPTER V

Henry

Henry Napier, an unemployed naval commander, had been lucky enough to find so many friends during his visit to Malta in the early months of 1829 that "every face received us smilingly", and the Admiral had sent the sloop of war *Meteor* expressly to Cephalonia in order to take thither Henry and his wife Caroline. After a gale and lowering sky at nightfall, and darkness spent with the ship bare of all but her storm staysails, running through "a cross, nasty and somewhat dangerous sea for so small a vessel," they were happy enough at dawn, "discovering the lofty mountains of Cephalonia looming indistinctly through the morning haze". "The sun rose in splendour and heat"; and Henry, carried away, quoted Byron:

Not as in northern climes obscurely bright
But one unclouded blaze of living light

Greece had captured his eldest brother Charles, and was about to get Henry.

Avoiding "the dangerous flat reef which extends itself a considerable way from the island" by a passage "excellent when once known, though strangers should not attempt it", the *Meteor* dropped anchor in ten or twelve fathoms. On the way in they had had time to admire John Kennedy's newly-built lighthouse, "in the form of a Doric column, rising majestically from the south point of Guardiana Island"; now, gazing around in the euphoria of safe arrival, they could equally admire the beauty of Argostoli harbour in the first blaze of morning. Life with Charles was rarely static, and on April 14th he and Henry were off for Ithaca: on the route Henry was touched to discover that one of the bridges Charles had had constructed across Cephalonia's numerous ravines was a copy of one they had known across the river Liffey in their childhood at

Castletown, and his thoughts turned to kindly nervous Tom Conolly and to their aunt, Louisa Conolly—"Oh, what a deal of happiness one or two benevolent people aided by riches can spread around them, and how long and deeply is their memory cherished!" Mule tracks brought them down into a beautiful valley with a shady village—"delightful shade, a rare occurrence on Cephalonia"—where the soil was richer and where "fine baytree and arbutus fringed the road with their thick and luxuriant foliage", and all the Romantic Age poetry rose in Henry's soul,—"Indeed the whole ride to Asso is singularly wild and beautiful, at least for those who love naked mountain scenery."

Far below them the town and fortress of Asso lay spread out like a map—"this singular and almost impregnable fort erected by the Venetians as a place of refuge for all the island population in case of a descent by the Turks . . . on a rock nearly perpendicular throughout its circuit". It stood on a peninsula joined to the land by a fortified isthmus, and must have been, Henry thought, impregnable. A bridle path brought them down to the town through gardens and cottages and olive groves; they were warmly received by "Signor Antissa and his two sons Dionysius and Antonio, one a ninny and both great bores, but extremely hospitable and attentive", and "their two young wives one of whom was beautiful, the other an odd good humoured thing about the size of a small fat mushroom and not unlike one, but with something so pleasing about her that it became difficult to say whether she were pretty or not". After supper they were entertained with Greek songs, which was as well, as a little Italian was the only tongue Henry had in common with them. The romance of it all was slightly dashed when the silver finger bowls were accompanied after supper by only one small towel, common to all; but Henry cheered himself; "concluding that the ancients did the same, it became classic dirt and therefore venerable".

Henry was enormously impressed with his brother's roads, blasted with such enormous difficulty out of the solid rock of precipitous places and laid with such skilled design. Word had gone out from Corfu that every island was to have roads; and that the financing of them must be achieved within each individual island. "In none of the Ionian islands was the difficulty of executing this order so great as in Cephalonia both from its poverty and mountainous character: Corfu and Zante are flat and rich, Santa Maura, Ithaca, and the others small." Yet, "for boldness of conception and mathematical accuracy in the execution through all its details, and for cheapness of construction, there are probably few hundred miles of road in the world which more deserve the notice of the scientific man and the Engineer than those of Cephalonia", Henry proudly thought. "It is necessary to be on the spot to judge of the difficulties overcome in making these roads."

The pass of Liberales over the Black Mountains had been planned and executed by Charles himself before Kennedy's arrival, the road rose 3,000 feet above the sea in three miles, with its maximum slope never exceeding one-foot in twelve. Kennedy had made the Asso and Guiscardo roads, "and right well has he acquitted himself," hanging between the cliff above and a drop of nearly 2,000 feet to the sea. "This road runs along the side of the mountain so beautifully parallel to the sea-level that from the offing it has the appearance of a slender line of white chalk just marked out to indicate where something was to be—a parallel ruler could not have drawn the line more accurately. All this may *sound* trifling, but the *execution* is no common work." The men who had held their horses on the route to Asso while Henry was sketching had waived all thanks, exclaiming to Kennedy, "Sir you have made our heart a garden by promising to mend our road!" Henry echoed Charles's opinion; the Greeks *were* very Irish: "Pat would have made a similar reply and perhaps thrown a bit of native wit in to season the compliment." In neither case could you believe a word that was said, but oh, the charming way of saying it!

As Byron had been five years ago, they were rowed across from Saint Euphemia to the beach on Ithaca by four young Greeks; the journey, Henry noted, took an hour and a half. Here Mr Parsons, Resident of Ithaca, awaited them with saddle horses; Charles departed on island business with him, and Kennedy to survey further roads, while his younger brother, Charley Kennedy, and Henry took off up Mount Aita, the Eagle's Nest, for the joys of some classical sight-seeing. Henry had enjoyed reading Sir William Gell's "plausible guesses" on the lay-out of Ulysses' palace spread on its summit; "but it needs much enthusiasm and more imagination to follow him through all the courts and chambers". Henry felt "only too happy to believe everything tradition tells about bygone times, whether it be the scenes of celebrated actions, ruined towns, or any other events of antiquity; I hate the dry accurate matter-of-fact investigator who meets one with a handful of doubts and difficulties and breaks into these very agreeable errors of the imagination . . . imparting a double interest to every spot, peopling a desert and doing no harm to anybody." On the way up they counted no fewer than five circuits of walls built of large polygonal stones: were they the massive foundations of concentric streets once standing on the slopes of the hill? "I see no other way of making streets in such a situation, unless they led straight up the hill in long flights of stairs as the small cross lanes do from the beach at Malta." How else could one build on such precipices but by streets in horizontal concentric curves, sweeping round the hillside and connected by small flights of stairs, or else winding about in a spiral form?

Not much remained of the palace at the top; but was that little island south of Guiscardo the place where Penelope's suitors lay in ambush to intercept Telemachus on his return from Sparta and Pylos? Homer was always accurate over permanent natural features, and this island was not on the route of any vessel; could it have been that near-island, off Samé, close to the ruins of the ancient town whence twenty-four of the suitors came, and commanding the Cephalonian channel? Homer had made Ulysses and Eumaeus come from Arethusa's sable fountain to a hill overlooking the palace before they met Antinous, and sure enough there *was* the hill: but the night must have been marvellously still for the sounds of music and revelry to have floated so far from the palace. Had it, therefore, in fact been further down the hill? Henry was lost in pleasing reverie.

They came down to find the Resident blasting his new road near Vathi: the echo was more strange than any Henry had ever heard; and he blenched with horror on being told that a previous Resident had blasted for a road right through what little remained of Ulysses' Cave, "for no earthly necessity or benefit". Morale was restored by an expedition next morning "to the fountain of Arethusa at the foot of that precipitous rock still called Korax, or the Raven, about three miles south-east of Vathi". Raven Castle! Here Henry beheld for the first time the shores of mainland Greece, free at last after four hundred years of subjection, "to the northward the shore of Epirus, the more distant hills of Etolia and the Focide; Leucadia, Meganese and Calamo. To the south Chiarenza (whence the title of Clarence) and the remote and snow-clad hills of the Morea, . . . mountain behind mountain in thick succession as far as the eye could reach, all brilliant with snow; one, the object of many but the prize of few, the lofty double-peaked Parnassus. Here too under our very eyes was the theatre of that battle where cool ambition won the world from love, of that other fight which saved half Europe from the Turkish sway." (Actium and Lepanto.)

Maybe that cool ambition would always win the world from love; so hot, confused, and uncertain a political driving force. Henry, like Byron, mistrusted the hoary system of imperial Europe and the cool ambition of its statesmen, and welcomed the movements of its young revolutionaries towards freedom; but here in Cephalonia Charles was authority, and that, in Henry's eyes, turned authority into a very different thing. Charles was much less a man of cool ambition and much more a devotee of human well-being; and if anybody thought different they were simply deceived by his loud voice. Henry looked on his elder brother with an uncritical devotion and admiration. A few questions might have been ultimately more helpful.

A scramble down the hillside through grassy woods of bay-trees brought them to Arethusa's fountain, hung with festoons of wild vine and ivy, and sparkling from a fissure in the rock. Well had Homer called it "sable", Henry thought, "from the shadow of the cave and colour of the stone it looks black as ink, but out in the daylight it shines and sparkles like a diamond, and thus it runs across the grassy plain into the deep ravine and bubbles to the sea . . ."

O fountain Arethusa! Henry was transported. "To me this whole scene was enchantment—the romance and classic interest of the spot; the natural beauty of the place; the heat of the day; the coolness of the Fountain; the shadowy freshness of the Grotto; the grouping of our party at its mouth; the green grass lawn watered by the infant stream, the music of the water trickling from rock to rock and splashing at the bottom; the bright blaze of ocean and the snow-clad hills of Greece against a blue and cloudless sky, and over all the glorious sun in all his majesty, made together one of those delightful moments in human existence of which remembrance clings to the heart." Here was one of those high places where the ancients so often, and so rightly, felt the presence of God. All Henry's sorrows, anxieties, disappointments fell from him as if they had never been.

Like many a man of imagination, Henry had been a bumbly little boy. Both his parents had been married before, and as the seventh son of his father and seventh child of his mother Henry should have been lucky; but was emphatically not. Four older brothers, agile, intelligent, and strong, had set too hot a pace for a dreamy little boy whose place on everyone's lap had been most rapidly usurped by two younger sisters, both delicate and in need of care. Although he rapidly improved, Henry had at first seemed a dunce in his lessons, as also in running and riding and leaping; his brothers had given him a nickname which he still in his late thirties could not bring himself to write down, and it had stuck. "This spread even to the domestic servants, who were too much our companions, both at Celbridge and Castletown", and in Henry's ears still rang the careless Irish laughter which his shortcomings had drawn forth. "I *was* comparatively dull, but this lowered me still more in my own estimation, it increased my natural diffidence, it destroyed the little boldness and confidence in my own powers which nature had given me." It had made him irritable and argumentative, he believed, inclined him to maintain his own opinions even when he knew he was wrong, simply to keep his end up: he thought it had done his temper and character irreparable harm.

"Neither my parents or brothers had any idea of the injury thus engendered, still less of the pain and mortification, or the thing would have quickly ceased; and children cannot, even if they are so disposed, fully explain their own feelings: they generally show themselves in tears, passion, or sullenness." In thinking thus, Henry sometimes wondered if he was simply "putting a varnish on my own deficiencies"; but did not feel he was wholly to blame for his comparative unsuccess in life. He thought that if it had not been assumed that he was as tough as his brothers, if anyone had found out what he really could do, and encouraged him in that, the necessary confidence would have come. The Jesuits in their schools were so wise, he thought, in their individual treatment of different boys. Boyish spirits had supported him most of the time; but he had suffered continual distress and sometimes sharp pain. "I have been behindhand in everything, followed, not led", Henry gloomily continued; but neither to his parents nor to the outer world did he, in fact, seem less up to snuff than the others. His mother had thought him in some ways the most charming of the lot.

"As an instance of how a single word will encourage or discourage youth—one of my first attempts at drawing was to make a copy of the ancient Roman Temple of the Sibyl at Tivoli. My brother Richard copied the print along with me, and when finished we showed them both to our Father: he examined them for some time and then said that Richard's was the neatest done, but that mine displayed a greater turn for drawing. I was surprised, because independent of being usually considered behindhand in everything, I really thought Richard's copy far the best; but this one observation gave me spirit to continue; and the only drawback to my pleasure was in seeing Richard so discouraged.

"I was of a weaker fibre than my brothers, though since strengthened by a sea life: I therefore never could equal them, and this gave me a feeling of despair . . . all [were] far more able than myself, and as they have since proved, rather above the common run in sense and talents. I was the son also of a man of lofty mind and powerful intellect, only lacking opportunity to blaze forth amongst the brightest spirits of the age, whose mind and body were equally beautiful and vigorous . . ." Perhaps he had been over-sensitive, Henry admitted: "My brothers were and are all love and kindness; they are the dearest friends I have or ever had, and therefore have caused me considerable indifference in seeking other friendships." All little boys, he thought, were in some sort tyrants—"The mischief was done in boyish pranks and all the thoughtless gaiety of youth, but I have never recovered from the joke!" He was probably right.

But blame he would not; and even felt moved to insert at this point in his journal an epitaph on his father that he had written earlier—

Reader, if worth or virtue e'er did move
Thy mind to honour or thy soul to love,
If strong integrity thy heart enclose
Or if that heart e'er wept at others' woes;
If brilliant talents play a noble game
In fields of science or the lists of fame,
If the stern virtues of the stoic rule
With all the mildness of the Christian school
Pervade thy heart, Oh drop a kindred tear,
For these and Napier sleep united here!

Lady Sarah has far more effectively captured the imagination of succeeding generations with her charm and her naturalness; but much as they loved her, it was Colonel George (Donny) who rode triumphant in the hearts of his sons throughout their lives. Nor did they ever forget the transcendent goodness and kindness of their aunt Louisa Conolly, whose beautiful house at Castletown had been for so many years their happy stamping ground.

Henry's life at sea had not been easy. He had been one of those ardent young naval officers who never seem to be in the right place at the right time, going through their long endurance of cold, hardship and storm without the compensating thrill of action or of glory. He had been on Whitelocke's failed expedition to Buenos Aires, and had then been dispatched to the East Indies, where he had succumbed to such an appalling illness that messages had sped home to tell that all hope was gone. Recovered, he was left the prey of life-long and increasing malady; was sent to Halifax; and, in command of the sloop of war *Rifleman*, narrowly missed capturing the Vice-President of the United States (who had ventured out on a boating picnic and had to make a hasty retreat into the shallows). Stranded at the end of the Napoleonic Wars without a ship, like many another he had been jobless since, for all his long service and his applications to Lord Melville; he was galled to see many men with more influence getting commands, though he himself had been commanding ships on active service when they were still in the nursery.

Somehow he had picked himself up and kept himself going; not without a final row with Melville over the latter's perfidy in breaking promises of promotion; had turned his attention to improvements in gunnery, in the design of ships, in machinery for stowing boats and lowering them swiftly, of none of which the Admiralty took note. The Royal Society, however, did take note, making him a Fellow in 1820. And three years later Henry had married Caroline Bennet, gentle and charming, and so beautiful with her bright complexion and her arresting combination of brilliant hazel eyes and pitch-black hair that whenever she arrived at a party everyone stopped talking and gazed at her spellbound.

So far so good and happy; but Caroline was delicate, and more dangerously still, she was Henry's first cousin. Only three of their eight children survived and those precariously; this trip south had been taken after the death of the latest baby. Henry's maternal uncle, the third Duke of Richmond, like many another gouty and lonely nobleman, had, after the death of his childless wife, liaised with his kind and handsome housekeeper, and Caroline was their child. The activities of Mrs Bennet thereafter become obscure; but she seems somehow in a light-fingered manner to have extracted most of Earl's

Court from her benefactor and out of the hands of his legitimate heirs and assigns, of whom the principal was his nephew Charles Lennox, heir to his dukedom. Earl's Court is no mean heritage, and some of it might, without unfairness, have gone to Henry and his wife, since Henry himself was half a Lennox, and a legitimate one at that. But not so much as a lamp-post had come their way, and they were living happily on moderate means; while Mrs Light, a younger Bennet sister, was, if rumour speaks rightly, at this time or soon after swanning joyfully round the Mediterranean in a large and very expensive private yacht, and otherwise living a jet-set life, to the permanent loss and detriment of all future Richmonds. Henry was handsome, lithe, and strong, with crisp fair hair and large mild blue eyes; but a harsh critic might have described him as a born loser, if anyone who appreciates the joys of life as much as he did can ever be so called.

Byron, though he had expressed his detestation of "antiquarian twaddle", had also felt "real Happiness in such magnificent scenery" when he came singing across the channel from Cephalonia to visit Ithaca those few years earlier: there was something in its air, so clear and totally wholesome. No wonder that Ulysses had reigned from here over both islands, free as Ithaca was from Cephalonia's malarial lowlands. Henry called his visit to Ithaca "a drop of honey in the cup of life", and all the way back across the strait to Samé young Charley Kennedy, fluent in Greek, had never once stopped joking with the boatmen, so that their way, apart from brief intervals for translation, was one of ceaseless laughter.

At Samé they explored the ruins of the ancient town—great polygonal blocks, squared, smoothed, and laid without cement, but so exquisitely fitted to each other that Henry had not been able to insert the blade of his small pen-knife between the joints; he had heard tales of this but never till now believed it. They rode past "ancient Pronos high on its steep and rugged hill" into a narrow valley covered with fine young trees; from here, at least, that firm ruler Charles had managed to exclude the all-devouring goats. All elsewhere had been dragged bare by them: "I would have no mercy on goats", the animal-loving Henry decided; and riding through this winding valley he hardly knew whether to admire more the brilliance of light and shadow or "a magnificent piece of masonry built by Kennedy to sustain the road". A few hours' riding took them out into "a wild bleak region of an opposite character; savage, rugged, and sublime", leading to the plain of Saint Gerasimo, floored in a fertile soil which centuries of erosion from the denuded mountainside had rendered deep and rich. Gerasimo, the patron saint of Cephalonia, "has it seems taken my brother under his immediate and personal protection, as the good people believe; so implicit a credit is given to this by the peasantry that some of them kneel to him for a blessing as he passes!"

And blessings, Henry considered, were what they had got—honest government, the destruction of bandits and oppressors, impartial justice, order, frugality and diligence in public office and public expenditure, good roads, improved agriculture, buildings, schools, commodious quays, a healthy prison, and lighthouses. If those were not blessings, what was? And he noted the long avenue which, in compliment to the saint, Charles had planted across the plain to the convent gate and around the saint's holy well, to shade the poor people who came in their thousands from all over the island on his day.

Coming into Argostoli in the after-sunset cool they crossed the bridge over a considerable creek; further up the banks were silting up, but there were old men living who would remember the Venetian galleys riding here at anchor. A clear stream fed an ancient reservoir; Venetian squadrons had regularly watered here, and so too perhaps had the inhabitants of ancient Kranea on the hill above, one of the four great cities which Cephalonia had boasted in classical times. Here too at Kranea was Cyclopian masonry, and Henry longed for excavation, but where was the money to come from? Stumbling through the great rocks and aromatic shrubs he and John Kennedy copied inscriptions—"clean and sharp as if cut yesterday". Palae, another of the four great cities, had been besieged by Philip of Macedon, and Polybius told how one of his generals had played him false, wishing to spare the city for the sake of a friend: the Greeks still called it Castro Palo.

Riding towards Heraclea next week Henry admired the Venetian fortress and capital of St George, "cool, high, and healthy, above the reach of malaria", the rich and populous district of Livato, and Charles's road along the face of the Black Mountain, "as level as a bowling green, seeming rather a tide mark than a human labour", and Jove's Island, far below in the blue water, with its chapel built on the ruins of Jove's temple. The Black Mountain itself had been called, long since, the Hill of Zeus; its dark immensity ended in the Scala, a drop down to a pretty little bay, where, so the Greeks said, a ruined town lay beneath the sand and the green clarity of the water. Near these shores still stood the convent where returning Crusaders would clank ashore to pay their vows on their long voyages home. The great displacement made by a recent landslide turned Henry's thoughts to the buried town; had such a fate sent it hurtling into the sea? His great virtue was to note and describe scenes of interest and beauty which Charles also loved but was too busy to record.

A road through well-wooded and mountainous country past the willow-fringed stream of the Racli valley brought them out onto Racli plain, different, but no less beautiful; a great stretch of fertile land long since abandoned through its vulnerability to Saracen attacks, and never since cultivated. Here Charles had planted his Maltese colony, on government land, to grow crops of "all sorts and all seasons", hoping that the Cephalonians would then take courage from the sight, and cease to confine their activities to olive and to vine, paying expensively with the sale of their currants—now greatly increased since the devastation of the Morea had removed competition—for all the corn and cattle they might so well grow themselves. Here was fine country for corn, for pasture, fruit, and vegetables.

But the authorities at Malta had taken this as an invitation to send, not the gardeners, farmers, labourers and carpenters for whom Charles had asked, but "many ragamuffins of no trade or calling"; everyone in short of whom they wished to be rid. "Just the sort of colonists whom Lord Bacon in his essays on Plantations warns people from taking, as 'a Shameful Unblest thing' ", Henry pointed out severely; and the scheme had not prospered in such hands. The government itself had had to take over as landlord, and the Maltese seemed happy enough to work for wages on land they might have had for themselves almost free. Elizabeth Napier, Charles's wife, had a great-nephew, Charles Curling, who had taken over as superintendent, and already "one hundred acres of as fine land as any in Cephalonia was cleared and planted with various and thriving crops". The Maltese lived in "a neatly built hamlet erected for them by Colonel Napier on the cliff overlooking the little harbour of Poros". The main road ran past their door, and Charles was building them a mole.

Flushed with satisfaction at all this, they rode on in the hot sunshine: looking up at the mountains from this pleasant plain Henry felt that they must have been "torn asunder by something more than an earthquake", so turbulent and broken-faced were they, and black as night in the afternoon light. "Fording the river we came to a narrow rocky pathway almost hidden by bay-tree, rhododendron, and oleander, with every kind of creeper and flowery garland hanging from the rocks, and ilex, oak, and plane shading the glen—the whole ride was enchantment, and our final issue from the gloom of the pass to a bright and flowery plain, level as a bowling green, and studded by nature with groups of beautiful trees like an English park completed our enjoyment."

Not less enjoyable was their host, Signor Cambici, receiving them "*en prince*; and after a good substantial supper *Al Greco*, that is to say, a whole lamb roasted; plenty of fowls; bread piled up on shining silver plates, and plenty of excellent wine with divers patriotic songs by our host, we were not sorry to go to our beds, tired from a ride of near thirty miles in the heat of the day.

"Cambici is a patriot, zealous, sincere, and enthusiastically attached to the cause of Grecian Liberty; he is rich too and maintained a hundred men commanded by his brother but all paid by him, at the siege of Missolonghi." His wife was handsome, but more *dame de ménage* than lady of the house. "She did not sing, but the patriotic airs were sufficiently interesting from the touching beauty of their music alone, independent of the place and the person who sung them. The struggle was not ended, the hearts of all were in it, and it was in itself glorious. Could we have understood the words we should of course have felt them more, but there was no lack of sentiment even in the sound, and assuredly none in our feelings", and Henry's heart swelled with love and revolution, with liberty, wine, war and song.

"Little Hanmer Bunbury who was of our party [he was a midshipman], having lost his arm by a Turkish shot at the Battle of Navarino became an object of strong interest, as well as of curiosity and respect, not alone to Cambici and his household, but to the Papa, or Priest, and many of the neighbouring people of every rank as soon as the fact became known. The fact of an English child losing his arm in defence of the cause excited deep interest and many a shaggy head peeped in at the door or window to see the young hero . . ." After which they got down to some tough talk about farming with their host.

Cambici had introduced lucerne into Cephalonia, and Charles had brought Guinea grass: Cambici showed them also a kind of couch grass which was native, "larger, stronger, and fully as difficult to eradicate as couch grass", which might do, as it did in Naples, as "a most nutritive food for cattle . . . We entered on this with great eagerness." Charles's black eyes doubtless shone, and Henry's blue ones blazed, his fair curly hair, naturally inclined to stand on end, fairer and wilder than ever from sun and wind. Had not Homer, somewhere, spoken of Cephalonia "black with lowing herds"? And if then, why not now? "There seems no reason why there should not be as fine beef, mutton, butter, milk, and cheese, not only in the Colony but all over Cephalonia as in England; at all events for a great portion of the year. Mrs. Napier has already made at Argostoli incomparable butter, cream so thick that I mistook it for clotted cream, excellent cream cheese; veal of the first quality and admirable bacon, put on the table, all charges included, for twopence half-penny a pound! This astonished her Greek and most of her English neighbours, but there was nothing to prevent their doing the same but indolence."

Most unindolently, Henry and Charles Curling were up at four next morning for a good close look at the ruins of Pronos, "for I had not seen half enough of the latter the evening before. Its excessive and peculiarly romantic beauty still hung about my mind like a first love, so that I could not rest without a second sight of it." Henry was on foot, but Charles Curling had trusted himself to a local pony, "nearer the size of a Dog than a Horse, and more like a Bear than either . . . my guess would be that Ulysses' old dog Argus fell in love with Penelope's donkey and hence the Cephalonian Shelties", Henry speculated. They climbed steadily, with Henry splashing in and out of the mountain streams and envying Charles Curling his local sandals, so much better adapted for rock climbing than his own heavy boots which allowed no play to the toes. Henry made two sketches, and they were on the way down when Charles Curling jarred his feelings by shooting a heron, "noble, stately, bold and proud, just alighted in the marsh . . . I have often marvelled at the recklessness with which really excellent and even tender-hearted men, when once the gun is in their hand, shoot right and left, and kill merely for the pleasure of killing. Nay, I have done so myself, but always with a dash of remorse, and hope never more to do so, for there is something so repulsive in the dying struggles of any animal as to paralyse all previous pleasure." He hoped a further step in civilization would "in time confine shooting to animals which serve for food, but there it must stop, unless we turn Pythagoreans or Hindoos . . . Why is man incited as it were to bloodshed even by the very construction of his frame and juices? This is God's work. But did he really intend it? A question for wiser heads than mine to answer."

Up on Pronos, as Henry and Charles Curling were standing among its gigantic tumbled stones, gazing at the distant coast of Greece, a huge eagle appeared overhead, "now sailing to and fro with a sort of disturbed dignity, now again bearing down on us like a three-decker . . . there is something peculiarly fine in the measured vibrations of an Eagle's wing . . . Cambici told us that there are many of them among these hills, and that he has known them, when people were near and seeking for their nests, clutch up a large stone in their talons and then hovering over their adversary endeavour to crush him by dropping it on his head." The soaring eagle in its strength, the high air of Pronos, so serene and beautiful, made Henry feel that the archaic men who made it their dwelling must at any rate have been extremely healthy, "running up and down these rocks like goats". Time was when he could have been as swift, but now Charles Curling had the legs of him. Perhaps even now, with practise? Across the strait and round Missolonghi desultory fight was still going on against its stubborn Turkish garrison, for Constantinople had held out for at least a nominal suzerainty; and Henry thought of those wiry Greek men who had stood so many thousand years ago where he now stood, and gazed across—with apprehension? with defiance? —at those distant hills of Greece, still now reverberant with the trumpets of a new-found freedom. He felt stirred and elated to his very depths, as if with Greece in its vanguard the sad old order were indeed changing, yielding place to new; and God were fulfilling himself in ways deeply satisfying to Henry's yearning soul. The fifes and drums of revolution were sounding from all over Europe.

CHAPTER VI

The Old Adam

They returned home to Argostoli by another route, passing through a valley where lateral streams "come glancing down the mountain and are here and there caught in their fall by wooden trumpet-mouthed spouts of several feet diameter and thrown almost perpendicularly on mill-wheels, which from the great height and impulse are driven with a very small quantity of water". The whole scene, with the falling streams smothered in foliage, the millers' huts like swallows' nests against the rocks, seemed to Henry "completely Arcadian"; and as they came into the narrowest part of the glen "Captain Kennedy, who has a fine voice, suddenly broke out into a famous song amongst the Greeks which calls on rock and hill and stream and mountain to overwhelm the oppressors. It had a beautiful effect in this valley so suited to its invocation where the words were echoed a hundred times"; and once again the *angst* floated out of Henry—the frustration of his long-delayed promotion, the fear of that recurrent East Indian virus that ate into his once powerful frame, the mysterious maladies of his young children, his wife's alarming delicacy, their far from abundant means. He was a boy again, catching John Kennedy's tune, sending it reverberating from crag and cliff and leaping stream and fall.

Next came a desolate valley, "frowning hills and deep chasms, a change from Paradise to Purgatory", which was the scene of the recent capture of the brigand Condremara and his six followers. These had been terrorizing the villages on this part of the Black Mountain, and the villagers had appealed to Charles for help. Charles first took into custody the brigand's family, "all those who would supply Condremara with food for love and family ties, the rest only doing so from fear or money, in both of which if necessary he could outbid the robber". He next marched three hundred soldiers into the Black Mountain, assembled all the threatened villagers and told them that he was turning them all out of their homes and on to the mountain—it was summer—and not allowing them back until Condremara was taken. "The villagers at first thought that Colonel Napier was not in earnest, but their empty stomachs soon showed them their error, and being further stimulated by a reward . . . the Peasantry finally determined on the chase and executed their purpose with all the acuteness and energy which belongs to their nation. They spread themselves in the most scientific manner village by village all around that part of the Black Mountain where Condremara was known to be, and the first man who got sight of him made the signal, then came on a general chase of the whole district, and when he escaped from that there was a shout to the next to take up the chase." Condremara had been captured exhausted, without bloodshed; and his balloon was further pricked by his being escorted to trial and prison at Argostoli by an Irish sergeant accompanied only by a single soldier, "to the astonishment of all the inhabitants who had deemed it as probable that the Black Mountain should be levelled in ten days as that the terrible Condremara could thus be taken and brought in a prisoner!" Inspired, Henry sat down to write a ballad. He did not question his brother's high-handed methods. Charles was the adored eldest who had saved his life when he was a four-year-old, the immediate chief of his clan, loyalty to whom was in the marrow of Henry's Scottish bones. Besides, he agreed.

He continued to enjoy his sojourn in Cephalonia to the full; writing, sketching, recording, with Caroline accompanying him whenever the jaunts were not too strenuous. He was no geologist, he feared, but he noted the red rock of the mountain, the black soil of the valleys, gypsum formations, stones veined in red and white and smooth and hard as marble, brescia, white and brown sandstone that he believed to be a kind of oolite. He noted the cattle, the diminutive native horses, the Turkish steeds imported from the Morea, mules, donkeys, the occasional jackal, and on Guardiana island, a few rabbits. Produce in the main came from the ubiquitous olive and the currant-vine. Amongst the plants he noted squill, sage, thyme, mint, and a kind of euphorbia. There were innumerable wild flowers, china-aster everywhere, hyacinths, stock, cyclamen.

As to the human fauna, Henry thought there were few pretty women in Cephalonia except at Asso, though he noted in both sexes finely shaped and well-set heads. "In Ithaca I scarcely saw an ugly man except from age", and as to the girls, "it is an island of beauties and not common ones, of the most delicate cast". The males of both islands were on the whole "handsome graceful figures with finely chiselled features and intelligent but often extremely ferocious expressions. Their motions are easy and graceful; their frame light, hard, and active, with much natural action and I am told uncommon eloquence in their discourse. There is a manly freedom and general boldness of demeanour quite at variance with the reputation for dissimulation and obsequience which Greeks generally enjoy. They live with much frugality and sobriety and a great deal of their food consists of wild herbs especially the dandelion which along with other vegetables they cook into a very good dish." On the other hand Henry was obliged to admit that they all loved idleness and gambling. But was it not after all, sensible to eschew hard labour, if they had all they needed? "The privilege and option of remaining idle or at leisure is the ultimate object of more provident and industrious countries. Should we not rather admire contentment in their present condition, without being disturbed by gain or softened by luxury?" They were improvident, but "Sufficient for the day is the evil thereof. If a man be content with the mere necessaries of life, why should he be blamed for not labouring to make himself master of its comforts and luxuries, both relative terms? Why should he toil for riches, acquire new wants which he *don't* want?"

All the same, it seemed very, very rum, to English Henry, for people to live on an island surrounded by fish and not fish for it. There was hardly a fisherman between all four harbours, Argostoli, Asso, Guiscardo and Saint Euphemia, to say nothing of Samé and Poros, "besides many other little creeks and bays invaluable to an industrious people". Charles was unable to let this be, and had established a fishery with a ten-year contract to supply Argostoli.

Henry was sad to see that the ladies of the islands were giving up their most becoming national dress and taking to French fashions, and he much admired the beautiful Countess Siciliani, who was a Macedonian and wore her native dress with an air of immense distinction, "instead of the cockatoo bonnets of the day which turn every woman into a Parisian Grisette and confound all ranks in one mass of execrable taste". At Santa Maura the ladies had stuck to their Greek dress, and all the peasantry still wore it, and so indeed did the men—"a close fitting waistcoat, a short light jacket, and a pair of petticoat trousers confined below the knee, and at the waist by a coloured silk sash". One night the Napier party had been picnicking on the grass under some olive-trees, and they had heard singing and asked the party to come nearer, which they had most happily done; and the whole lot of them, some Olympian and some local, had danced the Pyrrhic dance and sung songs, and the Napiers had poured out coffee for them and made friends, and all had been struck by their naturalness and dignity of manner, and the real pleasure with which they had performed. "How could one ever venture to ask a group of English rustics to come over and sing, except for hard cash and a previous bargain?" Henry had been impressed by the Greeks' total absence of awkwardness or bashfulness, "although in presence of the Resident, and two Captains of British line of Battleships in Uniform". The Pyrrhic dance was not, he thought, so pretty or warlike as the Maltese sword dance, but gained by the grace and freedom of the dancers. A night was spent camping up the Black Mountain in a hut which Kennedy had built for keeping an eye on the forests: they drank champagne and cooked on the open fire and rose at three in the morning to climb the 5,000 feet summit and see the dawn come up over the mountains of Greece. On the way up Henry's horse, which he was leading, fell off the path and down a steep slope, sliding alarmingly down the mountainside; he had kept hold of its reins, accompanied it for some way, and was able to haul it back. But when they arrived at the top the morning was cloudy and drizzling; they spent some while in the shelter of the cairn of stones which surveying Captain Smith of the Royal Navy had built there to indicate the highest point, but the day declined to clear, and the drama of sunrise over the tossing sea of the Greek mountains did not reveal itself. It had been delightful all the same, and Henry scrutinized the Black Mountain spruce—"large and beautiful and spreading, but I saw no straight sticks, none that would answer naval purposes or even make a Frigate's Topmast". Not for nothing had Henry been bred a sailor and taught to notice everything and to fend for himself in any quarter of the globe. Till very recently these hills had been so bandit-ridden that it was impossible to ride through them without an escort of two hundred men.

At Metataxa Henry saw Byron's house, finding it not without difficulty as he had asked for it by the poet's name, and here he was still universally known as Milordo. Byron had chosen Cephalonia from amongst the Ionian islands, Henry was told by some of the garrison, because he had heard "that Colonel Napier's opinions were not narrow, bigoted, or illiberal; but declined becoming an inmate of his home lest it might embroil him unpleasantly with higher authorities, which in those days were anything but liberal in thought, views and actions: they met as mere acquaintances but parted as friends." Henry admired the house's situation, "small, but in one of the most retired corners of this beautiful village, with a fine view of the rich plain on one side and on the other the castle of St George and Black Mountain". The road from Metataxa to St George invited Henry's disdain; very bad, and not laid out by Charles or Kennedy.

But at Lixuri Henry could admire Kennedy's Market House, "a noble edifice, strictly Greek, and of the Doric order"; this, with its sixty columns and well-proportioned portico had been dug from a local quarry unearthed by Charles and Kennedy. The lower part of it was let to tradesmen, the rent of whose shops paid most of the interest on the £5,000 that had been spent. Upstairs was the Lixuri school, "on the Lancastrian system"; the rest housed a court of justice. Over the portico was a terrace, and under it a cool and shaded walk for the hot months. Why, people asked, place such a fine building here and not at Argostoli? But it was Charles's plan, as far as possible, to disperse the island's prosperity and not concentrate it all in the capital. Had not ancient Cephalonia carried four great towns? The crab of Lixuri was a harbour unsheltered from the south winds; "a Mediterranean gale is up and down in a twinkling, but *lives hard* and does much mischief while it lasts", Henry knew well.

He and Caroline departed for a trip to Zante: they had longed to explore all the islands but settled for this one. On Cerigo, Henry had heard, there were peasants who still worshipped the Nereids and Naiads under a slightly different but recognizable name; if one wanted a side-line, how much better, he thought, to worship the spirits of these sparkling places, rather than a lot of gloomy saints incessantly being martyred in ways much better forgotten. On Zante, he noted, the people spoke a Greek so differently accented from the Cephalonian that it was instantly recognizable. Zante was sunny and lush, "like a garden and precisely exemplifying the French expression Riante". To add to its beauty, in the harbour were HM ships *Wellesley*, *Windsor Castle*, and *Rattlesnake*—"I do love to see a British Man of War, especially in a foreign port: besides I like the three captains."

Zante, Fior del Levante
Cefalonia, fa Melancolia

their Venetian conquerors and overlords for six hundred years had maintained; and Henry saw the point; looking back from this Eden on to Cephalonia's dark looming mountains and the wild clouds of her snow-clad heights. A certain peace and plenty prevailed in Zante: its assistant conqueror and first governor, Major John Slessor, had been given a handsome sword by the Zantiots on his departure, for being the first uncorrupt ruler who had ever come the island's way. Zante was undoubtedly sunnier and cosier, and next morning Henry joined a party of naval officers who were off to see the Pitch Wells, "a celebrated Natural Curiosity". "We had some difficulty in steering a steady course through a very intricate country, and soon got fairly out of our latitude but enjoyed a beautiful ride for our pains; besides we were a merry party of navy chaps to whom nothing in this way came amiss." The countryside was opulent and beautiful, the pitch lay below the surface of the wells but could be stirred up by a stick; the surrounding ground was so sticky that one of their horses lost a shoe, "by fair suction"; and Captain Walker, RN, however merry, was instantly able to translate the Greek inscription from an ancient altar at Melinado; not that it was very exciting, just a notice that a long ago Zantiot couple had dedicated their daughter to Diana. Henry and Caroline were staying with Lord Charles FitzRoy, the Resident of Zante, and they spent an agreeable evening dining on board the *Windsor Castle* with the Bouveries, Maitland, and Orlando Bridgeman. The surge to Greece had already begun.

Stopping a night or two on Cephalonia to say goodbye to Charles and Elizabeth, they took the steamer for Corfu, passing by "that part of the Leucadian coast so famous in classic lore as the scene of Sappho's suicide—the far-famed Leucadian Leap. It is a long point of land running out for some distance into the sea in white perpendicular cliffs of vast height and admirably adapted to cure love: the Greeks still call it the Lady's Leap." The whole coast of Epirus, and "the lovely channel of Corfu, like a vast and glassy lake enclosed by the richest and most romantic scenery" made Henry feel that here indeed was a land worth fighting for. "Our whole course to-day was enchantment", if only they had not been travelling in a sort of floating Birmingham, "choked and sickened by coal smoke, train oil, and candle-grease": Henry, bred in sail, did not take kindly to steamers. "It is bad enough to travel through Birmingham on shore; but to take it to sea with you amidst all the graceful deities of Greece! For Shame!"

At Corfu Sir Frederick Adam received them with courtesy and put them in a sumptuous suite of his newly-built palace; it was difficult not to like him personally; and Charles still trusted him; but Henry could not quite believe in him, all the same. He was right not to: Adam was already pursuing Charles with what Harold Nicolson beautifully describes as his "affable but tortuous malevolence". They departed in the government steamer for Ancona, and reached Brindisi in a fog—"I was up nearly all night with Lieutenant Kennedy [a naval officer in command] endeavouring to make out the land, and thus had an opportunity of observing the perfect confidence with which Italian sailors will try to persuade you that they see the land, while at the same time they are pointing quite away from its line of bearing." Kennedy had trusted to his charts and his own reckoning, and he had been right. Henry thought that in this respect Italians were like an Irishman, "scorning to be thought ignorant of anything; if he has not a reason or a story he soon manufactures both, and believes them afterwards".

At Ancona Henry had leisure to do his accounts, and reflected sadly that though he and Caroline had been guests almost everywhere and had had several free passages, they had still managed to spend an average of £7 a week, on tips and presents and so on. Quarantined for a fortnight in the lazaretto at Ancona, Henry recorded the Latin and Italian inscriptions, tried to translate Manzoni's *May the Fifth*, and complained of the exorbitant price charged for the bed-linen, cooking utensils, wooden chairs, knives and forks and spoons and tables and beds which they were obliged to hire for this enforced stay. The rent of these had cost far more than any hotel Henry had ever stayed in; and wasn't this supposed to be a Papal State, and not a conspiracy to rob strangers? "Extortion, deceit, falsehood, and holy humbug in every department of the Papal Government", Henry grumbled; but with his dogged fairness, argued his way to the conclusion that England itself was "rife in Napoleons of mercantile dishonesty—if ever there were one place more than another where Mammon is devoutly worshipped and reverenced in all his phases and aspects, it is good, moral, religious England!"

Inspired by Greece, Henry trod the shores of Western Europe with a certain exhilaration. He wondered how freedom could be brought to Italy, to luckless France back again under the stultifications of Bourbon rule, to his own country struggling in the unforeseen results of its industrial revolution. Let common sense prevail! and the essential changes be made without the bloody estrangements of revolution. He was getting old, was an invalid, a failure, a spectator; none the less he believed there were still things he could do to speed the good work along. Perhaps, by writing of their glorious past, he could help to stir the Italians out of the political apathy which endured subjection to Austria, division into innumerable tiny states, lethargic and varied administrations? Or would the future only afford a series of dreadful events at which he must stand by helpless?

And Henry's exhilaration was tempered by some apprehension as they drew away from Ancona; and he leant back in the carriage as he and Caroline swayed along the dusty roads to their home in Florence, the confidence with which Charles always infused him trickling imperceptibly from him as the sun-baked miles succeeded one another.

Back in Cephalonia the harbour of Argostoli was now well-founded, the swampy inlet filled in, quays and new houses built; a fine esplanade swept along the front, and in the middle of this, by order of Corfu, was placed a remarkably bad statue of Sir Thomas Maitland. King Tom was wearing Roman dress, and awkwardly posed; his right hand proffered a scroll, his left was behind his back, resting upon a backside to which the sculptor seemed to have given an unnecessary prominence. Henry had been contemplating this work of art with some amusement one morning, when an Irish soldier joined him. What, Henry asked him, was the statue supposed to be about? "Plase your honour, sir, the Gineral is giving thim the constitution wid won hand and telling thim to kiss his arse wid the other." This reply had delighted Henry, himself an Irishman by upbringing though not by birth: it was a view of King Tom's character and policy which he felt could hardly be better or more succinctly expressed.

In 1825 Maitland had been succeeded at Corfu by Sir Frederick Adam, a character without the intelligence and gusto that had made bearable the arbitrary ways of King Tom. Adam was a great one for little pomps and exactitudes, and soon instructed Charles, a very furry man, to shave off his whiskers. Charles complied, posting his harvest to Adam in an envelope. He was soon at odds with Adam about finances: Zante and Cephalonia were being drained of gold to pay for an alleged representative "senate" in Corfu. Charles thought it a pompous nonsense, a waste of money, and quite unrepresentative of anybody. King Tom in his day had once appeared in its midst more than usually pickled, stared round him at the senators, announced, "You can all go to hell", and stumped out. Nor, as Charles pointed out, did it fool "the acute satirical Greeks" into thinking themselves self-governed: why give its members enormous pay, exceeding the private fortunes of the richest inhabitants? In Cephalonia, by persuading the people to terrace more land, he had doubled the output of currants; would Adam forward a memorandum to the Home Government asking them slightly to lower the high duty on currants, so that more could be sold? "We can live by, but not on, our currants." No, Adam would forward no such thing, he replied, with a wealth of circumlocution: a refusal causing distress, discontent, and eventual emigration from Cephalonia.

King Tom's far-famed Constitution for the Islands, with its Senate and its advisory bodies and its wealth of safeguards for Ionian participation, had in fact been a masterpiece of humbug, as everybody who knew Old Tom, or was aware of the current demoralization of the Greeks after their centuries of enslavement by the Turks, had known it would be. The government of the several islands varied according to size: at Cephalonia the British Resident was assisted by a local regent and three judges, a treasurer, a secretary, an advocate fiscal, an archivist, and a weekly meeting of local magistrates. Law was administered by the old Venetian code, which as Henry said, was just as well, as it did not involve juries "and it would be a long business to make twelve Greeks agree in any single point". One of its disadvantages was that no evidence against an accused man was admissible from anyone even remotely related to him; so that if a man in company with two of his sons was murdered by a third, the murderer had perforce to go free. Other discrepancies made it difficult for someone like Charles accustomed to English common law not to interfere with the judiciary; as did what Henry called "the volatile and intriguing disposition of the litigants, their family feuds and jealousies, their love of self-aggrandizement to the exclusion of public morality, their incessant struggle for mastery over each other", which made "a mild despotism best adapted to their condition". Charles, on a much smaller scale, and with infinitely more care and attention to what actually went on, was as arbitrary as King Tom.

Greek divisions and hatreds were still savage. Charles once said that there was only one project in which every man, woman and child on Cephalonia would have followed him with heartfelt support and enthusiasm, and that would be on an expedition to kill every man, woman and child in any of the other islands. The Regent, he told Emily, was "a designing foolish old woman who hates me because I put a bridle on his rascally tricks". He had put too many bridles on too many powerful feudatories, though Countess Annina, a feudal lady powerful as any, had backed Charles up in quelling a disorder amongst men working on the roads and attacked in her territory—"even if he demands your sucking babes, deliver them up at once", she had crisply commanded her vassals. But among the upper echelons of the islanders this line was not widely taken.

Throughout the summer of 1827, when Charles returned to Cephalonia after his marriage to Elizabeth in April, the war on the mainland had dragged miserably on. On arrival in the island Charles had found Paul Marie Buonaparte, son of Lucien, and had had him to stay. This eighteen-year-old, a student at Bologna University, wanted to join the Greeks. Charles had "liked him much", and had always admired his father Lucien; "a man who refused sovereignty altogether, when most of the great crowns of Europe were within his choice"; he gave Paul Marie a letter of strong recommendation to Admiral Cochrane, but at Nauplion, sadly, the young man had accidently shot himself on board ship whilst cleaning his pistol. Charles regretted the departure this spring of Bathurst, "a good master, of whom we had nothing to complain, for he took a fair view, and a liberal one, of our small affairs". He rejoiced when Wellington became Prime Minister—"We are in too bad a state for any man but *old Douro* to save us. Weak men do not suit these times, and orators least of all . . . Is Lady Georgina Bathurst married? My love to her. Wedded or single she is the prettiest person I know", Charles wrote to Louisa. "Again let me say that the duke being premier delights me; the best chance for England is having the greatest man of Europe for her ruler. He has done all he ever had to do well, and we are too far gone to care about Whig or Tory, it is an affair of existence."

For many of the Greeks the war on the mainland, still trailing on, was also an affair of existence, bare and doubtful, under either Turks or fellow countrymen: no boundaries had yet been fixed, or definitive treaties signed. "Church has sent me an account of his plans, which appear to me bad", Charles wrote to his brother William in April of 1828. "He has spent money and food idly at Dragomestre, and now he has neither, nor discipline. He had but few men, yet has spread them on a chain of posts for fifty miles, and he is trying to stop the predatory excursions of the Greeks; but what else has he to look to? He threatens, he says, Lepanto and Missolonghi; that is, he sends ten or twenty thousand wild rascals to the neighbouring mountains who come back when they have stolen all the sheep and goats of their friends.

"Fabvier has failed at Scio [Chios], as he has everywhere. He is superior as a general to Church; but they have both gone the wrong way to work, and shew that they neither knew the Greeks nor their own lesson. To attack fortified places or positions is not of the Greek character, troops, or people, in their present state. They should take and fortify positions on the Turks' line of operations, which are few, and unchangeable because they depend on certain strong towns. The Greeks are bad for assailing such positions, but the Turks are worse; they would wonderfully dislike the option of starving, or carrying a Greek position: the secret on both sides is, that neither expects quarter, and therefore both defend themselves lustily. All the Greek generals have been bent on assailing positions; but neither they, nor Fabvier, nor Church, have thought of assailing supplies: they must change this, or suffer defeat.

"As to these islands, would that Lord Bathurst were our master again! We are going fast. Sir F. Adam has spent all our money, dribbled it away, and has nothing to show. He has no system, no general views; all is extravagance accompanied by mean savings, and the employing of too many people too highly paid . . . He has appointed a body called The Supreme Council of Justice. Kirkpatrick is the head, having under him two clever Greeks who ride Adam roughshod, and Adam does not perceive that they are tying up his own power in a sack, for they rule the islands . . ."

But Greece was now, after all, almost an independent country, and less inclined to have its compatriots pushed around, whether by Byron's fellow countrymen or not. And Canning's and Wellington's governments had been trying, in the later twenties, to move towards self-government in dependencies, as a sop to keep the Whig opposition quiet.

During the spring Adam was preparing a piece of legislation which would, he told a colleague, tie up Napier's hands. A right royal row was brewing.

His happy marriage did not seem to have softened Charles's rule, nor his belief that he was the Father of the Cephalonians, and that Father knew best. Henry's long visit, his brotherly admiration, his loyalty and enthusiasm for Charles's works and reforms, had deepened and strengthened all Charles's chieftain impulses, as did Kennedy and Curling's constant support. Henry was by nature even more agin the far-off government than Charles was, and encouraged him against Adam—why should a parcel of hangers-on in Corfu think they knew best? Capo d'Istria, now in power in Greece, was hand in glove with the Russians: to hand over power to locals who supported him was simply to encourage the ever-present menace of Russian influence in the islands. The Russians had one immensely strong lever: like the Greeks, they were of the Orthodox Church. In his impatience with the general folly of Christian divisions, Charles had insufficiently considered how the Orthodox priests would resent the settlement of several hundred Maltese, all Roman Catholics, at Pronos. Religious rage was nearly as deep and bitter in the eastern Mediterranean as it had been when Orthodox and Catholic split apart in 1054: to the Cephalonians, though officially tolerant, the Roman Catholics were only a more archaic form of Protestant, and equally beyond the pale.

But between Charles and Adam there was as yet not much more than the normal friction to be expected with a despotic high commissioner acting as suzerain over a series of despotic local governors. In his major row over Rhys's complaints, Adam backed Charles, and both together again fell foul of the Horse Guards. On Cephalonia a motherless thirteen-year-old girl whose father, a beggar, had induced the family of one of the garrison officers to employ her in their house, was taken thence by another young officer, seduced, and turned out on the town a fortnight later with a few pounds. The Cephalonians complained to Charles, who investigated, and asked that the young officer should be court-martialled. Adam sent home to the Horse Guards for permission, backing Charles's demand. The project was overruled at the Horse Guards, and a proclamation to this effect ordered to be read to all the garrison officers of the islands, reprimanding both Adam and Charles: they had "interfered in a private matter". "I don't follow the argument," one young officer wrote home from Zante, "are we to be gentlemen or not?"

"I still personally like Adam, he is only weak and misled, but I can no longer do the good I did in Maitland's time", Charles mourned in 1828. He cheered himself with the thought that the public works were going well, the lighthouses on Guardini Island and St Theodoro were all but finished. In time he might accomplish all he had planned, and leave Cephalonia on sound foundations.

In July a blow fell that left him deeply chagrined: Sir Frederick Adam had suddenly passed an act through the Ionian Senate for taking roads and public works out of the hands of the Residents and handing them over to the local authorities. "He had full right to do so", Charles admitted; but it was the death-knell to his road system and "my personal mortification is not slight". The Resident of Cythera chimed in with a parallel indignation—"All my exertions have been so much crime, and I walk about like a detected felon", he wrote.

Charles thought the islanders not nearly ready for this mild attempt at self-government. They were, he felt certain, still in need of a benevolent despot: law would be perverted by perjury. "Foster all institutions which educate the people, schools, a free press etc., but we have to do with an ignorant demoralised people, whose occupation is to rob and injure each other." "I have ruled Cephalonia for nine years", Charles grumbled; "changed the face of the island, increased the revenue and established justice." He thought of the drained marshes, the bridges he had built, the harbour busy behind its now completed mole, the contented peasants who before had gone in daily peril of their lives. He had made mistakes, but it seemed to him that he had done a lot more good than harm.

Going home on leave, he parted amicably with Adam. Some months later the Cephalonians declined to sign a loyal address to King William on his accession, having been persuaded by their priests that the new constitution for the islands would involve forcible conversion to Protestantism. Adam, visiting the island, was met by complaints against the Resident for oppressive conduct, and seems to have believed them: "He mistook the whoop of a faction for the voice of the people", William Napier afterwards wrote. The corvée system of road-building was not universally popular; but payments for exemption on the labour had been carefully graded, and the whole system sanctioned from Corfu. Adam had used the same method to make the Corfiots build him three palaces: one had been turned into a lunatic asylum, but had proved a failure: "It was not built for so many", Charles had rashly commented. (Like his mother, he could not resist these unlucky quips.) The Cephalonian roads had at least been built for the general benefit, and as the islanders easily made enough to live on by working for only three months out of the year, four days out of each of the remaining months did not seem to Charles a heavy requirement. But Adam reported officially that he could not allow Napier to resume office under him: Goderich had now replaced Bathurst at the Colonial Office, and he backed Adam.

One of the disadvantages of a military life as a training for public office is that it makes for belligerence. Charles had held a commission since he was eleven: it was to him axiomatic that attack is the best defence. Instead of resting on a record that was in the main excellent, he launched a burst of fire at Sir Frederick Adam. "I hope you will order Sir F. Adam to produce specific charges against me", he wrote to Lord Goderich, "limited to complaints made previous to his public attacks upon my conduct. Far be it from me arrogantly to assume that I have made no errors of judgment in the long period of eight years' government: but I am not guilty of what Sir F. Adam accuses me of; and the sweeping charges (unsupported by a single fact) of injustice, oppression, and conduct producing odium for myself and disaffection for my sovereign, I utterly reject as unfounded; and as a charge that I possess both the power and the fixed determination to repel." The fact was, he told Em, that he had "put the bridle on the Regent's rascally bribes . . . since I left Cephalonia Sir F. Adam has by filling various posts with this man's infamous relations whom I had chased from the public service for fraud or villainy, given a faction the upper hand"; and it was this faction who were raising the howl against him.

Charles then tried an interview with the Minister in London; but did himself no good. Goderich, soon to become Earl of Ripon, had waffled on for an hour. The victim of family bereavements, he was a tearful character; often trying as now, poor man, to make the peace between intractable subordinates, but too fearful to discover the truth or pronounce a definite judgment; his procedure was described by Charles as "descending to coax a poor colonel to be friends with a lord high commissioner . . . he said I was too stiff". He offered Charles the job of Resident of Zante; a move which lacked logic: if he had really oppressed the people of Cephalonia, why let him loose on the luckless Zantiots?

But Charles would not take Zante, to find himself under complete control of Adam, with no appeal from what he often felt were the Commissioner's daft decisions. "After standing a full hour of nonsense I said I am very much obliged to you, but no power shall make me put myself again under Sir F. Adam", he reported furiously. "Generals are sufficiently knavish but they can come to a point. Goody Goderich will not say Yea or Nay." Edward Curling had arrived in England with the cheering information that the Cephalonians were getting up a petition for his return: two thousand had signed it in the first week and it was going on fast. It would not, Charles thought, get any nearer London than the office at Corfu; and of course it never did.

Limping indignantly out of Whitehall, he went over in his mind the good things he felt he had done in Cephalonia, bringing horses and carts for the first time to the island, introducing spinning-wheels, terracing hillsides, opening harbours, building lighthouses, enforcing proper weighing and fair payment for the crops of currants on which most of the peasants lived. He thought of his hundred miles of road, forty of them blasted out of solid rock, the quarry of Lixuri stone opened, the spacious streets he had laid out, the market-place, the girls' school, the town hall and square with its colonnade, the swamps infilled. Then there were the Maltese he had settled on uninhabited waste in Cephalonia—"I feel proud of this colony", he wrote to his half-sister Louisa; "it is being of use to our kind to have taken 300 starving people, fed them and made them turn a desert into a garden." Handing over the roads and thus the *angheria* or corvée to the Regent and his colleagues had, as Charles foresaw, meant corruption, delay, and unfairness; the rich excused from contributions, the poor squeezed for greater ones. "To pay the forced labour", he had written in October of 1828, "is very desirable if it can be done", but it was no use doing it in an attempt to acquire popularity for British administration. "In the state things are in Greece it is vain to imagine that *any* government can be popular in these islands, history and common sense tell one this . . . the Ionians cannot be taxed more heavily without danger of making them emigrate to Greece" where, as yet, no-one had had time to organize any taxation.

Adam had forwarded a list of no less than seventy complaints by the Cephalonians against Charles's rule; at Corfu these had been sifted down into the dozen or so most important ones to be sent home to England, of which the major charge was that he had failed to pay one man compensation for a tree belonging to him which had been felled in the road-making: a complaint which, as Charles said, he could have had settled by application to a magistrate. Adam had repeatedly visited Cephalonia during Charles's rule: why had no-one appealed to him then, and why had Adam himself never then found any fault?

Much of what Charles had built would be undone by the 1953 earthquake that devastated Zante and Cephalonia; but the memory of him and his good works would live on in the island. He had learnt to speak Greek, he had made many friends, cherished the poor, never kept himself aloof. At Argostoli there is still a Napier Square, and Napier Gardens, and he is intimately remembered. British visitors still feel kindness from the islanders, which they attribute to Charles, who sailed away 150 years ago; and this indeed would have pleased him.

But the government treatment, and his virtual sacking from his post, freed in Charles an angry demon of fight, which was to grow over the years and land him in much trouble, like some terrible virus seeping into his veins as the long years of unemployment lagged by. The prickly, thistly dignity of his Scots blood would rise more readily in him. Most unwisely, as he afterwards realized, he published a book describing Ionia, and by implication, impugning the rule of Adam. Satisfying to himself, after the flow of Adam's calumnies, it also caused pleasure to some others. "You have turned him inside out, demolished and pulverized him", Thomas Gordon applauded from Paris. "It is a pity you do not spend your leisure on writing an extended series of military and political essays after the manner of Marshal Saxe, showing how troops ought to be treated and decayed countries improved. I do not think there is a man in Europe able to do it as well as yourself." Gordon had just been appointed colonel and ADC to King Otho of Greece, and sighed to Charles, "Oh that we had you in Hellas!"

But Adam did not forgive Charles, and was not without influence in preventing others from forgiving: and understanding between them became impossible. "Never embrayce dishonorabill agreyment", Alexander Napier, a sixteenth-century forebear had urged his brother; and such ancestral voices prophesied, if not doom, a deal of adversity. "Neither George nor Richard nor Henry are in the least revengeful", Charles wrote of his brothers. "William and I are, but only when resistance continues", he added imperiously.

He felt sure of having done good service, confident of being able to do better. But two feelings calmed and comforted Charles's riled heart as he left Cephalonia for his leave, thinking to return in a few months to complete the many things yet needing to be done. He did not know that this was farewell forever, as he sailed his last on these enchanted seas, past the little stone houses circling the crystal-clear bays, past the sentinel cypresses, the aromatic headlands baking in bright light. He had Elizabeth, he had his two beloved little girls, and all was well between them. And Greece was all but free: that long, long agony was drawing to the right close. At last the Christian powers had combined against the victorious Turks; Navarino had ensued; eventually a French expedition had bloodlessly ejected the Turks and the Egyptians from the Morea, and American generosity had fed its starving populace. After four hundred years the Greek people were their own masters again, set free perhaps for those triumphs of the spirit and mind that had once laid all Europe in their debt; even though at home Admiral Codrington had come within an ace of being court-martialled, and the battle had been referred to in the speech from the throne as "an untoward incident". For Turkey's weakness had been exposed, and Russia had been let into the Mediterranean Sea, and how that would end God knew.

Charles had not been the man who freed Greece. Byron, the dear fellow, had outgunned him. Tactlessness, intolerance of sentimental minds, crisp rejections of impossible schemes, had tripped Charles up; as had love, responsibility, tenderness. Byron, the impractical nervous poet, had succeeded where Charles had failed, for all his skill and energy, for all his confidence, warmth and magnetism. Mad, bad, and dangerous to know, Byron the bounder, the wild, moody, incestuous, sometime sodomite; Byron the mocker, the prince of good fellows, the generous kind friend; Byron the perennially fascinating, for ever trailing a scandal as glaring as a comet, had known at some deep, unconscious, poet's level, what to do. Simply by writing poetry, simply by going to the right place at the right time and dying there of fever, he had swung the great creaking, groaning apparatus of western idealism into movement, while practical Charles was still arguing about muskets.

Brilliance faded from the waters, the wind scudded across from the ashen mountains of the mainland, and the Dinas Bran of a world fame dissolved into the clouds.

Part II

England

"The flood of luxury and extravagance obliges many decent families to think of further migrations . . . and will drive them from place to place to the very Land's End . . . Here is now a mushroom of opulence . . . this portentous frenzy is become so contagious." Tobias Smollett, *Humphry Clinker*

CHAPTER VII

William

The country to which Charles and Henry would now return presented, for all its urban miseries and some rural hunger, at least the aspect of serenity. Looking back on its little-troubled continuity, its unchanged links with all that went before, the early nineteenth century seems calm and promising as some great inland lake with the morning mist rising off it and the world's stormy seas barred off by the stalwart hills of a general English contentment and solidity—a Morland country of soft woods and ruddy-faced sportsmen. To its statesmen, whose nerve had been broken in youth by the Terror of the French Revolution, it felt more like an earthquake area, which they felt in duty bound to stabilize (in everyone's interest), by covering it with cement and not listening to the rumblings from below.

In a long gruelling war Britain had triumphed through loyalty and cohesion; but after Waterloo came the divisive strains of peace. Napoleon had turned the British into a nation of warriors on a scale they had not known since the days when Louis XIV had done likewise. Unintentionally he had given the British a great chance for glory on land once more, by enabling them to fight the Peninsular War; to him a sideshow, but to Britain her finest hour for a century and more. In the face of a foe who they were told and believed, was intent on changing their way of life, on destroying their independence and their freedom, the great-hearted unity of Britain had never shone before the world more brightly than in those land campaigns in a priest-ridden and antediluvian Spain, where the Royal Navy and Wellington's leadership made it possible for them to hold out and fight for six murderous but inspiring years.

Napoleon's ambition had not only made the British glorious, it had made them rich; some of them at least. Metternich had told the French ambassador in Vienna that France, if she wanted to weaken Britain for ever, must make peace at once, for every day of war made the English richer. Landowners prospered, and the factory owners, the new class of industrialists, grew each year more opulent: while the rural poor whose crafts had been made redundant by the new factory processes moved perforce into the towns where they suffered bitter lack. Manipulated by the newly-risen captains of industry as so many items within a "liberal economy", they lived in tree-less slums, dwelling in exhaustion on the edge of unemployment and starvation.

John Wesley's movement was going far to soothe those few of them who were revolutionary-minded. In his own New Lanark Mills, Robert Owen was demonstrating that improved conditions of life and education in the factories would pay the employers and benefit the nation, aided and abetted by Archibald Hamilton, a young Scots landowner returned from the wars. The agnostics and the intellectuals, the Sidney Webbs of the epoch, rallied peacefully to the banner of Jeremy Bentham.

To the men who marched home from the seaport towns in 1815, accustomed by then to the rural poverty of the Continent which was so prevailing as to dull compassion, the tended countryside and prosperous villages of England seemed like another world. Poverty in England, eighteenth-century visitors had been wont to remark, was so scarce that you had to hunt round for it; but therein lay the danger: for what the eye did not see the heart was only too delighted not to grieve over. The rural poor had often kept themselves going by growing vegetables and keeping pigs and poultry: the industrial poor had vanished from the ken of all except each other. They starved unseen.

Far from those smiling fields and those lush woods sheltering neat cottages, those patriarchal villages where squire and parson for very shame would help them, a dreadful misery of stinking alleys and dark cellars held by the 1820s the many victims of mill and factory and of get-rich-quick employers. They were men and women of self-respect and intelligence, very many of them; cotton spinners who propped up Newton's *Principia* on their machine looms, or were amateur botanists who knew the name and habitat of every flower in range; who hungered for education as too often when trade was bad they hungered for bread.

For a kind of madness had possessed the victors, the desire to get rich and even richer at all costs, at no matter whose expense. Like children after nightmare they were desperate to suck sweets, to put war behind them and to surround themselves with life's pleasures and life's affirmations. Unlike the same universal post-war passion of our own day, exacted mostly at the expense of old-age pensioners, this was exacted at the expense of hard-working men, many of them old soldiers and sailors whose toil and dangers had made the whole festive grab possible, and of their families. And like rockets that cannot rise without pushing down the ground whence they spring, by none were working men more mercilessly oppressed and neglected than by those whose parents had themselves been working men; a new genus of boss far removed from all the old but still powerful influences of feudal obligation. John Bunyan's Sir Having Greedy rode again; and now not singly but in troops.

It was the fault of a great sloth of the imagination. The Industrial Revolution had moved so slowly that hardly anyone perceived its victims. Because few people of education and influence ever saw the miserable children herded into factory and mine, ever passed through the teeming slums, ever beheld the starving Irish, they were content to go on as if none of this dreadfulness existed; easing their consciences with a mild but effective mitigation of what came immediately to hand. As a people, the English are rarely cruel in intention, exposed as they have been over many generations to a mild climate and the sweetening influence of the gospels. But too many of them were busy being happy in the country, unaware that the rising competitive greedy middle classes, desperate to ape what were still known as their betters, were oppressing their fellows and handing England over to socialism on a plate; no less surely than the crusty wall-eyed monarchies of Europe, encouraged by churches whose major impulse was directed towards backing a frame of things which preserved their status and their wealth, were handing the Continent over with a lavish hand to communism and fascism.

"Do not you think that the tone of England—of that great compound of folly, weakness, prejudice, wrong feeling, right feeling, obstinacy and newspaper paragraphs, which is called public opinion—is more liberal (to use an odious but intelligible phrase) than the policy of the government?" Sir Robert Peel asked Croker on March 23rd, 1820. "Do not you think there is a feeling, becoming daily more general and more confirmed—that is independent of the pressure of taxation or any immediate cause—in favour of some undefined change in the mode of governing the country? It seems to me a curious crisis—when public opinion never had such an influence on public measures, and yet never was so dissatisfied with the share which it possessed." Peel might wonder, but Croker did not. "We should not give an inch to Parliamentary reform", he assured Peel two years later; and in 1832 the Reform Bill was to give him nightmares. "Once passed, and goodnight to the Monarchy, the Lords, and the Church" the aptly surnamed Croker told Lord Hertford on January 17th of that year. "She may live to be plain Miss Guelph", he brooded, after a visit to the young Princess Victoria a few months later; and to many like him, it seemed as if the world was about to come to a grisly end. Public opinion could go hang; it was, always had been and always would be, mad, gulled, and wrong. So thought many.

Soldiers, the reformer Cobbett thought, were less prone to hypocrisy and falsehood than most men; and certainly Charles and his brothers George and William raged at the complacency of England's rulers in these years; though not more than did Richard and Henry, barrister and sailor. The three eldest, half-pay colonels and Peninsular heroes, had little to live on but the fame of their early manhood, were racked with wounds, and pinched by sporadic half-pay. George had lost his right arm storming the breach at Ciudad Rodrigo, and sat uncomfortably from a Busaco bullet—"George was hit in the stern and I in the stem", Charles had commented: "That was burning the family candle at both ends." William still suffered from Alemtejo fever (probably recurrent malaria) and had a bullet lodged painfully near his spine.

Of George and William, the younger was the more vocal, the more rebellious. He had at least a well-to-do wife, Caroline, a niece of Charles James Fox, of whom William himself was a first cousin; although, twenty years on, the Holland money was less impressive than it had been in 1811, and the William Napiers had nine children. William had been a colonel since he was twenty-six, but the command of his regiment, to its furious indignation, had been bought over his head by someone else who could afford the ready cash. He and Caroline had been happy enough, living in a house in rural Sloane Street, while William eased his bitter war memories out of himself by learning to paint and sculpt. But as the twenties stretched towards the thirties, and no relief for England's or Ireland's miseries hove in sight, William came to feel ever more strongly that love and art were not enough.

Five years of peace passed, ten years: prosperity of even the most modest kind seemed further away than ever, for people in general. Charles had always enjoyed a laugh, "but at these things I cannot laugh", he told his mother in 1820; and William, who also had dearly loved jokes and fun, felt the same. He and Charles were bound to each other by the rarest ties of sympathy and like-mindedness—almost as if they had been identical twins. Their lives acted and reacted upon each other's, so that it is not possible to tell Charles's tale without including William's. Every blow that fell upon William repercussed in time upon Charles. Every injury to Charles was felt tenfold by William. In the end it would bring disaster upon both.

Possibly feeling that political influence lay that way, William had turned to writing. In 1821 his review of Jomini's book on Napoleon's campaigns was published in the *Edinburgh Review*: asked to a public dinner in the home of his clan, he thought Edinburgh a delightful city, "the air is cold and elastic". Everybody ought to be happy in such a climate, but for "the crushing tyranny . . . the detestable intolerance and cruelty of a Scotch ministerialist in power . . . exceeding the most determined advocate for despotism in England, the most bigoted priest-ridden wretch in Spain, the most violent ultra-royalist in France." But the success of this article sparked him off: walking in "the fields of Belgravia" with a friend, he was persuaded to write his Peninsular history. For the moment his rage at those who were now openly denigrating Sir John Moore exceeded his rage at government stupidity and mass misery. His wife Caroline encouraged him, and Wellington lent him the whole of Joseph Buonaparte's correspondence captured at Vitoria. (When the Duke learnt that clever Caroline had broken the code he said he wished to goodness he could have had her with him in Spain.)

Thus settled in purpose, William took on a keener lease of life. Painting, sculpting, dinner parties with clever men had been enjoyable, especially after the long haul in Spain; but here was a tough beneficial project to put his heart into—the long search after truth, the sorting, compiling, building up of his great monument to this now reviled hero of his youth. Pausing only to plead off a negro ex-soldier of the 43rd, rather shakily convicted of rape and sentenced to be hanged, William was away to France early in 1823. He chanced to cross the Channel with two acquaintances and agreed to share a chaise with them to Paris: bowling along the wintry roads they argued about politics without drawing breath. So freely had the adrenalin flowed that agreement came for the first time as they rattled over the Paris cobblestones to their parting: all were as one as to the enjoyable nature of the trip.

Fond as William was of all his family—"what a nice little twinkling thing Louey is with her songs"—he was stimulated by his enterprise and by being on the Continent again and in touch with military thinking. On a visit to Wellington, the Duke had promised to answer every question that arose in the course of the work; a promise he scrupulously fulfilled. He had also been very funny and mocking about some of his generals. Wellington would not give William his papers, having it in mind to write "a plain didactic history" himself, to be published after his death: he told William many a tale of "blunders made by generals and others acting under him who it would be harmful to expose". Yet, Wellington had said, he could not do justice to himself without "ungraciously affecting the fame of many worthy men whose only fault was their dullness".

No such inhibition hampered Napoleon's marshals. William saw Jomini—"he resembles Tom Paine so much, with that remarkably cunning look of knowledge so conspicuous in him"—who gave William a printed defence of himself which William found "very curious and very strong"; Soult, with his abrupt aloof manner and his "grandeur of mind; he received me very unusually well, he has four pictures by Murillo that are exquisite", and he had asked William to come again; Suchet, "who looks quick and clever": all had seemed pleased to be quoted. Then there was Madame Ney, "very lady-like and agreeable and rather handsome", and her four sons, one of them "with an air of great character", like his father. "I met at her house many generals, who all remembered Charles and apparently with interest." (Charles had been Ney's captive after Corunna.) Then, almost most useful of all, there was "my old friend Brossard, chief of the École Politechnique, and with access to the Depôt de la Guerre"; and he had also been able to see Massèna's and Junot's aides.

Sometimes it went less well, and Paris was "wet, luxurious, filthy, the women ugly to the last degree". Daru was agreeable enough, but his main contribution had been to send William his *History of Venice*; Jomini would talk endlessly about every subject in the world except Spain; and William was "assailed by half a dozen authors offering me presents of their works" if he would write *un petit mot* for them in the *Edinburgh Review*. Hope, frustration, joy, gloom; all the occupational diseases of authors beset him. It would take a year to sort the documents alone, some in French and some in Portuguese and all crossed doubly over their fragile pages. There were moments when the monumental nature of his task oppressed William. "My health is very bad, my spirits worse, and my expenses very great; books crowd on me": there were more and more that he must buy. By March 12th he felt better: kind Henry Bunbury, departing for Pau for a few months, had offered William his house in Suffolk to write in—"Delightful", he told Caroline, "three months with you in the country in a house without noise." Very good for the children too; "we will paint, and walk, and read and write history." "My information crowds thick upon me", and if peace lasted, which he doubted, "I hope to be able in time to make a history worth reading."

He was working six hours a day at the Depôt de la Guerre; he might never have such a chance again; he expected "to see another revolution while I am here". One such revolution was being suppressed in Spain with the aid of Bourbon France. Lady Oxford, the ambassador's wife, had typically put her foot in it, asking Soult what he believed would result from France's invasion of Spain: to which Soult, equally typically, had laughed and said, "I am like St. Thomas, I believe nothing." There was a report that the tricolor had been hoisted in the south by a Colonel Fabvier, "a very clever man whom I have seen; they say he is at the head of a band of refugees from France; at all events he is on the Spanish frontier, if he has not yet entered France". Next week William reported from his hotel Petit Montmorency in the Rue St Marc, "a conspiracy has just been discovered in the French army to place young Nap. upon the throne". Altogether, he must cull his information from France while the going was good: a renewed revolution seemed only a question of time, the ultras were becoming so violent and dominating, the Napoleonic element so frustrated.

William was relieved to find that peace had laid some ghosts at least, if not Louis XIV's and Napoleon's. The long war with France, "and the pains the papers took to brutalize the minds of the English people, gave such a turn to the mind of many a good man, that I hated them, when they deserved to be admired for their intrinsic good qualities. Campbell is one of them; he has since the peace lost all his ultra prejudices, and shines forth now like Bunbury, full of kindness and benevolence and gentleness to everybody within his reach . . . and goodness to a degree very unusual in a man of his age and experience of the world." Before such qualities William's heart instantly glowed and responded.

His heart knew other pulls. There was a certain stretching of the limbs to be felt in this sudden freedom from domestic routine. There was no-one in the world like Caroline, and he adored her; she was the light of his eyes, and yet . . . Having come so far should he not go further, perhaps on to Charles in Cephalonia? The struggle in Greece was just opening: the temptation to muscle in on it, to achieve both glory and spiritual satisfaction, was great. In earlier days William had laid aside a great longing to see Italy when two soldier friends bound thither in their coaches had wanted to take him, and instead he had gone home to Caroline and the babies. Now he hoped she would receive his latest refusal as "a handsome homage". "Captain Bacon and Lady Charlotte are going a cruise in his schooner to the Mediterranean, and mean to wait upon Lady Hester Stanhope, visiting Egypt and agreeable countries en route."

William was a very attractive man, still in his prime. He was greatly tempted: aside from Egypt and the agreeable countries, Lady Hester Stanhope had been in her exotic way a charmer of his early youth, and the idea of her still excited him. She was such fun to talk to, and would be more fun still, with all her strange experiences of life in the fabulous East. And in his heart William was again the dashing agile young redcoat who had only to cross a ballroom to cause every head to turn, every woman's heart to flutter, to hear that long excited sigh "I think I never saw a handsomer man!" But the seven hostages he had already given to fortune rose up in his mind's eye and regarded him with their round surprised eyes, besought him with their innocent parted lips. Not without a pang he wrenched his heart from travel, adventure, activity, a more daring fulfilment . . .

Paris in the spring of 1823 held qualified charms for William. He couldn't stand the political atmosphere, the ultras with their arrogance and their open boasts that they would very shortly put paid to England as a first-class power and return her to her rightful place, their continuous and powerful resentment of her victory. "A delightful place for rogues," he apostrophized it, "for conspirators, gamblers, intriguers, painters, sculptors, charlatans, gourmands, drinkers, speculators, but the devil for honest men and women . . ."

In March William's combative instincts were given a brief but exciting run. Manuel, one of the few liberal ministers in an increasingly ultra government, was in process of ejection from office. "I was engaged, the day that Manuel was expelled the Chambers, in a fine row in the Place Louis Quinze. I was riding with Lady Frances Harley, and as we came home she proposed to go and see what a French mob were worth in such a cause. This of course I acceded to." They found the mob not very large, and all composed of well-dressed people—"none of the real strength of France, that is the peasants and workmen, take the slightest interest in the party calling themselves Liberal . . . When Manuel came forth the mob shouted, and my horse plunged violently; and a sort of hat-on-one-side bully, so common in Paris, struck him in the head with a stick. Thinking it might be done from fear of the horse, I spoke calmly to him." The man's reply was far from calm, raising his stick for a further blow, he damned William "for an English beefstik, and damned all the English".

A prudent man faced with hostility in a Paris mob would at this point have retired, and particularly if he were an Englishman barely eight years after the victory of Waterloo. But Irish-bred William had never been a prudent man and was unlikely to start being one while still in his thirties and accompanied by a pretty girl. His faintly diabolical looks had some foundation in fact: plenty within him relished the situation.

"I desired Lady Fanny to ride away, and keeping up the conversation with my friend until I had fixed him, I suddenly rode upon him." Probably nothing would have induced William to ride at a ragged mob unless it was neck or nothing; but he could Cossack it with the best when faced with a middle-class one, hitting his horse's face and damning his country; and he struck the Frenchman across *his* face. "He roared, and the mob fell upon me, calling out 'À la lanterne, à bas L'Anglais beefstik.' My horse however soon cleared the crowd, and I found Lady Frances in the middle of them, addressing them in my favour. We afterwards rode slowly away pursued by the beasts, who were very noisy, but offered no more violence . . . I never saw so brave and generous a girl in my life, except one, and you know who that is", he assured Caroline. Frances Harley told him afterwards that she had been "considerably frightened", but this did not prevent the whole family, mother and daughters, from sitting down after dinner to copy out "all the different cramped French hands that my papers are written in. You will laugh at my despotism extending to them, but you must feel it is very kind of them."

Suborned as ever by William's looks and charm, Lady Oxford next asked him to give away her other daughter at her wedding; it was flattering and William felt he must, but what should he do for clothes? He wanted to go and see Black Charlie, his first cousin, and ask him how he was getting on with his steam boats, "but his boy has got the scarlet fever and I cannot worry him, poor fellow". Next William's wounded back was playing up and he was working full out, "sixteen hours at a stretch once". France had been made to disgorge many of her Napoleonic acquisitions, but "the Louvre is still superb: there are five or six paintings there that I study and gloat upon until I am ready to lie down and groan over my own want of power . . . there are two Coreggios, and one Titian, and two Rembrandts and a Raphael, and a Paul Veronese . . . then I shut my eyes and they swim before me in a vision. A propos, I think of Bessie and Johnny always, they rank with the Coreggios."

Back in England he was involved in endless correspondence; collecting information for his history. When he was staying at Stratfield Saye in 1824 his heart warmed towards Wellington for his praise of Sir John Moore. William was amused by the instant change in the company's attitude towards him when the Duke asked his military opinions—"silly people!" Charles had gone back to Greece again and left his horse in William's tender care—"the History has been cut up badly by twelve days of painting Blanco", who was due to follow his master by sea. But the work went steadily on all the same. William had "got a long description of Talavera out of the Duke, and would have had more, but for interruptions". He was copying some of the pictures and the Duchess had talked him into giving her one, in such a nice way that he had had to promise it. He liked both the sons—"Lord Charles I delight in; he is such a fine, laughing, playful, spirited boy, without the least pride or impertinence about him. Lord Douro is more grave, very amiable and gentlemanlike, very much resembling the Duke without his *devil*." William must have had a breeze with the Duchess; he clearly opened his mouth too wide with his radical views; "I was told that you had expressed yourself in very strong terms relative to me, and declared that you would never ask me inside your house again"; he wrote to her and an invitation to dinner had come in the Duke's name only, and William had answered it as such, and now Pamela Campbell had told him Kitty had thought this very rude.

William's reply, though measured, was not very likely to sooth the Duchess out of her pet. "You are the best judge of your own feelings", William allowed her. Like both Wellington and his wife, William was in some sense an Anglo-Irishman, and he had known Kitty Pakenham all his life and was disinclined to have any nonsense from her. "The expression of commonplace opinions in politics was not a just cause for you to take offence, and I did not conceive that it could last long upon that point.

"If it should continue," William went on sternly, "however unjust I may think you, my own part is very clear to me; and certainly rudeness or even anger would hardly enter into my mind, much less I trust be deliberately displayed towards a person from whom I have received a great deal of kindness, although mixed with some injustice; and least of all to the sister of Sir Edward Pakenham, for whom I had as much esteem and veneration as one man can have for another." Poor Kitty had hazarded yet another friend; but between William and the Duke, perhaps more used to her touchiness, all went swimmingly. He had answered all questions, in full, and stood up firmly for Moore: "Beyond all question the Duke is a noble high-minded man", William applauded, "and I never will believe a story to his prejudice again." What he had said of the much maligned Moore was "very noble in him, and very pleasant to hear, as I have not a single point of my own history which I do not find confirmed by his opinion". It had given the whole opus a great boost: "He has given me a long paper of conversation besides, and I shall make my way well and fast, I hope."

In 1826 William and Caroline left Sloane Street, now becoming rather less rural, and moved to Wiltshire, taking (suitably enough) Battle House, in the village of Bromham near Devizes, where William could write without urban distractions and where Emily, Fanny, Johnny, Bessy, Henrietta, Louey, Caro, and eventually Pamela and Nora could stretch their legs in the fields and gardens. They made friends with Tom Moore the Irish song-writer and his family, and with the Fitzmaurices at Bowood, read and admired Cobbett's books, grew Indian corn, visited the cottage people and helped them in their distresses; while William for exercise after writing would put on a straw hat and a smock and dig in the garden until his back cried halt to it.

Rarely was his large fund of physical courage called upon; once when a fire threatened to envelop the thatched houses and William organized a chain of fire-fighters, leading them from in front; and another time when he was away nursing Johnny, ill at Tonbridge, and the doctor called him in to deal with a very powerful young man, armed with a loaded pistol, who had taken poison and would not let anyone come near to give him an emetic; William went in to him and reasoned with him calmly, refused to let anybody threaten him, discovered and sent for his girl-friend and stood guard while she soothed him into a reconciliation, and when she eventually fainted, induced the young man to take the emetic which saved his life.

Aside from his implacable pain, William led the ideal author's life. "The time of haymaking makes this place more beautiful than you can imagine, and sweeter than spiced Arabia. I have weeded your garden", he told Caroline, and he was doing up Fanny's room. He seemed to have steered into a happy haven; family, friends, congenial work. His children flourished, he took the whole pack of them to Devizes Fair. Pretty as pictures, they tumbled round after him, and came back laden with cakes, gingerbread, drums, whistles, "and enough dolls to people a desert island".

At the end of the year the blow fell. Beautiful, silent, deaf Henrietta died of the whooping cough soon after her fifth birthday; and William was tormented with grief and guilt. Could they have found better treatment, done something different? Had she, unable to cry out, choked to death for want of instant help? Had his back been turned at the moment Henrietta might have been saved? His friend Rutherford wrote William a splendidly bracing and sensible letter—"How is it possible to act but for the best at the time, as we see and know it?" Grief always added to its torments by self-blame, but "I would fain prevent your aggravating your affliction by causeless and groundless self-reproach . . . Consider what you owe to the living, who, while they are partners of your sorrow, have a right to find support in your strength." Thus adjured, William raised his black head from his littered desk and bent himself to the task of consoling Caroline and the children. He was an extremely tender father, and would spend long hours nursing them in illness and comforting them in fear; one of his little girls, afflicted by wolf-terror, remembered how William would come and take her up out of bed, walking up and down with her in his arms for hours until she fell asleep. The memory of "the intense relief and sense of protection I felt" stayed with her all her life.

By day in his study he would unravel the intricate plots and campaigns of the Peninsular War, and tramp again in memory the icy hills of Galicia, with the French bugles sounding ever nearer in his ears, would march under a July sun to Talavera, ride through the cannon-balls on the Salamanca plain. Sorting the letters, puzzling over the battle maps, over conflicting versions of the same event, all written by honest men, he would make out fresh draft after fresh draft. Summer winds blew in from the hayfields again, wood fires crackled for another winter; the eight children grew taller, needed more food, grander clothes, pieces of music, French lessons, paint-boxes. Laboriously, painfully, often sleeplessly, William wrote on. Sweet-tempered Caroline kept the accounts, and copied out the drafts of William's pages, erasing out the spelling mistakes. As a small boy William had refused to learn to write or spell: this last omission he never retrieved.

Caroline was the pillar of his life, the joy of his heart; and his daughters a delight. They laughed with him, argued at him, sang for him, leant on him. They made far too much noise, and were told to pipe down; they made far too many demands, and were generally successful. Visitors remarked upon the glowing happiness of the establishment. Deaf and dumb Johnny—John Moore Napier—the only son, was clever and able despite his disability. For all but William, and no doubt Caroline, Henrietta's little ghost was laid: and both believed implicitly that reunion would come hereafter.

And yet domestic joys and a rewarding task were not enough. Perhaps some of William's inner frustrations might be laid at the door of his appalling fertility: his wife was almost always having a baby, or recovering from having one. Ten were born in fifteen years: even the cheerful and placid Caroline must sometimes have flagged. There were alarming moments when William's savage temper took charge. His son Johnny's beauty, fine physique, and terrible disability roused his father to a fever of protection. Caught fishing in a river, this speechless nine-year-old, unable to hear of what he was accused, unable to explain that he was fishing by permission of the owner, was cuffed and kicked by a water-bailiff, and his rod taken from him, broken, and thrown into the water. The spectacle of his helpless little boy thus abused was too much for William, returning from inspecting a higher beat of the river. The water-bailiff responsible was so mercilessly beaten up that he was fortunate to survive. Such actions do not make life smooth; and nor did William's life of constant pain. There were flashes of power, of activity, of danger—for William's fiery soul they might not be enough.

Yet slowly the six-volume history took shape. He had done his best, he recorded, to find out and recount the exact whole truth, but his book was "full of lies all the same". Confronted with different eye-witness versions of the same event, all given by honest men, what could one do but use one's head and guess? He sent out long questionnaires, with blank spaces for the answers—"What brigade of the 5th division first advanced? When were the volunteers let loose? At what time did the great explosion happen?" People were very good about answering, but it all took years; and several indignant characters challenged him to duels, which involved William in a great spill of ink, though not of blood.

In August of 1826 Lady Sarah had died. "The last link which held so many people is broken." He and George had both been with her: to both it felt like the end of a sunny epoch. William's health continued deplorable: the bullet near his spine pressed, with more or less of torment on the nerves of his backbone, causing him fifty years of pain which could probably now have been set right by a good surgeon in as many minutes. Once, climbing with some French officers, William had received a boulder on the foot which broke every bone in it, and made no fuss: the surgeon who dealt with it asked him how he managed to make no comment at the time, and William said he had not wanted to look faint-hearted in front of the French, and also that it had been a flea-bite compared with what he continually suffered from his back. His malaria, caught in 1810 in the Alemtejo marshes, was recurrent; so that, one way or the other, he was incapacitated for much of the time from the age of twenty-five years onwards. Nor was he free from lesser ailments. "Murray roars out for the manuscript, I roar out from the gout", William reported in 1827.

At last the great moment arrived; volume one was completed. "Author got to London well—dined with James Moore—quarrelled—Jones praised work too highly—slept at Gloucester Coffee House—damp bed, fever, no lodging—Murray praised book highly—offered 500 guineas for copyright—took no notice—gout, laid up, pain, fever, and irritation—unable to write—Cooke very kind—opened intercourse with X.—had hopes 1500 l.—X. could not manage the negotiation in person—agent made some mistake of little consequence—anxious to buy but tried tricks—enraged, kicked him to the Devil—wrote a peremptory note to Murray—he came forward handsomely—bargain struck, printed in three weeks or a month, but continued gout irritates and interferes dreadfully—1000 guineas for the copyright, Murray to have the option of purchasing the other three volumes at the same price—all the money yours darling—twelve copies, and the right of sending proof sheets to Soult, mine." After a difficult and tetchy birth, William's *magnum opus* was away.

Despite gout and politics, book production went on. "I am in town printing the first vol.", William wrote to Charles on January 30th of the New Year of 1828. "The Duke of Wellington is Prime Minister and all the old politicians are going mad for spite, calling him a fool as they used to do Buonaparte—poor devils! The King's speech made this day calls the Battle of Navarino an untoward affair. This country is going in a hand gallop to hell: stick to Cephalonia . . . They talk of an income tax, the revenue is short, the funds high, the people grumbling, the soldiers all Methodists, the farmers ruined, the landlords funked, and the Ministry changing every day." It was quite obvious that William's gouty misgivings wouldn't clear until he got back to Caroline.

The first volume was published by John Murray—one month after the delivery of manuscript (what a wonderful thing is human progress, the writer is now lucky if it's only a year)—and went like a rocket; a grand *succès d'estime*. "Nothing can exceed the unexampled success of William's book," Caroline exulted to Charles, "or the admiration it seems to meet with from all parties; it is much more than he expected and I do feel *a little* proud." Reviews were satisfactory, public opinion was more than satisfactory, only the *Quarterly Review* struck a sour note. The book even seemed to be selling, and money flowed in—"Feed some little children that are hungry", William instantly instructed Caroline. There was a lot of correspondence from people who felt themselves slighted; and William himself had said, when he finished it that even after all his care there were mistakes, though contemporaries thought it wonderfully accurate. General Guy Campbell, who was Pamela Fitzgerald's husband and had been through the war and knew what he was talking about, complimented William on the whole book, and on the beautiful writing, "free from affectation, short, pithy, and to the purpose". In France its reception was even better; Mathieu Dumas thought it a model of truth, skill and eloquence: "Your brother", he told George, "is the only man who has done Napoleon's genius justice."

For George was in Paris, and reported to William upon Soult's view of the book: the old Marshal had received George as kindly as possible. "Soult desired I would give you his best regards, and said 'Your brother's work is perfect; it does honour to his head and heart, and must be as satisfactory to the French army as it is to the English; it is the work of a just and honourable man whose sole object is to tell the truth without fear or vain boasting . . . Your brother is the most candid, fair and honourable man.' Most sincerely do I thank you my very dear William for your kind letter to him. He lives *en prince*. I like his daughter very much she is a handsome woman."

George had not, with middle age, lost his tendency to be fond of people, to look with appreciation upon members of the human race until he found some excellent reason not to. "The Duchess [Soult was Duke of Dalmatia] was very friendly indeed, and I rattled out execrable French without fear, jumbling tenses, genders and numbers in one confused mass", George continued. "All kinds of French compliments and sayings to dear Car., it would do her heart good to see how highly respected and esteemed you are my dear Podge by all the French. As to Paris itself, it is delightful, and I saw everything." George went on down to Bagnères to see old Alava, his and Wellington's favourite Spanish general, who had salvaged wounded William out of a bullock cart standing in the baking sun at Celerico and nursed him in his own house after the Coa action. "He swears you are blind to that coquin Napoleon's conduct in Spain, and believe in all the French rascals . . . 'I am angry wid William, but the military part is to me better and dearer than Polybius, by ——, George, I tell everybody no such book in Europe. William would make the best minister in the world, by —— he is equal to command any army. William is one damn clever fellow, but damn rascal to Spaniards' ", Alava had concluded. "He sends his best love to you."

All very fine; but a book so pleasing to France would perhaps not have an immense appeal to the many English who could not or would not see that a brave and clever enemy adds to the glory of victory. Many a copy of William's work has 'Thats right, run down your own country', scrawled indignantly on it in thin agitated Victorian handwriting whenever William mentions the undoubted fact that British soldiers were sometimes sozzled and British generals occasionally obtuse. Sales began to drop. "Small cares thicken on me", William wrote from London, "and I have had another gout for two days." That strange mid-Victorian passion for riddles was on him: he told Caroline of one he had invented which had gone down well at Crockford's. Next week he is "weary of life; I have been rolling in agony with the gout; the pain was incessant for thirty-six hours which never happened before".

In his disappointment and apprehension William could see no daylight. Even the Duke had been "near dying". France was heaving like an ocean in a gale of wind: what were those damned ultras up to? "War seems to be certain, and France will have Egypt, depend upon it." Charles, always a calming influence, had urged him to trust the people of France rather than the people of Paris, more than fed up with their Bourbon King Charles X; but "slipping one's king is like slipping one's shoulder, after the first time a trifle does it", William thought.

"I cannot stay away from you for long without pain", he still felt of Caroline, after twenty years of married life. He sensed that a blow to his book might be coming. It was cheering that Sir James Graham had promoted Henry to be post captain, and especially as Hal in his day had been exceedingly outspoken to the civil Lord of the Admiralty. "I bear so much malice myself", William admitted frankly, "that I feel an esteem for those who do not."

On May 13th, 1829 the blow fell; and soon even calm Caroline was having hay fever. William's impatient hands tore open the publisher's letter. "Upon making up the account of the sale of the first volume of the History of the War in the Peninsula, I find that I am at this time minus 545L. 12s.," John Murray wrote from Albemarle Street with a deathly accuracy.

William skimmed through the next words "At this loss I do by no means repine . . . much gratification . . . a work so intrinsically valuable . . . so generally admired" till he came to the nub; for there were five more volumes still in preparation. The words fell like a knell ". . . recommend that you should, in justice to yourself, apply to some other publishers . . ." To all intents and purposes, his *magnum opus* was a flop.

His temperament had armed William's black devils, his ailments had reinforced them: there were moments when they crowded in upon him. Superannuated soldier, intermittent cripple, mediocre artist, failed author—who now would listen to his urgent political views? But William was fired with resolution: not John Murray nor a whole legion of canny publishers would halt him in his enterprise. His History was a masterpiece and he knew it. Physically he might be increasingly out of action, but he felt himself full of fire and purpose. Somehow they would save up, nine children or not, and he would publish the History himself. Somewhere, amongst the upheavals of Europe there might come occasion to stretch the limbs of his manifest abilities in some great and good cause.

Charles's return from Greece buoyed William up, his brother's cavalier treatment by the authorities enraged him. Official sense had acted nohow: official justice was nowhere. Family and friends alone were true; and to these both brothers increasingly clung, as if still battling on the Border, or along the Highland line.

CHAPTER VIII

Revolution in France

The summer of 1830 was a stirring one for Europe, and Henry Napier was moved and excited by the news that flickered through to Florence. After two years here—Italy was cheaper to live in than England and its climate easier for Caroline and for Henry with his recurrent Indian fevers—they were off home. The news made it increasingly difficult to know which route to take. Henry came back from a visit to Pistoia (whose soft-eyed and pretty women had pleased him after the hard, bold looks of the Florentines), to hear that Bourbon Charles X of France had annulled the election of deputies, deprived the electoral colleges of the better part of their powers, and established press censorship—"If the French bear *this*, and *him*, they are not the lads I took them for." Perhaps the King counted on aid from Austria and Russia, "the two great mines of European tyranny; but England I trust will spurn the tyrant!"

And things were on the move in England itself. "Nobody regrets George IV," Henry insisted cheerfully when news of his death had arrived the previous month, "except those that lose office by his death." Such friends as the King had once had, he had long ago worked through. The sailor Duke of Clarence succeeded as William IV. "What will William do?" Henry wondered. "His whole life has been wild and his shameful part in Queen Caroline's persecution gives small hope of good": impossible though she might be, there was no sense or kindness in this public bullying of the wayward queen, poor foolish woman. And her trial had given the London crowds, with plenty to complain about, a cause into which to channel their rage. King William might find a better course for their energies. It was possible to believe that a new king would have the grace and common sense to avert what was beginning to sound increasingly like an English revolution over the need to widen the electorate and to mitigate the hardships of the poor. And Henry hoped that quiet

Queen Adelaide's respectable relationship with her husband would be a pleasant change from George IV's matrimonial and extra-matrimonial goings on. Also there was one great hope—"William IV is a sailor, brought up in the Navy, knowing it, liking it, and commanding it with spirit and impartiality."

By August the 7th the rumours were rife in Florence. King Charles X of France was dead. King Charles X had routed the rebels in a bloody battle. All France was up in arms. The trouble was confined to Paris. Finally came definite news that after three days' bloodshed the royalist *gendarmerie* were defeated and the tricolor flag of the Republic floated once more over the Tuileries. "What next?" Henry demanded. "This is a fearful question. The passions of men are up, a great energetic and powerful but enlightened nation has been moved to a tempest and 30 millions of excited men do not easily subside into a calm . . . I am glad that this burst of French liberty has come just before our elections." He hoped it might awaken some kindred feeling in England and drive out the corrupt self-aggrandizement of the new rich and the sleepy lethargy of the old rich there prevailing. And how it might stir up Europe, held in a lifeless but powerful grip by its series of exceptionally stupid monarchs! Henry was carried away—"What a day for the cause of liberty throughout the world! The French have nobly won their freedom, let them guard it well and use it wisely, and may God prosper them!"

He wondered how much of the Napoleonic spirit was still alive, as his carriage rolled over the Var bridge into France two months later. He and William had always had a curious feeling for Napoleon as a man who, for all his errors and horrors, was somehow supernatural. As the family equipage had rolled out of Spezia—"the harbour is superb, it ought to be a great naval station"—and up into the Appenines towards Bracca, the road had suddenly rounded a bend and opened up a vast expanse of glittering cloud-flecked sea, with one tiny ship visible between the clouds from the great height; and Henry had been hit by an enormously powerful I-have-been-here-before. After a moment he remembered where it was he had seen such another breath-taking plunge into infinity and just such another tiny object solitary within it. Twenty years ago, high on a mountain in St Helena, ashore from his ship, he had gazed down on the plain where one solitary man was imperceptibly moving; and had had that indescribable feeling of being a god, of looking down on something as small as an insect, and yet of being within that insect, of feeling with its feelings and understanding its own tremendousness and of yet being infinitely remote from it. "There was something sublime within its insignificance", he had known. The feeling had been so strong that he could not keep it to himself and he had shouted out to his companion—"He looks insignificant but he might have that within him which could turn the world upside down"; and his companion had doubtless thought him quite daft; for this was a small remote place in the south Atlantic that scarcely a soul in Europe had yet heard of or thought about; and the little Emperor was still triumphant in the Tuileries. But four years later Napoleon had been that little man walking on that distant green.

To Napoleon's country they were now come; and to be in France was a tonic and a relief. "The Genoese beat even the Venetians in knavishness and every sort of imposition, they are sharp as needles and cutting as razors, it requires great knowledge and quickness to compete with them"; and though Genoa was still the superb, with its palaces and its Veronese, and the magnificent house of Andrea Doria, yet the "long straggling suburbs of dusty dirty houses in that half-delapidated or rather slattern state of small negligence so common in Italy and so disagreeable to the tidy mind of an Englishman" had made a sad send-off; and were "what to me always gives Ireland the look of a foreign country". Commander Viri had very kindly taken Henry on board his ship, "very clean and apparently in good harbour order, what the squadron may be at sea and in bad weather I cannot say, but the Genoese have always had a good naval reputation and they look sailor-like". He thought the sailors were splendidly treated as to pay, food, terms of service and conditions. "How different is all this from our rigidity and niggardliness, our vast powers of chastisement and slender means of encouragement and reward, our severe discipline, small pay, long periods of service, cruel system of impressment, and scanty recompenses. Verily the British Navy although the finest in the world is by far the most illiberally treated, both officers and men, by their country!" Viri had taken them both to the opera, and Henry had gone back next day to be entertained again by Viri, and had heard Mass on board his frigate the *Beroldo* and was amazed, "never before happening to see the Mummery of it so near. I am far enough from disposed to ridicule the Religion of any sect or people, more especially when I believe them sincere, and it is anything but fair or in good taste to shew one's contempt of their rites and ceremonies, but I could hardly contain myself to-day, more than once I was on the point of laughing right out. The whole affair was so utterly irreligious in appearance, the Priest so like a Chinese conjuror, the performance of Mass altogether so like a ridiculous game, that I give myself infinite credit for my forbearance."

The good manners of the French *douaniers* across the Var seemed to indicate their happiness at recent doings in Paris, and Henry saw the tricolor flying from several buildings. They drove rapidly on to Cannes, "under the guidance of a wild young postilion who dashed up and down every hill", but Henry liked French postilions and always spent much of the day on the box talking to them; no-one better from whom to discover what really was felt in France. "They are always lively and intelligent, and generally sensible; they have ever been favourites of mine", and no-one of them had ever asked Henry for a sou beyond the tip he habitually gave them, "none were sulky, and all thanked me. From these postilions I learned that there is in this part of France one great and compact mass of enthusiasm in favour of the present government." There seemed to be no purely republican spirit, and people were "peaceably inclined if unmeddled with, but confident, and ready for war if forced to it". He was struck, as ever, by the contrast between France and Italy: the Italians so apathetic about politics and bent on doing the best for themselves; the French "so full of spirit and energy", whenever they started talking about their country and its future.

At Brignolles the landlady told Henry that in her parts at any rate they were far from happy with the revolution, and feared that worse was to come; her view perhaps was swayed by having suffered the use of her hostelry as a Buonaparte barracks for twenty years, and by the loss of the Prince de Condé and the Duc d'Enghien, whose magnificent fêtes at their local chateaux had coloured her childhood and youth. "Mais après tout pour moi c'est égal pourvuque le pays soit en paix et que les Anglais voyagent", and she had said it with such charm that Henry bought a box of her dried "plumbs" and they parted friends.

At Aix Henry refreshed his mind with the thought that Caius Marius had here defeated the Cimbri; and admired the town's spacious central avenue. At Nîmes, which he spelt Nismes, all faces were scowling and gendarmes were everywhere: there was some sort of local revolutionary row boiling on, which involved martial law and was complicated by a Catholic-Protestant undercurrent—one might be in Ireland! But the Maison Carré was one of the most perfect buildings Henry had ever seen or imagined. His taste in architecture was firmly classical. "This temple and the Pantheon at Rome I call the Venus and Apollo of architecture." At Avignon, where "a view opened of antique towers and no less ancient churches", Henry's passion for the poetry of Petrarch took them on to Vaucluse, where so much of it was written, in a valley "beautiful, retired, and romantic", and Henry quotes him at length. As for the Pont du Gard, it was "really a fine monument of Roman art and civilization", and he longed for time and skill to paint it—if only one were Turner!

On his restoration in 1815 King Louis XVIII, though lacking star quality, had at least tried to heal the wounds of France, to induce royalist emigré and displaced landowner to live in concord with defeated soldiers of Napoleon's revolutionary armies and to accept the continuance in office of his officials. Louis had been outwitted by political excess from both sides and by the assassination of his nephew the Duke of Berry, which had swung the reactionary royalist "ultras" into power. Louis' death in 1824 had allowed his younger brother Charles X, the great hope of the ultras, to inherit the throne, where he had done his utmost, with nervous persistence, to put the clock back to pre-revolutionary days. This July he had been swept into exile, in favour of Louis Philippe, his more liberal cousin of Orléans.

The actual fighters in the Paris revolution had wanted a republic, but Thiers, the guiding spirit, had decided otherwise, and Lafayette, the hero of the crowd, had foxed them by propelling Louis Philippe on to the balcony of the Tuileries with the adored tricolor in his hand. Eighteen hundred revolutionaries and two hundred gendarmes died, but the people would find that they had settled for a bourgeois and decidedly boring monarchy instead of real change. The respectable figures of this businessman régime were to be thrown off eighteen years later: a French people still heady with the fumes of Napoleon's triumphs dearly liked life to be exciting and glamorous; and preferred things to happen, even if people were killed in the process. Almost the most fatal thing to do with the French was to bore them—nearly preferable was the desperate drama of Marie Antoinette's "Let them eat cake" to a people clamouring for bread. "We are creating the most sublime poetry!" Lamartine would declare as the 1848 revolution rolled on: and Henry, driving north through the flushed cheeks and sparkling eyes of France in 1830, would have fully understood him. Had the revolution looked in any danger he would have been sorely tempted to shove his wife and children into the nearest British consulate and join in.

But in spite of the political shortcomings of Kings Louis and Charles, the children of France looked remarkably well and sturdy, Henry noted. Whatever the political disturbance, there could not be anything basically wrong with a country whose children thus flourished. Henry and Caroline had loved life in Florence; yet it seemed clear enough that the French, who had had their real revolution and were now but confirming it with another, were very much happier, materially and in spirit, than the long oppressed and divided Italians who had not yet had theirs.

All the same they had been sad to leave Italy. After a few months in Florence they had taken the Villa Capponi on a hillside in the direction of Fiesole—"Our terrace is a morning and evening enjoyment of no common sort, country sounds come floating up, the lowing of cattle, the deep tolling of the city bells, the distant and solitary bark of a dog." They were out of the fogs of the Arno valley and the view was a delight; they made many friends, Italian and English, and improved their Italian, already good: Henry appreciated the way in which everyone in city or country was so ready to converse. They had enjoyed the New Year Ball at the Pitti Palace, where the pictures, Henry thought, looked even more brilliant in the candle-light than they did by day—"a fine assemblage, no unnecessary ceremony, the sovereign moved about as a private gentleman"—and had, in their turn, given a ball themselves to a hundred local peasants in their best room; and although it was furnished and curtained and lined in yellow brocade and they had supplied plenty of good wine, none of the *contadini* had damaged anything and none had got drunk, though the party had appeared to go with a swing. Leaving in late July, they had been given a warm-hearted send-off as the carriage swung down the long avenue. Of course it didn't mean much, but how pleasant and mannerly it was!

Impossible not to like the Italians; and the longer one stayed the deeper into close knowledge of Italian friends one came, and the more the top-dressing of national difference disappeared. Henry greatly liked the scientific and literary men, and admired the good humour and politeness of the peasants. "English travellers are commonly far too prompt and decided in their judgment of foreign nations"; and the Italians differed so greatly from each other that it was foolish to lump them together—the Romans were fiercer and more energetic than anybody but the Milanese; Naples was "Greek all over still"; Venice was as commercially astute as ever and had kept some of its ancient spirit; the Lombards were perhaps the most generally admirable. The Bolognese and Senesi were different again: Henry liked the latter much the best. The Pisans "show some remnants of a nobler race", the Lucchesi were "quiet and industrious and generally speaking good people", the Florentines, he thought, were too ready to exist on ancestral fame: their farming and rural industry flourished but in the city "expense, idleness and vanity prosper". Like them he did; but, speaking cautiously, as he only had three years' knowledge, one had to admit that they were tortuous and secretive in their dealings—"they do nothing off hand and above board as we do"—and he must really condemn their heartless treatment of their old people; from the moment when these ceased to be useful their lot was total neglect.

The relics of their ancient grandeur had given Henry unsearchable delight. He had always been more moved by natural beauty than by the finest works of art—but Florence had converted him. His bouts of fever left poor Henry very low: faced with house-hunting during his first August in the city—"never in either East or West Indies did I suffer so much from heat"—he had poured it all out to his journal (perhaps a better plan than pouring it all out to his wife). He was good for nothing—"I feel a lassitude, a want of my usual energy, a languor, a failure in my powers of continued and persevering exertion, an irritability about trifles and a sinking under difficulties which tell me plainly that my day is past, that I am no longer fit for public service or for public life and can scarcely bear the little worries of a private one." Why, he wondered, were our spirits so much the slave of our health? "Are our souls the spirits of higher beings incarcerated for a time in these frail and feverish prisons to pay the penalties of crime committed in a higher sphere of the invisible world?"

Yet the instant he was on his legs again he had whistled round Florence with the speed and concentration of an American tourist on a package trip; reading all he could lay hands on in Italian history, literature and poetry, visiting, listing, describing each church, palace, monastery, statue, museum, picture, library, manuscript. Surely and persistently he sorted out in his mind and came to know and appreciate every artist, major or minor; learnt the story of their lives, the story of the lives of their subjects, of the political interplay between their rulers. The slightest coincidence gave him courage. The statue of Abundance in the Boboli gardens struck him as being remarkably like his mother, with its expression "peculiarly engaging and beautiful", even before he knew it had been modelled from the head of Giovanna, daughter of the Emperor Ferdinand I, and hence an ancestress.

Aside from its extreme beauty and interest, Henry took a faintly proprietary pleasure in Florence: his (four greats) grandmother had been a Medici. Rome, he felt, was grander, Milan more dignified, Venice twice as exciting and romantic, Genoa more brilliant. But Florence had a little of everything, was "individually interesting", was fractionally his; and the germ of an idea kindled in his mind.

His visit to Charles had infused him with some of Charles's cheerful energy and purpose. Henry had no wish to be Garibaldi (at this moment still plying his trade as a seaman out of Genoa), no dream of leading the necessary Risorgimento in Italy. But could he not, by a powerful and lucid exposition of the glories of their past, by bringing to mind the intelligence, vigour and political skill of past Italians, stir them in some way out of their political apathy, out of the deadening preoccupation with money-making which was all the outlet that the system allowed them?

Travelling through the Papal States was still frustrating, like returning into some jealous and serrated medieval past. There were customs posts at each frontier (nine between Florence and Genoa), whose officials, each one wilier than the last, had their methods of extracting money unofficially from unwary travellers; and if you arrived too late at a city like Florence you were apt to find the city gates shut, and no entry till morning. At the gates of Lucca Henry had been obliged to adopt "a haughty, angry and determined tone", which went much against his grain; but which had worked with a customs officer bent on squeeze. Sight-seeing all the way, they had crossed the frontier into France at the River Var, just past Nice, which was still called Nizza and was part of Italy.

Henry had not thought much of the newly-built Corniche, winding and indirect as it was: after eight hours of hard driving away from

Genoa the city had still been in sight—"altogether a burlesque in the art of road-making": they needed a lesson or two from Charles, and John Pitt Kennedy! Two vehicles could hardly pass each other without the most careful man-handling, and at one point, to the dismay of Charley and Augusta, the nursery hamper had been jolted off the carriage by a passing cart and gone bumping down to the sea, scattering its contents over the sand and rocks—"a silver saucepan although thick and strong was a flat as a pancake." (An English nanny was clearly already boiling that dubious foreign milk for her charges.) "The books were fairly spread out for the perusal of interested fishes!" Henry grumbled.

The evening drive between Monaco and Nice with Charley and Augusta safely nodded off in the swaying carriage had soothed him. "I was alone on the Box, all were asleep within, the Postilion jogged leisurely on heedless of anything but his horses, so that I felt completely isolated, severed from all the world in the midst of these vast and savage solitudes, I like the feeling." The quiet had set Henry off on a train of philosophizing; while the night grew so thundery that he might have had need of that immortal phrase still current in the Anglo-French phrase books a hundred years later—"The postilion has been struck by lightning!" What with pettifogging customs houses, knavery, and bad roads, Henry had felt a lift of the heart on crossing from stultified and divided Italy into the fresh air of revolutionary France.

There were some things which France had not accomplished either before or after revolution. On the great route from Avignon to Lyons, the going astonished Henry by its roughness. After a look at the Roman theatre at Orange, with the large slum village then occupying a small part of its huge arena, they pressed on for Lyons, hampered by the extraordinary badness of the road, which "nearly shattered a very strong London-built barouche": there was so little traffic compared with England that it was hardly surprising that the road was nothing but patches of loose sand scattered in the hollows of bumpy rocks; but Henry wondered that Napoleon had not, for military reasons, done something about so important a route. Before crossing the Isère, "a beautiful river of clear water" they had caught distant glimpses of the Alps; but along the "dusty, jolty, dry and chokey roads" they could only very occasionally see the Rhone, with its "cool, blue, and glassy look". Hot, dusty and thirsty, they were overjoyed to join the river at Tain. "The hills closed in and formed with the adjacent isles many a striking point of view." At Vienne there was much to see, "but a family of young children on the road is a sad impediment to sight-seeing", Henry mourned. He managed a good deal, all the same.

At Tarascon he was uncertain which to be more interested in, the curious old square fort with four massive towers or the magnificent suspension bridge over the Rhone, opened only a month earlier and a fine piece of engineering: he thought the use of "bundles of strong wire tied firmly together by other wires, what we on board ship called a Selvagee", was better than the chain used in England, and safer. Lyons, at length arrived at after a fourteen hour drive, was bustling, smoky, dirty, noisy, clammy, and altogether reminded him of an industrial town in England. "All is commerce and manufacture; what a contrast to the Dolce far Niente of Italy." Henry spent a happy few hours with the pictures in the Musée: Lyons was an impressive town, commercial or not: situated on two such rivers as the Rhone and Saone, it could not fail to be magnificent. And its people were so clever, so full of taste and energy; they looked well fed and well clothed and were "far less cheating than Italy".

Signs of the times were here too; every shop in Lyons stocked muskets, bayonets, accoutrements: people seemed equally contented with the new government and determined to defend it. The velvet manufacture produced the most superb stuff, all made at home in the piece by men working fourteen to sixteen hours a day and getting half the value of the finished piece: the work was highly skilled and they made about a yard a day. Far too many looms were idle: Henry was told this was "in consequence of the Revolution which stopped the demand of the Clergy for rich silks and velvets, who were their greatest market. This to be sure is not absolute Christian humility, but give the Devil his due, the Roman Catholic Church was ever a most bountiful patron of the fine arts and richer manufactures."

At Maçon there was moonlight as they rolled into the town over the long bridge across the Saone: less peacefully there were swarms of troops. One heard drum-beats, saw National Guard uniforms, the fluttering of tricolor, bustle and military movement everywhere. French soldiers *looked* sloppy, yet the instant they got into action "one easily perceives that they are perfect masters of their trade". Loyal to his brothers George and William, Henry thought that their Light Division alone of both armies combined English precision and well-set-upness with French liveliness and expertise. Maçon to Autun was rich but not pretty country though it had its compensations—"I never knew what fine Burgundy was until I drank it on the spot." By Avallon all was grass and corn and wore the look of a northern country: Verlanton was charming with its steeply pitched roofs, but the road again was "such as to destroy the strongest iron work of the strongest carriage". After Auxerre the surface was better, and there was the river Yonne, dreaming between its green meadows and feathery banks, but even here the road was indirect and ill-planned, and "really disgraceful to a scientific people like the French", Henry commented sourly, as his tired wife and children bumped and swayed along it.

All the same, the people of France all along the route continued to look well and flourishing, particularly in the south; and their children were splendid, with ruddy cheeks and strong limbs to rejoice the heart. And Auxerre was beautiful with its site and its steeples and its romantic, almost novelettish antiquity—"Why is it that age imparts such charm to almost everything except horses and women?" he wondered, as the fields of corn and hay increased and the vineyards dwindled and the inns became markedly cheaper as they neared Paris. After Sens Henry marked the great divide: rivers ran north and west instead of south and east and he reflected with some gloom that "in short, weather, country, and all, give tokens of the black north and all its clouds and storms".

Driving through the forest of Fontainebleau, "beautiful, dense, and almost interminable", Henry dwelt once again upon the little man from Corsica who had dominated the landscape of his whole life, of his brothers' lives, and who had changed the face of Europe since the day when Marie Antoinette of Austria and Louis XVI of France had first met in this same forest. He believed that for all the blood and misery of the French Revolution, for all the war and destruction that had since followed, it had sparked off something ultimately good "to Europe, to the world, to the great and immortal cause of human nature, to the undying dignity of man! Nations will gradually awake, people after people will assume their position in the universal family, God's gifts will be better understood, more fairly used, more justly distributed: mind will become more free, elastic and comprehensive, and the great family of man approach more nearly to the intentions of its Creator! It will be long, it will be through struggles, time, labour, perhaps blood, but it will come. Knowledge is power, the knowledge of the world is rapidly increasing, spreading, fermenting," and it would lead to "an intelligence that sees and feels the necessity of peace, order, religion, and general morality, even as a matter of policy, and will try to establish them: habit and expediency will soon unite to confirm them, and reason and religion will ultimately render them permanent."

Coming down to earth, Henry noted that postboys in England were cheaper—threepence a mile—more efficient, and had better horses, but were not such good company as French postilions, who charged fourpence a mile and took double the time to go the distance. He was not sorry to be at last in Paris, safely lodged in the Place Vendôme, after a long journey "in which I became tired of being Lackey, Hostler and Courier"; not perhaps foreseeing that the brave new world of his dreams would include a situation in which gentlemen like Henry Napier would permanently become Lackey, Hostler and Courier to their own journeys.

Paris still seethed with convalescents from the fierce days in July: it was a town unlike the Paris Henry had always known. The Parisians looked much more thoughtful and serious and less lively than he had ever seen them—"less fun in the streets and a steady business in the crowd":—it might be London. On the Champs de Mars there was a great review: Henry thought there were not fewer than a hundred thousand men under arms: in the midst were two crosses standing over two vast graves, one of the citizens who had fallen there in the Revolution, and the other of the defending *gendarmerie* who had died opposing them. More graves outside the Louvre, and crowds of people looking bitterly at them, "sorrowful, discontented, and even sulky: they were far too sombre to question, it would have been intrusive"; but Henry would have dearly liked to know what they felt. There was, he knew, a tussle going on between Louis Philippe, who wanted to spare the previous ministers, and the people of Paris who wanted them executed. Lafayette was against execution: but the continuing deaths of the wounded kept feeling at fever heat, and the Parisians had sworn that in the event of acquittal they would take the law into their own hands, seize the prisoners and massacre them. The Luxembourg Palace was accordingly being fortified for the trial by steel blinds, and lodging built for a hundred and fifty officers and cavalry, musketeers and firemen and their horses. Henry heard that the Prince de Polignac had succeeded in calming down the national guard at Vincennes; whatever the ministers deserved, "one hates to see blood flow for political offences and especially on the guillotine".

The "Court people" were gloomy and desponding, and thought the troubles were by no means over. They told Henry that Louis Philippe was *reluctantly* on the throne. *Je m'en doute*, thought Henry, but if so, so much the better; it would make him act more constitutionally. France was a marvellous, fair country, how incredibly stupid Bourbon Charles X had been to learn nothing from the Revolution and throw the whole land away again! He met de Rumigny, an aide-de-camp of Louis Philippe, and took a great fancy to him and wished to know him better. "I do not often take seriously to Frenchmen but I have met some that I think I could have become sincerely attached to on better acquaintance and Rumigny is one." He had given Henry a ticket for the Chamber of Deputies where he heard a debate on the liberty of the press: Benjamin Constant spoke well and Sebastiani better, but otherwise the deputies lacked conviction and spoke badly, Henry thought—too much drama and over-emphasis, and too many "broken unconnected effusions". But they did at least all look clean and tidy; their dress had "none of that slovenly affectation of freedom so conspicuous in the English House of Commons".

There was a visit to Soult and Soult's beautiful Murillos: people said he had come by them dishonestly, but one couldn't always believe what people said: Soult himself was not the least interesting part of the show—"a strongly-built fine looking man with a soldier-like expressive countenance, unexpectedly mild and benevolent". The Veronese in the Louvre made Henry wish he could do nothing else for six months but gaze at it; and the opera, *La Muette de Portici*, was made still more moving, and very much more popular, by the fact that the leading singer, Nourie, had been "one of the most active and gallant combatants in the great week of July". Henry and Caroline went to a party or two, at one of which there were some of the most agreeable Americans Henry had ever met, and where he marvelled once again at the unbeatable skill of French women in giving parties; a little music, a little dancing, much conversation, and the whole made delightful for everyone by the ease and "native gaiety and unconstrained manners and conversational powers" of the hostesses. No-one could have guessed that their city had been drenched in blood only weeks ago.

They told him how extraordinary the silence of Paris had been after the Revolution: no-one moving, not a single cart or carriage on the streets—"Concevez-vous, Monsieur, *Paris sans voitures!*" There was an exhibition of modern pictures in aid of the wounded, very bad on the whole but Henry found many of them moving—the young man putting his tricolor on the statue of Henri Quatre on the Pont Neuf and exclaiming, "Ce n'est pas toi, mon vieux, qu-aurait fait tirer sur nous!" and the boy of thirteen refusing to be sent home and pulling a pistol at the leading officer of the *gendarmerie*. Henry felt moved to visit the Hotel de Ville which had been taken and retaken no less than three times, and after ten hours of fighting had finally been captured by the people. "The carnage was dreadful; twelve hundred Patriots are said to have fallen in this conflict alone, while their opponents lost six hundred men, four guns, and forty horses. Here six pieces of cannon played with terrible consequences on the revolutionary masses who had daringly advanced almost to their muzzles. Then they checked, when suddenly a young man, waving a tricolor flag, rushed forward crying out, 'Mes amis, il faut apprendre a mourir!' and almost instantly fell!"

Not sense, maybe, but how glorious a piece of non-sense! To Henry he seemed a second Leonidas. There had been many incidents of individual gallantry in this desperate battle of guns against people, and so often they had come from the very young; like the young man Arcole, undeterred by the incessant showers of grape-shot that swept the narrow suspension bridge and stopped reinforcement from crossing the river, who had led the way across when all others had faltered under the deadly fire. Henry had been under cannon fire himself, and knew what it was like: his admiration for those virtually unarmed men who had confronted it all day was boundless. He felt a pang that was almost of envy. How clear-cut, how uncomplicated, how sublime was such a life—twenty-one years and then death in such a cause! How noble was this disdain of life set against the freedom and the future of a country and a people! Not only the courage and resolution that made it possible, would render this overthrow of Bourbon tyranny immortal, it was "immortal for the undiminished force of reason which was still felt, and obeyed too, in the midst of blood and carnage, of destruction, wounds, and death! This Revolution, *so* accomplished, is perhaps one of the most glorious incidents in the world's long history, and a bright example of the rational nobility of man! The human race is honoured by it!"

*

Thus it seemed to Henry, standing in the autumn sunshine of 1830 outside the Hotel de Ville. But he had been disappointed to find that his compatriots in Paris did not see it in at all this glowing light. They were in a fuss; "and our own King's speech is not adapted to allay the ferment", either amongst the French or at home. "We somehow *always* manage to displease foreign nations; and they cannot be *all* wrong, all prejudiced, all unreasonable", Henry mused. The English in Paris seemed to Henry to view the entire future with fear and apprehension: he thought them lacking in faith, and lacking in guts. While he was standing in the Place, lost in "emotion, admiration, and deep sympathy", a party of his countrymen swept by him in a manner to underline these thoughts.

"An English travelling carriage rolled by in all its greatness, rich, full, and strikingly comfortable; there were the muffled Abigails, the laced footmen, the pompous courier, the proud inmates, the emblazoned bearings, trunks, cap-boxes, imperials, and all the trappings of luxury. Onwards it rolled, rapidly, smoothly, silently, as if all were silk about and beneath it, so admirably poised and fitted was every part; it was the very essence of refinement and opulence and pride." The sight had disturbed Henry, "nay almost disgusted me, it formed so strong yet so insignificant a contrast to the glorious doings that then occupied my mind. It seemed the very personification of selfishness, as the other was of unselfishness."

And yet, Henry told himself, there were probably people in that coach with ready sympathy and warm hearts, who would feel just as he did if they would switch their minds on to it. The trouble was not hardness of heart but sloth of imagination. Would people never learn not to swish their Rolls-Royces through slum areas, and particularly not through heart-stricken countries immediately after a shattering national disaster? If they didn't it would end by there being no Rolls-Royces. With its aura of serene stuffiness, the coach typified for Henry all that was wrong with his fellow countrymen.

And yet no Englishman, Henry thought, could fail to feel pleased at being home in England again; and certainly he could not; though he wouldn't answer for how women felt. It was true, as Cobbett said, that the first person you met when you stepped ashore at Dover, was likely to be tax-gatherer; and the second, Henry considered, was dead sure to be one of Robert Burns's 'unco guid', some sort of Holy Joe or moralizing hypocrite. All the same, how comfortable the houses were, how well suited to the sort of cosy family life that their occupants enjoyed! Italian houses were furnished in a way that displayed far more taste, more grandeur, and more beauty: French houses were unsurpassed for elegance, and again for good taste; but give him England for comfort, warmth, snugness, ease. French houses suited the French; they were for social life, for splendid entertaining; Italian houses were for being grand in; English houses were for living in!

But he was shocked and incredulous as the carriage drew them through Kent, where "the peasantry, especially the children, have a sickly starved look in painful contrast with the ruddy cheeks and healthy aspect of those in France. All through Kent the people had a look of misery and squalor and general suffering. A sad change for old England!" What had happened to the rosy stalwart English children that had rejoiced the heart of the returning Peninsular soldiers only sixteen years ago, sickened at heart as they had been by the wan, matchstick-limbed little objects seen in Portugal and Spain? Henry felt a pang of shame and horror. He did not know that four successive bad harvests had been followed by a bitter winter and a late spring.

He had been born into England's land-owning aristocracy and brought up in it. He knew very well that under the casual arrogance, the toughness and careless self-absorption and easy vitality, a fund of sense and goodness existed also. There were horrors amongst those rollicking and earthy fellows, as in other walks of life: there was also a strong core of men who loved their wives, cherished their children, were kindly with boring old mothers-in-law, patient with cross old fathers and pernickety old sisters. Many patronized art and literature on a generous scale, educated poor boys, gave steadily to charity, and lavishly at Christmas to every tenant and employee. They served the community according to their lights. But they lived within the ethic of their day, in which inequality of chance and of opportunity was accepted as unquestioningly as winter and summer. Driving through Kent, they would certainly have noticed the children, but would simply have commented that old so-and-so was a shocking landlord and always had been, and what a good thing that his nephew was said to be more promising. To question the right of old so-and-so to *be* shocking, to assume the responsibility of anyone else to people who were *his* tenants, rarely occurred to them. And pushing up through this calm acceptance, like couch-grass through a smooth and ancient lawn, were new standards of opulence and show, an arrogant set of values imposed from below by newer arrivals upon the scenes of wealth and grandeur. Was rat-race the only alternative to hierarchy? And revolution the outcome of either?

Henry's heart sank at the horrid novelty of undernourished English country children. Pragmatists rather than fatalists, Englishmen whose children hungered were disinclined to accept this as the will of God. They were apt to do something. The barricades of Paris were an accepted French tradition: cannon and bloodshed outside the Hotel de Ville were one thing: in long-peaceful Parliament Square they would be another. Rick-burning in Kent had started in June; the breaking-up of the new threshing machines that deprived men of work soon followed. The atmosphere, said a French visitor, was just like France's in 1789. As Henry and his family drove up from Kent through the mild stillness of the autumn days there were more rick-burnings and machine-breakings, while at Ash this month the local magistrate had his property destroyed for "unfeeling conduct" towards the poor. And behind them, across the Channel, the recent French outbreak had encouraged the Belgians, who in mid-October rose up against their Dutch masters and the House of Orange, and would soon be a separate state. Here was French opportunity: all Europe might soon be in flames once more.

As they neared London its familiar and revolting phenomenon came out to meet them, "an oppressive and most sickly effect of coal smoke". All felt ill, even Henry—"I was worried and ashamed of this delicacy after roughing out a life at sea." They had left Florence in mid-July. It was now mid-October: the coal fires were burning in the metropolis. "A thick and continued yellow fog received us in London"; and as it closed over their heads, it seemed to Henry that England too was lost and choking in a near-lethal fog of indifference and incomprehension; blanketing a rising river of conflicting claims, of dire purposes—Sweet Thames run softly till we get things right!

CHAPTER IX

Near Revolution in England

"How greatly people in general prefer opinion to truth", Charles thought, landing in this seething England; and, unemployed for ten years after his Ionian service, he had leisure in which to gather indignation. Having failed to get a job for five years after the end of the Napoleonic War, with his six wounds, his known skill and intelligence, and Wellington's recommendation, he was unlikely to commend himself to the Horse Guards fifteen years later, in the aftermath of a flaming row over his superior, Sir Frederick Adam, and smarting from his unsuccessful brush with Goody Goderich.

Bidding Charles goodbye on the quayside at Corfu, Sir Frederick Adam, affable to the last, had told him to stay on leave as long as he pleased, "but remember the longer you stay the worse for us"; and then briskly despatched two emissaries to Cephalonia to gather evidence against him. The truth is Charles was a difficult subordinate, unless he admired you, when he became mild as a lamb. Like William he never ceased, all through the disillusioning aftermath of Napoleon's defeat, to be fired with the glory of the Peninsular spirit; but like William, he was at a loss to find full expression to his ambition for prominent service and bold reform. Their Peninsular wounds and their besetting physical ailments did not soothe their temperaments or make their adjustment to ordinary society easy. In a Britain whose public men cherished repose and liked things very well as they were, these pensioned half-pay officers appeared virtually unemployable.

With waffling Lord Goderich Charles was hopelessly at odds, and with neither Wellington nor Melbourne was he wholly in tune. Wellington he deeply admired; but the Duke was the oak that could not bend, the statesman who believed that "beginning reform is beginning revolution". Though he shared both Melbourne's eighteenth-century wit and his occasional shafts of mysticism,

Charles was all activity; while Melbourne was sceptical about the value of all positive political action. Neither Charles's failure to obtain clearance from London for the leading command in the Greek war of liberation despite the support of Byron and the Greek leaders, nor his insubordinate conduct as Resident to his superior in the office of Lord High Commissioner of the Islands, had sweetened his relationship with the cautious and bothered administrators in Whitehall, from the Prime Minister to the Horse Guards. Back in England he found himself amongst the great unwanted.

His political views were wanted still less. The landed interests, which included almost all his friends and relations, were going to fight stubbornly for their own, for the political power of which reform of Parliament would deprive them. Reform would come only, they said, if it was clear that revolution was the alternative. Why allow the government of England out of its proper place in the hands of gentlemen? Fair enough, Charles said, so long as the gentlemen *are* gentlemen, and don't callously allow the poor to starve. What he couldn't see, the *status quo* supporters answered, was that power would not in any case spread far; it would simply switch from squires and landowners into the hands of the industrial middle class. And the middle class, as Melbourne patiently pointed out, was "all affectation and conceit and pretence and concealment". Anyone fit to rule would in due course float into the upper class anyway. Charles's birth and proclivities on one hand, and his poverty on the other, kept him out of either category. In any case he believed in the human race in general, which neither Wellington nor Melbourne did.

In 1830 Charles was forty-eight, and had a semi-invalid wife and two small children. His need for employment was great, and he felt himself more than able to contribute, in a society so dearly in need of helpful contribution. To an active man unemployment is a kind of slow castration, day after empty day chiselling away at manhood. What, he wondered, was everybody doing about the miseries of the British Isles? In 1827, when home on leave, he had told Louisa that men who merely speechified were not fit to rule. The Prime Minister, Canning, had proved less active than had been hoped. "The Duke's return as commander in chief is delightful"; but earlier in the year Charles had been amazed at the all-pervading prestige of Canning—"the whole country seems wild about him. Why is Canning such a great man all of a sudden? One man who directs several steam and gas companies assured me that Canning won all the battles of the Peninsula: the utmost grace to be obtained for the Duke of Wellington was that he was present at some of them and did not always run away."

By 1831 Charles's great desire was somehow to take a hand in Ireland, the country of his upbringing. In both countries he gave largely to charity, urged more drastic action. "We are here starving nearly", he wrote in September, "and in Ireland a whole nation starves as a matter of course . . . because what might be done is not done, and a little corner of a newspaper is all the notice taken of the wide-spreading tragedy." His anger mounted as months went by and nothing happened. "Oh the Whigs! Oh that Stanley! Oh that Lord Grey! They are the men who are sending more bullets and bayonets to Ireland. God forgive me, but if one did not know the King is a good fellow himself this is enough to shake loyalty. Reform tithes, establish poor laws, and drive absentees home to do their duty to starving labourers, and Ireland would be quiet and happy. I am of no party, but when I see people starving in the midst of abundance, my blood first runs cold with horror, and then boils with indignation."

It was not as if the experts had not all pointed out how Ireland could be cultivated. "These five millions of acres could support fifteen millions of people, and all Ireland has but eight millions. Yet they are left barren, and the Almighty who has sent such means is accused of over-populating. Grant me patience, oh God. Fifty millions could be well fed and happy in Ireland." Could he but go there, with authority to do something! By the end of September 1831 not even the matter of his return to Cephalonia had been cleared up. "I hear nothing from that What-in-the-world-shall-I-do, Lord Goderich." And Ireland was not relieved. When there were starving villages on his island he had sent corn on mule-back and caused them to pay for it when times were better, or partly pay for it. Could not something of the same kind be done on a huge scale for Ireland? "The ministers are in their way good men. Yes, but nations want results not motives."

If they would make him ruler of Ireland he would start by feeding everybody; and go on by sending all the Protestant priests to New Zealand, where, he trusted, the cannibal Maoris would eat them; and if any of the Roman Catholic priests started to pipe up and throw their weight about, they too would get short shrift; and then maybe Ireland would cease to learn hate and could gang its own gait and be happy. "I have had ten years experience in governing, which is something, and in six months not a man should starve. Stanley would make blood flow to produce love!

"Coercion, damnable coercion, which these Whigs have been crying down for forty years, and now cry up, being in office. O'Connell is called a devil, but he is doing an angel's duty. Fools that the Whigs are! Can they put down famine with bayonets!" To sit tight and see it all happen, with no power even to get a hearing in the press, was more than he could bear. "If my wife were young," he wrote next year, "I would go to New South Wales to get out of the way and rear young kangaroos to play with Susan and Emily."

But his wife was very far from being young; she was now well into her sixties. Such a marriage, even for a man in dire need of a mother for his two little natural daughters, was a curious one for a man who all his life had rejoiced in pretty women and continued to do so; and it was liable to provoke scorn and opposition. This duly appeared, and from an unexpected quarter: even his happy marriage had involved poor Charles in a ludicrous row. Elizabeth had a son-in-law, Samuel Laing, married to her daughter Agnes. Agnes had died, and Laing was assisted in bringing up his children by his two sisters-in-law, a couple of unmarried Miss Kellys, daughters of Elizabeth. Laing had been furious with his mother-in-law for marrying again, on the grounds that Elizabeth's marrying a man of his age made Laing himself look ridiculous. He wrote and told Elizabeth that he proposed to separate his children from all contagion of such an unsuitable grandmother; and he succeeded in working on the natural jealousy which unmarried daughters might be expected to feel upon the marriage of their mother to an attractive man more their age than hers, to a pitch where they too broke off relations. Elizabeth was thus distanced from all her previous family and affections. Unwilling to upset his poor wife any further, Charles made all efforts to secure a reconciliation; and a plan was made whereby the families should meet at Tours on the way home from Cephalonia. "Colonel Napier is much too anxious for my comfort and peace of mind, and is too liberal and kind-hearted to recriminate in any way whatever that might give pain to any of us", Elizabeth Napier hopefully wrote. "He has fully made up his mind to meet in perfect cordiality. Have no fear. Peace is our aim and desire."

Unhappily it was not Laing's. He wrote to Charles demanding money from him for the expense he would be at in removing his children from Tours to avoid meeting their grandmother. He also wrote to Elizabeth, enclosing a duplicate letter for Charles, to say that he had helped her with various sums of money over the years, and with capital and interest this now amounted to nearly three thousand pounds which Colonel Napier must send pronto. Charles got his cousin, William John, ninth Lord Napier, and head of the family, a naval captain who had been one of Nelson's midshipmen at Trafalgar, to answer the letters, "as having a cooler head". He was also canny enough to keep the next dozen of Laing's letters; his flowing and indignant handwriting inscribing across the packet—"or after my death he will traduce my character". The succeeding dozens were sent back unopened, but it had all made poor Elizabeth so very ill that they had had to leave Cephalonia in a tearing hurry, entrusting Susan and Emily to be brought on later by Edward Curling and his wife. To add to the gloom of this absurd fracas, Charles's beloved horse Blanco, who had come round by sea, had dropped dead suddenly in the Bay of Biscay—"my poor old Beast". The inordinate love for which Charles had blamed himself to Emily was extended also to animals.

Emily too was in a late-matrimonial tizzy. Now forty-four, and lonely now that George's little girls had gone back to him, she had been at Pau, staying with friends, when she had received a sudden and totally unexpected proposal of marriage from Sir Henry Bunbury. This kindly and benevolent man had been a friend of all the Napiers for many years. As a young soldier in Sicily he had married Louisa Fox, daughter of his General, Harry Fox; she whose younger sister Caroline had been the admired of Sir John Moore and had subsequently married William Napier. Bunbury had thus an in-law relationship with the Napiers and had also married their Fox cousin; in addition to which the uncle from whom he inherited his baronetcy and his property in Suffolk had been that same Sir Charles with whom Lady Sarah Napier had made her first marriage. It had ended disastrously and in some enmity; but the quarrel had been made up; and the Bunbury family, including Sir Charles, had treated Sarah's eldest daughter, legally but not actually his, with great kindness.

So that Emily knew all about her suitor, and liked all that she knew. It was a good and an eminently sensible match for a woman of forty-four who had nothing but charm, beautiful eyes, a small inheritance, and an even smaller pension as a soldier's daughter to recommend her in a worldly society. Louisa Bunbury had died two years ago, and lonely Sir Henry had been left with four sons, of whom the youngest, Hanmer, was one-armed since Navarino. Henry Bunbury was forty-nine, a general, and as an MP for Suffolk had held government office for some years. His need for a kind good wife was obvious and crying; and yet Emily, sitting down and trying to think things out calmly and rationally, had succeeded only in bursting into floods of tears.

In her forty-four-year-old spinster innocence, Emily felt that she had nothing but a sisterly affection, interest and kindness either to give or to receive; and how could she possibly begin at her age to switch this on to Henry Bunbury and away from Charles—"my own dear ten thousand times best loved Charles. Sir Henry has written to you; if I ever love half as well as a wife as I have done as a sister he may be very well satisfied." Should she marry Bunbury? "If I was young and in love it would be very different but how can I at my age begin an affection that will equal one that has 'grown with my growth and strengthened with my strength'?" She had by no means decided to marry, though common sense suggested that it would be a good idea. She had a distressing feeling that Charles might not have got her letter, and "my spirits are at their lowest ebb and I cannot bear the momentary appearance of having neglected the friend and brother I love most on earth."

Charles replied with his usual crisp common sense. Dearly as he loved Emily—he had once told her frankly that if she hadn't been his sister she would have been his love—he was probably not ill-pleased to have some of her affection switched on to someone else. He urged the marriage: he had always liked Bunbury, and was not, maybe, above the notorious brotherly conviction that all their sisters need to ensure happiness is a really good fellow. Things did not go very glowingly at first. On March 1st of the following year Charles was writing to his dear Em to say that he knows he can cheer her up. "I am at high war with that sneaking rascal Adam" and he "could not leave London till I see Lord Goderich", but "when we have a chat I know it will do you good—we are alike and our nerves jar alike, which convinces me I can talk you into better health and spirits." And talk her into them he did; Henry Bunbury and Emily enjoyed thirty years of happy married life, and she survived him by only two years, dying at the age of eighty.

Charles too was happy. Elizabeth was someone with whom he shared his ideas, someone peaceful and good, and intelligent enough to understand him, someone from whom he could evoke the laughter he needed as he needed meat and drink. Marriage with this elderly delicate woman had put paid not only to his hope of sons to carry on a name of which he was inordinately proud, it had also put paid to ambition: after her desperate illness in Cephalonia he would never dare to take her abroad again. In this same year he still thought "When death comes there is perhaps more comfort in love than in glory."

Not even the long-awaited serenity of life with Elizabeth could quite soothe Charles's intractable soul. For her sake he refused Lord Hill's offer of a job in Canada, though grateful for the kindness with which it was made. When in the fateful autumn of 1830 Wellington, the admired of his early manhood, opposed the Reform Bill, Charles thought him utterly at sea. "To serve under the Duke would be agreeable, but he has opposed himself to every just feeling of the age, and a man who tries to stem the feeling of the world acts like a madman." Louisa Napier, his unmarried half-sister, had met Wellington and reported the Duke not in spirits.

"The Duke has reason to be low," Charles told her, "for he is the cause of all the troubles which may fall on this land. Had he understood the English people he would have known that they may be led even to absolute starving, but if bullied, will hardly endure a look of taunt or defiance. Had he spontaneously given a fair reform England would have been at his feet. He was, before that blunder, popular beyond any man in the country: now God knows what will happen."

What happened, as the year ended, were burnings, maraudings and machine-breakings by ignorant and desperate men who felt that any action to express their plight was better than none. In December, 285 prisoners were brought to trial at Winchester; many were transported for life and six condemned to death, though two only were actually hanged. Later the Tolpuddle martyrs, who had not actually burned or bashed anything, were despatched from Dorset as convicts to Australia. Melbourne, now Home Secretary, did not interfere with what were then the due and accepted processes of law. He believed in containing revolution while reluctantly discussing reform. Slowly, the fires burnt up, the bitterness increased.

Groping through the London fogs of his first arrival, Henry too had wondered what would happen next. Near Christmas of 1830 he reported "a moment of great excitement, the whole country alive, bustling, eager, and anxious for events; hopes, doubts and apprehensions flitting about like swallows before a storm". Clubs and pubs and streets alike were humming—"so that all my latent political heat soon kindled up in despite of fog, cold, and an almost cimmerian darkness, the blessed odour of coalsmoke and the round dim looming of something like a new copper farthing called in England the sun!"

January of 1831 came in with louder murmurs from the have-nots and gloomier forebodings from the haves. "The question is not reform, but in fact *revolution*", Croker croaked on the 11th; and there were moments when he felt himself without even his staunchest allies. "Even the Quarterly Review talks for *Moderate Reform.* Moderate gunpowder!" The *Quarterly Review* and Croker had between them killed the poet Keats; now it seemed that the paper was about to desert Croker in his attempt to kill reform. Every section of the community was buzzing with alarm and dispute.

Even Sir Edward Codrington, with whom Henry dined, was stirred out of his naval calm by Wellington's calling his victory an untoward event, though privately the Duke had acknowledged to Sir John Gore that Codrington could have done no differently. "He certainly has been shamefully treated", Henry considered. "I asked him why he did not double on the Turkish fleet *inside*, and he answered that he had no idea of being obliged to fight, and his success a short time before in driving sixty sail of them from Patras back to Navarino with only the *Asia*, I think two frigates, and a sloop of war, justified this belief; because after so recent a proof of what intimidation could do, even by so insignificant a force, he had full right to count on the moral effect of three combined Fleets being sufficient to prevent immediate hostilities and secure ultimate obedience. He showed the Turkish commander his orders and the alternative he was put to in case of any attempt being made to sail, when he would have been compelled to give battle outside the harbour." Henry did not think his defence of Captain Fellow's conduct was "quite so unexceptionable": Henry himself thought it had been "injudicious, rash and hasty", but Codrington himself had endured five guns blazing away at the *Asia* before he fired one himself. The French admiral, Regni, had been "rather disposed to be tricky until he once had him fairly under his command, when he behaved admirably"; but this was understandable.

Henry had come home to England in yet another effort, but without much hope of success, to get his promotion from the new government. On January 1st, 1831 Henry received with delight and astonishment a letter from Sir James Graham with—"the gratification of testifying my sincere regard for your brother and yourself. I have this morning signed the very first commission I have had, in your favour, and you have now obtained that promotion which I think you so well deserve." It was a miracle of relief, "after all my disappointed hopes and Lord Melville's unjust, malignant and deceitful conduct"; for Lord Melville had twice gone back on his promotion promises. "And to get it from an able, honest, independent man and Minister of the Crown at the head of my profession." Henry's cup was full; but he could not help thinking there were many older and better officers than he still out in the cold—might they soon come in!

"Here then I am at length a Post Captain after all in 27 years with the blue coat on my back in all its various stages, from the wild unfledged Reefer to the staid Post Captain with starred and anchored swabs, gold laced coat, and iron-bound scraper!" Henry thought he had done his best to earn it, bar a few youthful pranks, with no private fortune and "very limited talents"; and when next day he went to thank Graham at the Admiralty, the First Lord had been more than friendly, had complimented Henry on his war record of service and assured him that "he was proud that one of his first acts should be the promotion of a Napier". Henry couldn't help glowing, however little it was to do with him, for "if I shine at all it is by a reflected light"; proud to hear his brothers praised "and see them and my cousin Charles [Black Charlie], who is a brave long-sighted clever fellow, justly appreciated".

Even a piece of "abominable literary malice" on the same day, by which an unknown character had sent a letter to *The Times*, signed with William's name, accusing Captain Sherrar of poaching from William's volume one (of the *Peninsular War*) in his *Memoirs of Wellington*, could not damp Henry's spirits. He and William had gone together to explain to Sherrar in Portland Place—"a nervous person and was a good deal agitated"—and on to *The Times* where "the Clerk seemed conscious and frightened and William immediately sat down and wrote a flat contradiction to be published in to-morrow's newspaper". The worst of it was that it was done by someone who was "evidently aware of the extreme nervous excitability of Captain Sherrar". How malign could you get?

Coming home from a club celebration at one o'clock on the previous night Henry had seen a family—father, mother and four children—sheltering on the steps of "one of those great houses of Piccadilly near the Duke of Wellington's". They were "alone in the frosty night in an empty street, and a more wretched group of worldly misery I never beheld". They had asked for nothing, but told Henry they were on their way back to Barnet and had already slept two nights in the open air, and Henry had put his hand in his ready pocket and given them a handful of shillings (each worth rather more than what a fifty pence piece is now), and in the morning found that he had, "deceived by the moonlight", given them a handful of guineas (about £50 by current values). "Thus the year has begun prosperously with that poor family." Coming home to "every comfort and happiness that man can enjoy" and, thinking it over, he forgave himself for folly and was "pleased to have done by mistake what I would willingly have done from reflection", though it was a drop in the ocean of England's misery. "My promotion deserves a return which could not be better paid than to the poor."

"Perhaps before the year is out I may get a ship!" The promotion would make Caroline as delighted as he was, more pleased maybe. "What joy it would have given me fifteen years ago! and how much does long disappointment chill the feelings . . . Now that Emily is so much better and Louisa at Barton I think you had better come up", he told Caroline; "Louisa's goodness of heart shines out most clearly in a sickroom." She could surely leave unless Emily made a great point of it—"My dear Car I want you here infinitely." She must be sure and have the carriage wheels greased and had better start not later than seven a.m. To say truth he didn't really like her out of his sight; and how would she fare when he went to sea?

His luck made Henry feel profoundly thankful, and he prayed deeply to do better and complain less, "to love all I can and hate none". His good fortune sparked off a fifty-page dissertation upon the right way to read the Bible, and upon religion in general with special reference to the pros and cons of belief in the Trinity, in which he quotes Moses, Christ, the apostles, St Paul, Irenaeus, Theophilus of Alexandria, Origen, Alexander of Alexandria, Sabellius of Ptolemais, Athanasius ("poor man, on whom years after his death was saddled that strange jumble of words which is called his creed"), Caesarius, Jerome, Cyprian, Dionysius of Alexandria, Cerinthus the Gnostic, Tertullian, Novatian, Chrysostom, Basil the Great, Lactantius Eusebius, Paul of Samosata, the MS. in the Ambrosian Library at Milan, and Hilary of Poitiers—"Every year, nay every moon, we make new creeds to describe invisible mysteries . . . reciprocally tearing one another to pieces, we have been the cause of each other's ruin." Henry heartily agreed with him.

Taking a deep breath Henry goes on to Dr Clarke of St James's Westminster, and Bishops Jortin, George Bull of St David's, Jeremy Taylor, Porson, Stillingfleet, Mills, Mede, Tillotson, Pearson of Chester, Dr Payne, and William Wake, a seventeenth-century Archbishop of Canterbury: it was a comprehensive list for a Hornblower.

Henry was delighted to find that he was in distinguished company in not believing in Hell: Origen and Gregory of Nazianzen hadn't believed in it either. The whole notion arose from a mistaken view of punishment; in days when mankind hadn't got around to seeing this in terms of helpful strictness and thought of it as vengeance. To believe in eternal torment was to deprive God of his attributes of justice, goodness and love—"Such notions are abhorrent to my feelings, my reason, my belief, and my whole conception of the great father of lights." Who could logically believe that God created man full of frailty and then punished him eternally for sins proceeding rather from frailty than from wickedness? No: this world was a first step in an existence gradually progressing towards perfection. Characteristically, Henry visualized Heaven as a state of ever-increasing knowledge, culminating in knowledge of God.

In the middle of all of this an old friend called Bourchier came to dinner, and although his unnamed companion wasn't very bright, between them they deepened Henry's conviction that "knowledge, though superficial, still spreads"; and would lead to clearer views and a better understanding of the physical world's true nature, of man's true nature and interests, thus gradually giving him a fuller life, and greater unity to nations. Pending these happy developments, which Henry felt certain would arrive in due course, he urged his children in a final valediction to love all men as fellow creatures though it wasn't possible to love them all as familiar friends, to behave honestly to enemies, to be charitable to other people's faults, to be rationally religious and follow religion's forms; "but do not live on forms and fancy you are religious—to spurn all worldly advancement that may not be had with honour, all wealth that may not be gained with honesty, to let no specious or plausible arguments blind your eyes to the truth, to guard yourselves against the insidious arguments of covetousness, they are sweet and slippery and prone to deceive".

They would not do themselves much good by listening to modern sermons which were far too often cant and hypocrisy: they should study the gospels and not just read them, "endeavour to penetrate to the pith and heart of what is there written". Christ's doctrine was "on the vast scale of human nature, one great extended universal scheme of regeneration, to 'live through all time, extend to all extent', whose full operation demanded the zealous cooperation of every being". Which didn't mean throwing oneself into missions as now constituted, most of whose members went to people in the direst poverty, "and sang hymns instead of planting corn". Henry's children were not to be put off by St Paul's "eastern figurative style which is more poetical than persuasive at least to us gentiles of a more simple tongue and country"; for "through it all runs a pure stream of refreshing water". The other apostles seemed to differ at times from St Paul, but when you looked deeper, their real agreement became clear.

The times were such, Henry thought, that everybody needed all the faith and strength and clarity of thought they could muster; and, coming down to earth, he reported a letter from Paris this January: "there all is snow, hail, and gunpowder." England might with wisdom still be saved from bloodshed, "but we are on the brink of a precipice, and in a thick fog . . . No work; distress, sickness, starvation, general discontent; incendiaries everywhere; insufferable taxation; extreme poverty, state, show, pomp and feasting—such contrasts are against nature, a violation of God's laws".

"Parliament meets to-day", he recorded on February 3rd. "Reform is the first, the great, the all-absorbing subject; the stream from which a bright or bloody river will flow." So much depended on the ability and resolution of so few men, "but the whole nation is now awake and calls out with a giant's voice". But would little Lord John Russell be big enough to respond? The ministers had again promised

6*

reform, and he was to bring in the Bill on March 1st, but "surely this bit-by-bit reformer, who talks boldly but steps as delicately as a cat crossing a gutter, will be scared at the work entrusted to him, if it be worth the people's acceptance! Lord John is greatly cried up, and he is an industrious plodding man, but no statesman." Henry thought his bold speeches contrasted strongly with the timidity of his actions: perhaps now at last he would act up to his words. "The King and Cabinet I hear are unanimous on the subject of Reform and the former pleased. It is thought that Lord Grey cannot propose a less extensive plan of reform than his own of forty years ago; this would indeed be good; and in truth from Lord Althrop's speech there is great hope of its not being niggardly." There was even talk of some minor reforms in Ireland, but good things for Ireland invariably hung fire, while any coercive measure "ran through Parliament like lightning through stubble".

Though still holding his breath politically, Henry had time for diversion. It was still *When* he got a ship, and not *If*. At a party at Lansdowne House he and Caroline had seen Talleyrand, arms akimbo and looking exactly like his caricatures: he had survived so many wars and revolutions; could he be about to survive another? Samuel Rogers was as ugly as ever, but his kind and welcoming manner and his conversation made up for it; and they had seen a lot of old friends, Francis Baring, Chin Bailey, Fox, Vernon-Smith. Henry had then been lucky enough to see Turner's picture gallery, "a great favour granted to but few; I however had an opportunity of being civil to him once in Italy, and he with all his uncouth roughness does not forget it". Henry was struck by the boldness and power of his painting, "yet he is very unequal; it puts me in mind of Byron's poetry, a curious mixture of the beautiful and careless." But the words magnificent, wonderful, astonishing, real, beautiful, vigorous, original, star Henry's comments. He thought the sea-pieces equalled Vandervelt's, "except in the technical accuracy of the shipping". Turner's ships were always admirably placed, and sat well in the water, but anyone, even half a seaman could see they were about to run into each other. His talent was extraordinary: Henry thought no painter had ever come near Turner in his skies and atmosphere.

Jones had taken him to see Chantry and his works—"a rough, frank, outspoken man, with a bluff English countenance in which spirit and benevolence predominate", but you would not credit him with the imagination and taste his sculpture showed. What charmed

Henry most was its extreme simplicity: his portrait of Banks was magnificent, and so were those of Pitt and Grattan, Washington's better still, and Elphinstone's best of all. The British Museum had just been given George IV's magnificent library and had built a fine room to house it, though with "something too solid and heavy looking in the centre part". But on the whole it was "a fine structure and well worthy of the great establishment to which it belongs. Everything is here well arranged, the attendants civil, and the public curiosity gratified without any expense or difficulty, a new era in the history of English public buildings and institutions!" The pictures at Cleveland House gave him equal pleasure: among some indifferent ones there were magnificent old masters, and Henry was once more entranced by Turner's vigour and vision. There was really a lot to be said for life in foggy London; though William, visiting him, reported to Caroline that Henry's children were not well from the change of climate, and that Henry was almost sorry he had come. "The boy is the nicest pretty little thing in the world, and Gougou a nice little girl, though not so pretty. The account of your party pleased me, though how you got fifty-four people in the house I don't know!" Life went on, revolutions or not.

William and Henry alternated between brave hopes and troubling fears. In February of 1831 William was seriously thinking of sending Caroline and his children to France to be out of the way of a revolution that seemed inevitable when the Commons threw out the Bill: all that stopped him was "the dangerous state in which Louis Philippe and his cursed faction have placed that country". America was too far off; but he urged Caroline to start training the girls for privations and teaching them to look after themselves. Even Wellington urged Mrs Arbuthnot to "provide Means of Subsistence for yourself in another country". "Here in London men speak sedition openly in the clubs and secretly in the streets," William wrote. Both brothers feared a weakening in the reformers when it actually came to the crunch. Visiting William near Devizes—"about 11 hours by the Emerald, a Bath Coach"—Henry had been surprised to find "little Tom Moore beginning to be alarmed at the bright spirit of liberty which has been invoked". This in one "whose poetry has perhaps done more than anything to rouse the free spirit of his own oppressed ill-treated countrymen". If revolutionary Tom Moore was windy, what must more conventional souls be feeling?

People were so worked up "that what would, a year ago, have been received with joy and gratitude will be insufficient now". The Reform Bill, when published, was "far more liberal in some parts than I had hoped, but not so liberal in others; it is however great, glorious and efficient as far as it goes and will do wonders if not modified but will scarcely get through this Parliament. The debate still continues, Ministers deserve infinite praise but they will be hard run." If they resigned, Henry thought they would be returned in a hurricane: if they made a bold appeal to the country they would be swept back on such a wave of popular opinion that they might find themselves going further than they meant! When one thought of the growing intelligence of men, their growing aspirations, it was clear they would never, never stomach defeat now. We were on a precipice with a strong wind blowing towards revolution, thought Henry: only national good sense, and the fact that a great mass of people had a lot to lose, could keep us on an even keel.

The debate had been going on for five days, "with much railing and small argument against reform: its opponents prove nothing but their own selfishness, folly, or prejudice, or else unmitigated fright". Peel's speech had been "solid and powerful", Hobhouse's "good but rather fillagree", Baring's "bad and dirty". After nine nights, leave was given to bring in the Bill; the second reading to be on March 21st. Ministers, Henry heard, had no hope of succeeding without a dissolution: this they might safely ride, with the whole country behind them, "and although Englishmen are slow to rise, when once they do, they are indomitable!" But would the King dissolve Parliament? Or would the Tory old guard be too much for him?

Amazingly, the Bill was passed by one vote. The Tories seemed unworried; they expected "a reaction in the public feeling". Reaction? They must be out of their minds, thought Henry. What blindness and obstinacy: there would be no reaction until "they can feed starving multitudes, clothe myriads of naked families, employ numberless miserable families, reduce taxation, curb a rich, grasping, overbearing clergy, reform an ignorant and partial magistracy, equalize taxation and the franchise, unfetter commerce, un-tax food, and render justice cheap! . . . The present steady, calm, universal determination to have reform has been the growth of fifty years and is not the excitement of the moment, it is the stern voice of a great people who know their rights and will assert them." And on the anniversary of the day thirty years before that he so well remembered—splashing ashore through the shallows under the French cannonades from Aboukir Castle as a sun-browned thirteen-year-old boy in a cutaway coat who had landed with Abercrombie in Egypt and seen that great man die—he thought how totally different the people of England now were. "A new race has sprung up, and with it a far juster notion of political rights." Humbug was on the way out, and he hoped cant was too. Thirty years ago the very word "change" had made people think one was a Jacobin and start looking round for their pistols. Yet even as early as 1819, when that infamous old Sidmouth had fired on the crowd at Manchester, "even Lord Castlereagh, cold and comfortless as he was, and fond of coercion, was utterly shocked and astounded at his colleague's act, and all England execrated it".

On March 25th Henry's hopes were high. Lord Grey had made an excellent speech the night before, calm, manly, and determined; it seemed that so many converts were coming in "between fear and necessity" that a dissolution wouldn't be necessary; "swing and fright have made this revolution". April came in with "cold, blighting, searching weather . . . but damn the weather as long as we get Reform!" Everything was still in the balance, and as chilly morning succeeded chilly morning Henry "Longed for the newspaper as a wounded man longs for water". Let there be no more speeches, "I want results!" Yet even the King's inclination to dissolve seemed now in doubt; the government had been out-voted on an amendment, and Henry had "little faith in Johnny Russell's firmness" when it came to the crunch.

Unable to sit still, he walked into the middle of London to catch stray reports and rumours on which to hang his hopes—"saw Lord Cochrane, Sir Robert Lawley, Rogers, Sir Gore Ousley, and several others all in great excitement; all seeking news and getting nothing certain". It was April 20th, the Cabinet council was sitting. "Our choice seems to vibrate between dissolution and revolution and we may perhaps have both . . . Everybody is asking questions to which nobody can reply but by conjectures." Who would come in if these Ministers went? "Wellington cannot, for he is opposed to all reform, and even his colleagues acknowledge that a moderate reform is necessary. Who else is there bold enough to propose any course short of Lord Grey's Bill?"

If the King would be true to himself and stick to his guns all would be well—"There is no question about him or the Crown, no republican spirit." If he didn't allow himself to be jostled by the Tories he'd be the most popular monarch since Alfred! If he did, "he and his family will be run hard and England will be convulsed from end to end". Machine-breaking and murdering had already begun in the north: even the Duke, Henry heard, had said he had never been so alarmed in his life before; nervous and anxious before battle he had often been, but was now possessed by "unmixed fear" at the state of the country and the probable effects of this Reform Bill. "Early prejudice will blind even the strongest minds . . . His opinions are honest, but reform must come, whether in storm or shine."

"Still restless, and impatient of not knowing how events thickened I repaired to my club [the Travellers] where I met Sir Gore Ousely who told me that the King was gone down to prorogue Parliament." Henry hastened thither, "overtook Alexander Johnston and Mr. Milman the poet and joined them: from the suddenness of the King's determination there was no great crowd assembled and we soon arrived at the House of Lords: the King passed us on our way and was loudly cheered: Hunt had passed us a few minutes before and was hissed and groaned at. This shows how willing Englishmen are to be led by the great *when* the great will act honestly and patriotically; and how little they care for Demagogues except in great suffering and when nobody will listen to them."

The crowd by now was too great for Henry and his friends to get into the Lords, but "the scene both in the Lords and Commons was described to me by members of both houses whom we met as one of intense violence. In the Commons Peel made a most violent speech and a bitter attack on the Government; then the Row, for it could not be called a Debate, began and proceeded to such lengths that the Speaker could no longer keep order, one universal hubbub continued til the Usher of the Black Rod put an end to it by a message from the Lords."

Not that they had been any better. Lord Wharncliffe had moved an address to the King against dissolution which had been opposed "steadily, boldly, and directly by the Duke of Richmond, and supported by Lord Londonderry"; after which a violent debate had produced "such confusion that the Chancellor lost all control, was totally unheeded, and finally quitted the Woolsack. Upon this Lord

Shaftesbury was instantly voted into his place as Speaker and Lord Mansfield at once got up and delivered a most violent but remarkably eloquent speech against Ministers which he artfully concluded just at the moment the King was entering, by crying out: 'This Bill, my Lords, will bring eternal ruin on the Country; but God protect the King!' " People in both Houses really seemed to have gone slightly mad. Lord Mansfield at one point had denounced the Ministers for advising the King to dissolve Parliament, saying it was unprecedented: Brougham (Lord Chancellor) had had to shout back at him "What ! Unprecedented for a King of England to exercise his undoubted prerogative of dissolving Parliament, when the House of Commons in a manner unparalleled in the most factious periods of English History have stopped the supplies?" And in the Commons, over the Irish franchise, Sir Richard Vyvyan had only just been stopped from his avowed intention of raising what Henry called "the detestable and ever mischievous cry of 'No Popery' ". Members' excitement had to be seen to be believed.

In short, Henry reported, there had "never been anything like it since the days of Charles I. Lady Bute, who had hold of her husband's arm, was pushed into the body of the House amongst all the Peers, with her bonnet on, and remained there during the whole of this short but stormy scene. Thus at last, to the whole nation's satisfaction, has this Parliament been dissolved . . . The Bill, if carried out, will in fact be Revolution, but Revolution of a most wholesome kind." There must now be an election, and "only let the Nation respond boldly and honestly to the call of its Sovereign!"

Whitehall was seething. "I found the whole town in agitation, a perfect state of effervescence; the Clubs full and noisy; the people in the streets collected in knots and groups eagerly discussing the events of the hour, for the whole affair may almost be said to have passed in that time; some were laughing and merry, others sad, but the greater portion was serious. Palace Yard and Whitehall were thronged and busy with gazers, shouters, and talkers. King William had come out in his admiral's uniform, and been greeted with a storm of cheers." Henry thought it had been a long time since any King of England had heard that noise, a full-throated roar of approval. "There was the brilliant procession, the gaudy liveries, the splendid equipage, the tramp of horses, the wave of plumes, the flash of helmet and cuirass, the clang of arms, the roll of coaches, and the deafening cheers of the people! It was a stirring scene . . .

"This day however, thank Heaven, is not mere show; it is big with the fate of millions . . . and for the first time in my life I can say with sincerity God save the King!"

CHAPTER X

Reform or Revolution?

Checked but not halted in his History, William had turned his mind since Murray's letter to the burning politics of the day. Even if the money were forthcoming to fight an election, he did not seem to fit into any particular party. He had been a follower of his Whig first cousin Charles James Fox, but since Fox's day the Whigs seemed a bit humbugging and ineffective. Radical he might be, but "I like not republicanism, I desire to see men of all classes as God designed them to be, free in thought, unabashed in mien, but virtuous and obedient to the just institutions of society." Hunt and his fellows were demagoguish, too far out for a sensible man to take seriously.

Radical pacificism too seemed to him a nonsense. "If you have democratic institutions not calculated to support a standing army in the midst of other standing armies and nations hating democracy, then you will be trampled upon; you must conform to what the world forces you to conform to." Round his home politics went on unexcitedly, but when William came to London in January of 1831 looking for a printer for his second volume he was amazed to find people talking treason as if it were nothing—"You will be surprised to learn that I am reckoned too moderate", he told Caroline. By February he was sure that "reform must be granted or civil war will ensue . . . It is really time to do something; my heart is sick at seeing the miserable children starving in the streets, and the squalid wretches that are spread in all parts crying for food, amidst the rolling of carriages and the most insulting and selfish luxury, which rich people seem to pride themselves in displaying."

But to do what? By the end of February, when "the printers are again delaying until they almost distract me", he was being sought on every side to write political pamphlets for newly-sprung political societies, "and perhaps for one I will, but at my age I will not lightly *join a faction*. I am become an object of political catering": people had started offering him parliamentary seats all over the place: and very alluring it was, in this time of stir.

Common sense had to prevail: but there was nothing to stop him speaking; and on an evening in early May William was on his legs at a political meeting on the Reform Bill election in Devizes, spell-binding them all as he well knew how to do, and sweepingly repudiating the notion that Parliament's dissolution spelt anarchy and chaos, as the Tory candidate had maintained. "King William IV dissolved Parliament: the first monarch of his family that honestly acknowledged the full rights of his people . . . To dismiss such a House of Commons was a wise policy, an act befitting an enlightened Monarch, and it deserves the admiration and the gratitude of an enlightened and high-minded people . . . Countrymen, are your hearts so full of gall, are your minds so perverted, your judgment so clouded, that the frank and just conduct of your Sovereign will only excite your worst passions?" Were they thinking of bloody revolution? No! "Will you at once repay him with ingratitude? and drag down ruin on your heads? No!" Here the cheers shook the room, and William, shifting his weight from one long leg to another to ease the pain of his back, rose to them.

"I thank you for that loud and honest shout: I knew you would repel the calumny . . . The people of England are more energetic, more ingenious, more industrious, than any other on the face of the earth; and yet in the midst of plenty created by their own toil, they are scarcely able to procure bread for their sustenance, while a certain number of persons, a privileged few, are gorged with wealth and swollen with power . . . This, Sir, is an unjust and oppressive state of things, and therefore a degraded state . . . Aided by the King, we have braved the denunciations of false priests . . . we have dared to look into the innermost recess, and we have found not a sanctuary but a sink; not holiness, but corruption; not God, but Mammon", William declaimed, slightly carried away by his own gift of the gab.

"The English are a bold and persevering people; they may be deceived, they may be blinded for a time; but with their eyes once open they are not to be frightened." William's black hair was wilder than ever; at the best of times it sprang from his head like a turbulent sea. His eyes flashed fire, and his battered powerful frame looked as if it might take off from the platform at any minute. "The English people will make their power be felt. It is their King who leads:

millions of honest-hearted and clear-headed men will follow him, and they will prove by their conduct how false, how calumnious is the assertion that anarchy and not good government is their object!"

It was fine to hear the cheers, it was intoxicating to sway the hearts; but what did it actually do? Little children still trudged in the mines and sweated in the mills, women still starved and men stood idle, frustrated, and uncomprehending, outside the smoky factories of the north which Blake had so truly seen as hellish, for anything that William could accomplish. No Reform Bill could change these horrors overnight. He and his brothers were those not unusual specimens in English history, reformers in search of a party. What was the use, thought Henry in his day, of anchoring oneself to a formula, when life changed so rapidly, tying oneself down to a slogan or cry which sounded profoundly silly in a year or two? Organized left wing parties, then as now, seemed to get themselves tied up in doctrinal knots and obliged to worship willy-nilly at the shrine of some sacred cow called Laisser Faire or Nationalization of the Means of Production and Distribution, some unalterable political Koran or Talmud, some manifesto of Karl Marx or Thoughts of Chairman Mao, while the objects of their exercise went hungry.

Radicalism at this time, according to G. M. Trevelyan, was "not a doctrine but a spirit—indignation at the wrongs of the poor". It was shared by many, and in this passion the Napiers heartily joined; William moving as actively as he could while reform still hung in the balance. It was no use thinking of standing for Parliament. "My dear Evans," William wrote in April of 1831, "I have eight children, and scarcely enough to feed and clothe them; it would therefore be madness in me to stand an election", but he continued to speak; and to Henry in London it seemed that his speeches were having considerable effect; people discussed and admired them. Like many another before and since, Henry had sought an outlet in a letter to *The Times*, urging those in favour of reform to use a bit of energy and organization in fighting the election. The *on dit* was that on the anti-reform side Peel had subscribed £20,000, and the Duke of Northumberland £100,000. "Would the people of England be bribed, or stand idle in this crisis?" To his surprise and delight Henry's letter against sluggishness and apathy appeared prominently in *The Times*: he followed it up with another, also printed, and commented on in a leading article. There were no signs of a ship up to date, but this was something!

All Europe seemed to be stirring; there had been revolt in Spain, in France, in Belgium against Holland's rule, and now in Poland against her foreign masters, good luck to her! Henry talked to Foley Wilmot, back from the embassy in St Petersburg, who told him that Diebich, the Russian general in charge of suppressing the Poles, was not clever though a capable soldier, and so short and ugly that the Czar Paul had turned him out of the Imperial Guards, and that Jomini and Butterlin were thought to be mere theorists and no good in the field: they hadn't even courage enough to answer a duel challenge! Adulation at the Russian court was carried to a pitch where Russian nobles wouldn't dance even at a private party if the Czar were in bed with a cold: since the Polish insurrection they had refused a ball at the British embassy, and then, hearing the Czar would not after all object, had arrived in hundreds at the last moment. Nicholas was open and straightforward, "without the Greek cunning and falseness of Alexander", and was therefore unpopular; but all kow-towed before him just the same. "Can this state of things go on long in the nineteenth century?" Henry wondered. William, to whom planning military campaigns was as fascinating as seeing Dutch masterpieces or painting pictures himself, had been unable to resist sending Caroline an imaginary letter to the Poles—"fix a bridge and tête-de-pont at Seirock, beat the force that will come by the left of the Bug . . ."

Election excitements continued; Wellington's windows were smashed by the crowd—though they went away at once on being told that the Duchess was lying dead at Apsley House—and Lord and Lady Walsingham, perhaps carried away by the general incendiarism, had accidentally burnt themselves to death with all their household in Harley Street. Henry switched off politics to give the Academy pictures a run-through: Constable's "Yarmouth Pier" was fine, Walcott was affected, Jones's "Esther" was wanting in expression, Landseer's "Highland Deerstalkers" was good, Turner, as ever, seemed to Henry magical, little behind even Claude, but nobody bought him, except two other artists, the architects Soane and Nash —"English people on the subject of art were always gulled, are always gulled, will be always gulled, and what is more, dearly love to be gulled, by the soi-disant artists, the second rate." He and Caroline took tickets for Paganini, two guineas each and away beyond their means, but how heavenly! Carried away, Henry quoted Milton's "linked sweetness long drawn out"; and if he, "a poor earless unmusical brute" were thus transported by the hidden soul of harmony, what must it be "for those of more delicate and congenial organization!"

Charles was in London, and he and John Kennedy wanted to meet Admiral Cochrane and hear his side of the Greek war; Henry went with them to Hanover House to introduce them. They found the admiral, now stripped of his naval rank and his orders, planting out his garden: his house was full of books and fine sculpture and his manner gentle and rather shy, which astonished his guests. He opened out at once, however, on the Greek war. No-one had told him of the truce of June 1827 and he had sunk and burned some Turkish ships off Patras, so that the Turks, thinking the allies were not intending to keep the truce, had rather naturally fired first at Navarino. The Greeks were maddening to command, so terrified that their neighbour might be beforehand with them and not doing a proper share of fighting that they themselves often stopped fighting at the critical moment; they failed to fire broadsides through disobedience; and none of the fireships he ordered into Alexandria had got further than the outer harbour, where there was only one small brig, instead of pushing on into the inner harbour where he had sent them to destroy the Egyptian fleet. Although Cochrane didn't say so in so many words, they gathered he had been the planner of Church's attempt to relieve Athens, a dismal failure; Charles and Kennedy came away thinking Cochrane was no general, however expert an admiral.

People complained of the English Sunday, but in London Henry rather enjoyed the unwonted silence after the week's hubbub, with only the very occasional carriage rumbling in the distance. Even when the church bells rang, and almost everyone in London went to church, they were nearly all walking: it was peaceful, silent, uncompetitive. The beggars knocked off work, even the poor were adequately dressed, everybody appeared to be enjoying themselves, and that painful weekday contrast between ostentatious magnificence and squalid misery no longer glared. Henry was reading Tom Moore's *Life of Lord Edward Fitzgerald* and thought it fascinating, partly of course because he had known Tom Moore since they were small boys at Moira House in Dublin, with splendid spacious Lady Moira making everything fun; but also because he remembered

Edward, who was his first cousin, and his jokes and games and kindness, his general entering into the joys of childhood with all the little Napiers. He could just remember the tragedy of Edward's death, how carried away this young rebel had been by "the romance of political liberty and the detestation of oppression": he had been "imprudent, but noble!" The book contained letters from his parents, and he rejoiced at the well-remembered essence of his mother Sarah, her sincerity, impulsiveness, tenderness, and acuteness: and his father's sound judgment and deep feeling, Aunt Louisa's goodness and humility. Henry had heard that the now immensely respectable Holland House cousins had not been best pleased at having a first cousin's treachery raked up again, and Henry himself felt a faint pang at the inevitable disinterment of his mother's old scandal; but she rose above it, goodness how she rose above it! George's memoir was a delight too, though not written for publication but only for his children: Henry hoped his own children would read it too: it was "simple, natural, and even homely in style, though everywhere full of sympathy and strong feeling, which often rises into poetry. It is in fact George himself."

Meanwhile revolution was temporarily distanced and the election was going on splendidly. Dover had already returned two reform members. "These are great days for England and indeed the world, we are now fighting the battle of national liberty for all", rejoiced Henry. "The Lowthers have lost Cumberland and are likely to yield Westmoreland, Hart Davis cannot show his face at Bristol, the Duke of Newcastle has lost Newark, Northumberland will no longer obey its duke, Gascoigne will be hard pushed at Liverpool, the sailors at Portsmouth have nicknamed the King 'Reform Bill' . . . William's speech at Devizes is universally admired." He heard that various parties were after William, and not only as a political leader. He was known to be a first-class soldier, a thorough radical, a born leader, and eloquent as they come. But if anyone thought William would put himself at the head of armed insurrection they had, considered his brother Henry, another think coming.

William was potentially a dangerous man. He had all the demagogue gifts, was easy on the eye, easy on the ear, combative, quick-witted. He shared with Wellington a quality he had himself described as "the duke's devil", an inspired driving force which could equally well operate for good or evil and was formidable whichever route it took. As a young man William had had a touch of fire and brimstone about him which had proved devastating to the girls, and it had not yet deserted him.

In spite of the academic brilliance of his brother Richard, William was the cleverest and most able of his family, the most charming and persuasive, and in a kind of unacknowledged way, he knew it. He was the third son of song and story, with every gift in the world except luck. In this wild summer and autumn season of rumour and excitement the devil, within or without, tempted him to use these great gifts in the way for which he had been trained, and let them bring him the fame he deserved. These fiendish apparitions wore the sober forms of Messrs Erskine Perry and Charles Buller, the violent forms of two extreme malcontents Sharpe and Place, and much more surprisingly, of Tom Young, the keen-witted and breezy vulgarian who was private secretary to that unexceptionably pacific statesman Lord Melbourne.

How greatly tempted William was we do not know, and he would probably not have admitted, even to himself; but the pull must have been powerful. It was the supreme opportunity of his life. Violent through the circumstances of his upbringing, outraged by the delays and uncertainty of reform, frustrated by his intermittent helplessness, William was a sitting target. He had been tormented all his life by the demon of ambition and the strong desire for the martial fame to which he knew his powers entitled him. Long, long ago, when he was a twenty-three-year-old in the Peninsular War and had "no military position", older officers would watch with amazement and perhaps envy while Wellington, "most secret of men", would hold long confidential discussions with William about the war. Instinctively, he knew the form, and Wellington knew that he did.

The misery he daily saw about him gave a moral justification, if anything could, to violent solutions. He might even have felt that an experienced soldier would save bloodshed. Those daft civilians who had never seen a strewn battlefield, attacking wildly and having no notion that once they began armed strife, human life grew cheap as a barrowload of winkles! As he grew older and iller William's arrows would fly higher and wilder, until at last they laid low the brother he loved most in the world. But it is to his eternal credit that now, underneath that wild black hair, that agile restless frame, he kept a level head and an understanding heart; that he could perhaps have wrecked England, and did not. He had signed on; and when it came to the crunch, was a faithful soldier and servant.

"I am tormented daily by letters from people I don't know and from some I do know to step forward and raise a national guard, and I can scarcely convince them that I don't mean at once to turn traitor and begin a civil war," he told Charles early in 1831. "It is very dangerous for me to be marked out in this manner; I hear secretly that all the poor people look to me as their leader when the row begins, and nobody here seems to think that anything but civil war will be the end of the Reform affair. I however hold back from everybody, but if things get worse I must think of removing Caroline and the children to France or Guernsey. I hope sincerely that the Duke will yet take the reform question in hand."

Like others, William was distressed that the Duke, the idol of all, had come down against the Reform Bill, declaring in the Lords in November 1830 that the English representative system could not possibly be improved upon. There was no give in him: as Charles said, he was like an old oak that bent before no wind. "One cannot but deeply lament he should not have read more justly the spirit of the times", Colonel Shaw Kennedy wrote to William, and he thought that the whole tenor of the Duke's life prevented his seeing how opinion had progressed in a different direction: he could have had the whole country behind him if he had advocated a reasonable reform; as it was, everyone one met talked of it "with regret, not anger". In December William had met Douro again: like other young men he had reacted against his Papa—"His politics are decidedly adverse to his father's, and he is for a thorough reform. He dislikes London society for its heartlessness . . . and is keen in observation." With so many diverse strands of the English world wanting reform, could it not be achieved without a bloody civil war?

The political offers made to William became increasingly tempting. His election expenses would be paid, he could have a free hand. In due course William was asked to stand in the Radical interest in Bath, Devizes, Birmingham, Glasgow, Nottingham, Westminster, Oldham and Kendal. The people of Bath did not want "a smooth-tongued adventurer" to represent them, and begged William to stand; they would find even the additional expenses, help in any possible way. What they couldn't do was to restore William to his native rude health, or finish his History for him. He had an enormous desire to take part in politics in a meaningful way, but not even "that accursed spirit of ambition which torments us all" would make him sacrifice the children; or indeed the History on which their future largely depended and which was now absorbing all his energies between bouts of pain and illness. How fairly represent anybody when a good soaking in a shower of rain prostrated him with ague and fever for weeks?

His political speeches were bringing him great *réclame*; and the radicals wanted a man of education and standing to speak for them. The delay in the necessary concessions was building up an ever-increasing body of men whose ideas were far more extreme than William's, and there was talk of a National Guard against armed insurrection. When the Lords threw out the new Parliament's Reform Bill in October, Erskine Perry wrote to William about the new "Union" of which Sir Francis Burdett was Chairman: would William join, and "if a crisis should arrive" take on as military leader? Emphatically not; reform "will be gained, I hope, without the necessity of any appeal to arms".

Undiscouraged, Charles Buller wrote to William a week later—"In this age of eunuchs it is delightful to look up to one respectable man of undoubted virility . . . every man in England knows you to be a determined friend to the people . . . I am convinced of the utter incapacity of the known leaders of the people . . . One bold, honest, wise man could save the country." William might be that one, but again he pointed out his crippling ill-health, his eight children, and above all his fear that "we shall only widen the breach, already too wide, between the different classes of society". Very different in tone were other letters that came his way this hectic autumn. Did they imagine he would sign on as Jack Cade, Wat Tyler, or who have you? Never would he lead a revolution or foment a civil war: a youth spent in Ireland had taught him this much. If reform was to get anywhere they must tame their wilder notions, he told his correspondents, and enlist the support of men of property and influence, men who would listen to and encourage a rational scheme of reform. He would not, repeat not, lead a faction of half his countrymen to fight against the other half.

At this moment of extreme political excitement, William received a letter from the private secretary of Lord Melbourne, then Home Secretary, suggesting that he, William, should put himself at the head of the hard-core malcontents, Sharpe and Place, and march on

London at the head of fifty thousand men. Was it likely, William furiously wrote back, that he would join up with "a Birmingham attorney and a London tailor" and march against Wellington and every single one of the old friends by whose side he had fought through six years of bitter war, quite apart from breaking his service oath of allegiance? The letter, as its author pleaded later, had been written "in a giddy moment" and without the knowledge of Lord Melbourne, whom William came to respect; but it was worded in such a way that it could be read as an attempt of the Whigs to enlist William as *their* general in a show-down with the government. William was so outraged that he announced he would keep the letter and twist the tails of the Whigs by producing it whenever an innocent man were indicted for rebellion in either England or Ireland.

Later in the autumn he was up in London again about his book, and thought people there were quiet on the whole, except against the lords and bishops who had thrown out the Bill. Lord Londonderry had been knocked off his horse by a thrown half-brick; the Duke of Wellington was narrowly missed by another one crashing through the windows of Apsley House; trade was at a stand; there was a rumour that Belvoir Castle was burnt to the ground; and the funds had dropped like a stone. The crowd had tried to tear down Wellington's image, the Achilles statue—"but he was too heavy for them".

Too heavy indeed, both in image and in fact, and would the "timidity and faction of the Whigs" talk the whole reform away? "Delay, and the fell monster anarchy will waken", William dreaded. There was "an excellent possibility that Wellington and Lord Radnor would together with other rational Tories bring in a good reform bill . . . What I fear most is the sudden rising in arms of Scotland or Manchester". There were mass meetings going on everywhere: "the plot is certainly thickening and getting very bad, *mais courage*", William told himself.

In the midst of all this King William IV was crowned: "The train of carriages meagre," William thought, "the prettiest things by far were the horses. The coachmen looked like great diamond beetles; the Duke of Sussex like a great ton of flesh; the Duke of Cumberland like himself; the King like a very honest good-humoured fellow; and the Queen like a little gingerbread queen, so pert and well-satisfied with her glory." Sir Francis Burdett was too ill of gout to go to the

House; "the Duke of Newcastle's castle at Nottingham has been burned by the people"; he still believed in English sense; but at times it seemed not so much *if* as *when* Revolution would come.

At midsummer political feeling had still been blazing like a bonfire and Henry was amazed, at the June party at Lansdowne House, to see how "the most inveterate Tory, the most corrupt borough-monger, and the wildest radical" could meet and mingle; not to mention Count Woronsow the Russian and Valesky the Pole, whose two countries were at each other's throats, "and none of them out of sorts". On principle that was a good thing; never should political opinions divide good friends. Yet the day before they had been abusing each other like fishwomen, imputing base motives, yelling at each other as tryants or cut-throat Jacobins: was there any point and sincerity in social meetings and greetings when such basic feelings were involved? The guest to whom Henry personally would have shown the door was "that villain the Duke of Cumberland". His cousin of Cambridge might not be very bright, but at least he was good, and full of a rather innocent and simple sort of fun.

At Sir Matthew White Ridley's first ball on opening his new house in Carlton House Terrace, Henry was fascinated to see the frescoes he had brought back from Pompeii and Rome: how did really rich people still manage to buy and extract such things from foreign countries against every law and regulation? Ridley also had a Dürer and a lovely Rubens sketch of a woman's head. Henry was hoping for a meeting of the Royal Society, of which he was a Fellow: he had greatly enjoyed Sir Joseph Banks's soirées in the old days, where this President's "kindness of manner and natural urbanity", as well as his love of science and liberal patronage of scientific enquiry, had made it all go well. "Slightly conversant with many branches and deep in some, he could converse with all, and yet had neither sufficient talents nor profundity of knowledge to excite jealousy amongst the savants of his day." At Sir Humphrey Davy's gatherings there had been "far more formality and less cheerfulness, with a strong dash of jealousy through all: Mr Gilbert's I never attended, but the Duke of Sussex's are agreeable and interesting enough". It was "surprising and pitiful to see how many airs and pretensions and how much foppishness of manner" there was amongst really scientific men: one hoped for wisdom to match their brains. Herschel and Brand were free of this, as was the great mathematician Dr Wollaston:

others were inclined to go on and on about their own thing and never listen to a word said by anyone else. And it was a bit futile, at a Royal Society ball at Gorhambury, to find Lord Verulam not even knowing who or which Dr Wollaston was: Henry felt that the marble bust of Francis Bacon would come alive with indignation at the ignorance of his fat but kind-hearted successor.

Even the continuing political delay was dangerous. People were getting to expect far too much from the Reform Bill—instant Paradise—instead of a step towards starting on improvements, which was all it was. "Will any *immediate* good accrue to the mass of the people? I think not." The excitement had distracted people from buying, made less trade, more unemployment. Would "the Englishman's proverbial sound sense and love of order prevail over the momentary delirium? . . . Good sense will not stand against an empty stomach." Henry hoped the Reform Bill would lead on in time to shorter Parliaments, vote by ballot, and universal suffrage and stop there—but would it? One could only trust to "the natural steadiness of England".

The unsteady Continent was still agitated. "Holland has broken the armistice with Belgium" Henry reported in August, "and Leopold has demanded aid from France. The *on dit* is that Prussia excited the King of Holland to this step, or I should rather say Russia, in order to keep France sufficiently occupied to keep her from succouring the Poles. There is surely a great political crisis about to come in the world, and a great moral crisis will follow or accompany it." Henry, the most unwell and the least successful of the brothers, was the one to hope most from some great political change.

CHAPTER XI

Reform

At last October came and the new Parliament was sitting, an ungentlemanly bunch whom the old hands deplored. Henry and Caroline were with the Bunburys in Suffolk, where his sister Emily and her Henry were now comfortably settled at Barton, the house where his uncle Charles and her mother Sarah had so long and so vainly endeavoured to arrive at married bliss. It was Sunday morning, October 9th; crisp air, yellowing leaves, an autumn stillness over all, a feeling of peace and of hush, of church bells and rooks and the immemorial calm sameness of the English countryside. In the hall they were assembling for church—top hats, gloves, bibles, prayer books for the visitors.

Church-going now was different, was almost universal. Whatever Henry's boys might think, they went to church when at home with papa. Gone were the Georgian weeks when the French terror of the 1790s had sent every carriage in England rolling its owners to the village church to beseech the Almighty to avert the fate which had befallen their like across the Channel; and the sight had been so unusual that startled villagers had demanded to know what on earth was the matter. The churches had then been crammed; and war, hunger, and the general uncertainties had kept them crammed.

Sir Henry Bunbury had had four sons by his first marriage; elegant upright young men in frock-coats, contained and amusing, and housing God knew what within. Emily bustled affectionately round them: Henry's Caroline, black-haired, gentle, with brilliant hazel eyes and rose-petal complexion, more their age than Henry's, could hardly fail to be the observed of all observers, and especially of young men. She had the additional fascination of having been born on the wrong side of the blanket, even though the blanket was a ducal one. This was a world that had missed the scrutiny of Jane Austen, was coming under the romantic gaze of the Brontës, the calm summings up of

Mrs Gaskell, and would in due course be immortalized by Trollope.

At the back door the servants had likewise been gathered. The life and death of a young man living at the far end of the Mediterranean, ages since, had ensured that for this one day in the week all alike would be free of business, of potato-lifting and cub-hunting, of earth-stopping and of sitting on the bench, of wheel-turning and of pheasant-shooting, of all those interdependent activities of estate and village life which bound them together and gave each of them a known and valued place, of washing the linen and ordering the dinner and mending the roofs and taking the great red Suffolk punches down to the smithy to be shod. Church on Sunday morning, though the skies fell.

Even the rooks, out in force on the stubble, seemed to know that it was Sunday; the blessed day of no ploughing, no hustle, no back-breaking. In the church, there since no-one knew when, there through storm and tempest and medieval armies and civil strife, the incomparable words in their supreme translation fell on willing ears: for a moment all were simply human beings, were humble, were as one. Son, be of good cheer, thy sins be forgiven thee. In spite of the vicissitudes and fallings off, this was the faith whose depth and buoyancy had held them for four hundred years, had taken them unafraid to the ends of the earth, and would do so for another hundred more to come.

There was a certain nobleman, whose son was sick at Capernaum. Nobody except the gentry, and not all of them, had seen the sea, or even a lake with fishermen, or could imagine a town like Capernaum, but everybody had read or heard the Bible. A scraping of fiddles accompanied the choir, misty sunlight slanted in, the motes dancing in it. A smell of stone permeated, and of lavender water, a smell of the whole assembled village, of Sir Henry's caped top-coat just out of its summer camphor. Sir, come down e'er my child die. And that, it seemed perhaps to Henry, was what half of England was saying to the other half.

Back at Barton there were letters in the hall. "The Post is come: the Reform Bill Lost! Lost by an infamous majority of Forty One in the House of Lords", Henry announced dramatically. "Thus are long cherished hopes, just and rational expectations, natural and undoubted rights, and the excited feelings of 22 million people blasted and trampled on by 199 ignorant and selfish men! Perish their oligarchic dominion forever if it cannot exist but to the detriment of every other order in the State. The House of Peers is intended as a moderator between King and People, now King and People are united and the House of Peers is the enemy of both." Were they daft enough to imagine that there was a choice between reform or no reform, when in fact the choice lay between reform and revolution? Henry thought the people would soon refuse to pay taxes, "and then begins the fray! How is all this to end? I feel much excited", he ended, superfluously.

By the 12th the agitation was spreading, and there were huge meetings everywhere. On the whole Henry's famed English steadiness prevailed; but how, in the midst of all this, could you expect there not to be some wild elements who would start something? Henry was saddened when "the fine old ancient Castle of Nottingham, the scene of so much history" was burnt to the ground. "This is sad work, and injurious to the cause, and I fear that some poor ignorant misguided creatures will be hanged, besides the loss of life in the fray." Henry had heard of at least two parishes where the congregations had left the church in a body when their bishops came to preach. The whole bench of bishops had voted against the Reform Bill and this was perhaps where the Church of England began their long, slow, sad separation from the people of England. Henry thought that the King, with the Lords and the Bishops and the whole of his family against him, was being marvellously "sincere and resolute" for reform.

November came in with a terrible riot in Bristol, whose Recorder, Sir Charles Wetherall, had long been making a buffoon of himself in and out of the House by his fanatical anti-reform speeches; and having worked up a terrific head of steam against himself in this city, had chosen, quite unnecessarily and irresponsibly, to come to Bristol to sentence some prisoners and walk from the court-house in a public procession—"to show that he could not be intimidated". This had sparked off appalling riots, as anyone could have told him it would. Wetherall himself had escaped over the roofs of the neighbouring houses and left Bristol in a hack post-chaise; but the rioters had burned down the Mansion House and destroyed the city archives with it; the Bishop's Palace had had a like fate, as had most of Queen's Square and College Green, and the Customs House; three gaols had been broken into and all their prisoners released. Then of course the dragoons were brought in, and people, though not many, had been killed or hurt: this, Henry thought, might well be "the spark to explode the great magazine of suffering and discontent"; all because Sir Charles Wetherall wanted to show how brave he was—"and then to run away in a fright from his own work, and desert his post in the moment of danger!"

As if all this were not enough, a new and lethal menace appeared. "The Asiatic cholera which has lately loomed so fearful in the distance, advancing over the earth like an eclipse" had now reached Britain. Sailors from a Hamburg ship had jumped quarantine and come ashore to a pub at Sunderland, and soon it was rife in the town. Henry had had some experience of Asiatic cholera in the East Indies, where he had come across a type which literally killed people in ten minutes; this, he heard, was a less virulent though very often fatal kind. He had had Asiatic cholera himself, on board HMS *Pelorus* in Plymouth Sound long ago; "it brought me to the brink of the grave in four hours with the most excruciating torture"; at the end of which the doctor had assured him that this was spasmodic cholera and not malignant; but if that wasn't malignancy Henry hated to think what was. He remembered that he had had some sickness and diarrhoea the week before, when, if he had taken any notice, he might have nipped the cholera in the bud. The great thing was to take it in time; and he hoped to God the medical men were alert to this, and greatly feared they were not. If this searing plague were now to add to civil ills, God help them all!

The bitter seriousness of life ate into Henry as January came in and all was still undecided. The Whigs seemed to be falling over their own feet and each other's: could King William, under such pressure, stay firm? The redistribution of boroughs was being worked out by a young man called Lieutenant Drummond, who seemed to have a marvellously clear mind: Henry decided that although he talked and thought endlessly about reform, he had never really seriously set about reforming himself. Had he "truly striven to cultivate his mind and heart" to its fullest extent? "There cannot be true wisdom without moral rectitude, nor moral rectitude without deep religious feeling; I do not mean of this or that sect or persuasion, but a feeling of the existence and goodness of a supreme Being, who for the wisest purposes had placed us here as instruments, intelligent beings capable of aiding his work . . . The flesh and every passion and propensity of the human constitution are as necessary, when confined to their proper sphere, as the spirit." The thing needed was more effort, more knowledge; and Henry urged himself to remember Bruce and the Spider.

These new year resolutions were faintly dashed by a meeting of the Royal Society in Kensington Palace in February. The Duke of Sussex was President, a circumstance which swelled the ranks of the attendant scientists more than a little, Henry noted. He went with Sir Alexander Johnston, found it amusing as well as interesting, was introduced to an American called Macaulay, over to engage English miners for working the gold mines lately discovered in the United States, a student called Omar Offendi sent to England for scientific education by Mahomet Ali the Egyptian Pasha; and Ram Maun Roy the Brahmin, "here for a twelve month and watching with acuteness the signs of the times." The Duke of Sussex was a well-read, well-informed man with a scientific bent, and there had been various wonderful new inventions on view; but suddenly Henry felt what an amateur he was—how slight his own accomplishment in life had been, "between ill-health, ignorance and natural stupidity. I try my best, and fail; others I see succeed in all they attempt, and some of them, I occasionally think, are not wiser than myself." One could not judge exclusively from results; yet for the moment Henry felt he was one of those people who spent their time in life doing no more than sleeping and eating and creeping into bed at last. If the ship-of-the-line of his dreams were to float out of his reach for ever he must leave some memorial of his mind and heart within this interesting world.

March came, and still nothing was settled. Staying again with the Bunburys, Henry soothed his mind in the Mildenhall plantations, wondering whether it were *Ilvesimus Destructor* or *Bostricus Typographicus* of the Hartz mountains in Germany which was destroying his brother-in-law's trees; and weighing up the pros and cons of an application of tar and train-oil. Here one of the woodmen came and asked him what he thought of the Reform Bill.

"I do not think it will do you any immediate good, but in the end I think it is calculated to lead on to better times for everybody. What do you yourself think of it?"

"Well, now, I don't exactly know what to think. But after all I do think it must be a werry good thing for the poor."

"Why so?" Henry pressed him.

"Just because they be so plaguey long about passing it." Henry was struck by the truth of this comment. He noticed that the other farm workers with whom he talked lamented the old times; the days when farmers were not gentlemen, when their wives and daughters made butter and cheese and looked after poultry and took their eggs to market on horseback themselves; when farmers lived and ate with their men, and gave enormous harvest-home dinners, and thought of them all as part of their own family. "But now they are estranged, enemies in fact: the farmer drinks his port, sometimes claret and even champagne, and the wife and daughters have pianofortes and music parties while the labourer's wages are diminished, half the number unemployed, and the rest bundled off to the poor house.

"I remember the old customs well in Sussex when I was a boy: they produced a mutual feeling of kindness between master and man and drew the cords and links of society, high and low, more closely together: there was no burning of farmer's homesteads then . . . There is now little of that identity or congeniality of feeling between landlord and tenant or between farmer and peasant which formerly existed; on the contrary there is now enormously increased wealth, accompanied by ambition, love of power, and unbounded extravagance, on one side, and wretchedness, starvation, general suffering, exasperated feelings and excited passions and consequently law-breaking and wickedness on the other. But I trust that much of this will *in time* be modified by Reform."

Visiting the parson near Charles's house on business Henry felt strongly how very much more clergymen could do to mend matters if they "only fulfilled their vocation in the true Christian spirit and kept down ambition and eschewed politics, and discarded that profound admiration and reverence for rank and wealth and power . . . I approach them with respect as a first impulse." But how often they let one down with "their eternal struggles and intrigues for preferment . . . and the sort of clerical devils whose name is legion". Why did they not attack the greed, instead of sharing in it? On the other hand when one did meet good parsons, which was *not* infrequently, they were "really estimable and liberal minded men: I doubly honour them, first for their inherent goodness and next for having preserved it pure from the contamination of their sect". What an opportunity the Church as a whole was missing, though "our own Church of England has perhaps stood prosperity as well as most others or better".

Spring brought the long awaited, the unbelievable news. Reform was passed by the Commons on March 23rd and by the Lords on April 14th "at 7 o'clock in the morning after a long and sharp debate in which Lords Durham and Grey lashed Bishop Philpotts of Exeter as he deserved". The Bishop of London however had said he would not only support the second reading but would not allow the Bill to be modified. The King had refused to create more Peers, Lord Grey was thought to be infirm of purpose; and, after all the hubbub, they were still only one step on, fourteen months after starting the whole Bill! The Ministers had resigned—what now? "The news has turned me sick; the cholera is child's play compared to the evil that may come of it!" Would the Commons stand firm?

On May 12th Henry reported that London was in a state of extreme agitation and that a hundred thousand people at Birmingham had signed a solemn declaration—in what they called "this awful crisis of our country's fate"—that they would not pay taxes to a government headed by Wellington, "a pensioner of foreign despots and as such exposed to their influence and unfit to govern a free people"; and the City of London had sent an address to the Commons urging them to refuse to vote supplies; and there were grim purposeful political meetings everywhere "in perfect quietude, a solemn and earnest, and perhaps dangerous calm" Henry had thought. And then Wellington had failed to form a ministry, Grey was back, reform was through; and the church bells of Mildenhall, peeling and crashing like demented cymbalists, echoed from tower and steeple all around as far as one could hear; and it was suddenly and absolutely spring!

Relief and victory ran through Henry like wine. England was through, and without revolution! "The English are deeply religious and they feel and are thankful for this happy change which has saved us from civil war; no blessing Heaven has sent could be more generally or sensibly felt." No need for any order for a general thanksgiving, a huge crowd at Birmingham had offered up "simultaneous and voluntary prayer" on hearing the news. Not much would happen at first, but it would give people "cheerfulness under existing difficulties, and the heart to go on. The struggle has exhibited in glowing colours the union, strength and spirit of Englishmen, their bold determined purpose, their intelligence, perseverance, and wise resolution" to do the thing in a legal way, however long it took. Three cheers for common sense!

"The effect produced on the country by the favourable change in our politics is like magic! All now is still that was so lately in agitation; angry spirits are calmed and good men rejoice." Of course it wouldn't bring unmixed good; but nothing could be worse than the state the country was in before. Ireland was still with us, and mistakes were bound to be made there; Henry went to the Commons on June 18th, where O'Connell was arguing that a £10 franchise in Ireland was a very different thing from a £10 one in England; and of course he was right, thought Henry, in spite of the violence of his speech; a £5 franchise in Ireland would be the equivalent. Now was the moment to give Ireland a proper franchise, but would she get one? No! And, Englishly, he lamented Ireland's lack of that one great quality which Englishmen, though less talented, so superbly exercised—"Ireland that unlucky, misdirected, unmanageable land where great talent and a thousand amiable qualities abound and *Common Sense* is wanting!" His father had always insisted that England and Ireland were married by geography and circumstance; they were complementary and necessary to each other; they might score off each other like a sparring man and wife, but there was no future in such quarrels; they were temperamentally and indissolubly bound.

"I have not I believe been in the House since Fox abolished the Slave Trade in 1806; but I attended that debate. Those times and those people are still fresh in my recollection, their eloquence still tingles in my ears and the impression then made is not yet obliterated—'there were giants in those days'! I heard nothing in this debate to equal that." Often, while reform was hanging fire, had Henry longed to have Charles James Fox, his first cousin (and one of his mother's dearest friends as well as being her nephew), back at the head of the Whigs. The present-day Foxes were well enough, full of bonhomie, Lord Holland was kindness itself; but was there real heart behind it? "Charles James was all heart." By February of next year Henry noted with sharp sadness that "Lord Grey has at length unfolded his coercive measures for poor Ireland, and they are in point of fact a complete suspension of the constitution and introduction of martial law. Let grievances first be redressed and the common law will do." He noted with approval O'Connell's address to the Irish people, in which he adjured them not to use force.

Not everyone shared Henry's elation. The Duke of Wellington had done what he felt to be his duty: but he and many others were left low-spirited, and cheerless for the future. "The revolution is made," he told Croker on March 6th, 1833, "that is to say that power is transferred from one class of society, the gentlemen of England, professing the faith of the Church of England, to another class of society, the shopkeepers, being dissenters from the Church, many of them Socinians, others atheists."

What with the dissenters being so active, and "the practice of requiring candidates to pledge themselves to certain measures, which is but too common even amongst the best class of electors . . . you will see reason to be astonished that we should even now exist as a nation." To his mind, and to the mind of many others, disaster had irretrievably befallen; and it will be a few more hundred years before we know whether in fact he was right, and that England's power for good was here laid low. Casting his mind back to the chaos and corruption he had seen in India, and the revolutionary atheism laced with a crusted Catholicism that he had known in Europe, Wellington declared that it was England's religion that had made her what she was—a nation of honest men. (It remained to be seen, how long, without her religion, her honesty would endure.) To educate men without religion would be, he held, only to raise up a crop of clever devils.

People had expected great things from this reform: Sydney Smith said that every unmarried woman in England had expected the Reform Bill to produce her a husband: as 1833 went on it became ever more clear that one of the things the Reform Bill would not do was to supply Captain Henry Napier with a ship, or a shore job. The Admiralty were probably right: his health was too far spent. He had been two years and a half in England now: Caroline and the children were no stronger: he baulked at exposing them to yet another winter. They travelled back to Italy by Mont Cenis and Turin—"one continued summer even to this last day in October". In the autumn they were again in the Villa Capponi, hearing the bells of Florence, seeing the bright valley spread below them. Caroline and the children seemed better at once—they had now added on Arthur and Richard, their future admiral—and Henry, inveterate traveller as he was, was planning a spring and early summer journey with John Charteris to the Maremma and to some of the more remote and unvisited parts of Italy, when a letter from William came.

"My dear niece Fanny died on the 28th of last month at ten in the forenoon!" Henry wrote with a trembling hand. "I have just received the news: my poor brother was too late to see her alive. I can scarcely trust myself to write what I now feel for that dear girl and all around her. This world is not for happiness. But that to come? Aye, that to come! That where she now is; where so many are that I have loved! What and where is it? How can we ensure it, reach it, be happy in it? The troubles and inequalities of this life say plainly that this is not all; the belief in a just and merciful God tells me that it is not all; the fearfully delicate piece of mechanism by which I am known to be, tells me that it did not come here self-existing; the mute eloquence of nature assures me of higher spirits, and the sounds of universal life confirm the tale. That there is a great and good Creator I believe; that he did not put us here to suffer without our fault and then to annihilate us I also believe; but why he placed us here at all is beyond our ken."

Why, why, why? In sober unhappiness Henry concluded that such tragedies were tragedies of ignorance. "God made no law to produce evil, if properly studied, comprehended and obeyed. The sufferings of man are for the most part attributable to man, not to God: he gives man reason to discern and free will to choose between good and evil . . . Yet much natural evil, or what appears such, over which man has no control is for some wise purpose allowed by the Almighty, and we search for the why, and wonder, and are lost. But this very interest, this thirst for the hereafter, this strong deep-seated curiosity, this yearning and longing after the secrets of another world, prove our connection with it . . . The spirit recalls a confused, faint and mysterious image, a dim shadow of other scenes and of a more etherial being; it feels itself in trammel and in mist . . ."

William and Caroline's beloved Fanny, just nineteen and pretty as could be, the second daughter born to them in the last desperate years of the Peninsular fighting, had died of a consumption which they were powerless to cure or halt. This blow to the brothers was not the only one of the Reform decade: it was as if something they so deeply desired must be paid for in the tears of bitter loss.

Part III

The Storm Blows Nearer Home

"The spirits and good humour of the company seemed to triumph over the wreck of their constitutions. They had even philosophy enough to joke upon their own calamities; such is the power of friendship, the sovereign cordial of life—I afterwards found, however, that they were not without their moments, even hours, of disquiet."
Tobias Smollett, *Humphry Clinker*

CHAPTER XII

The Proud Waves

Charles, usually immune to contagious diseases, was the first to fall into the grip of the Asiatic cholera that was sweeping Europe. In March of 1833 Elizabeth had been very ill: two goes of pleurisy left her too weak to sit up without help. "I can never tell you half how much I feel your kindness in offering to come and nurse me", she told Louisa. "May *you* never want a kind affectionate nurse." In her weakness Elizabeth had told Charles she felt very useless and could not bear being a weight to all she loved. He felt thankful to have answered her with warmth and reassurance, but "Oh if she can see my heart now she will see all she was to me." For in July of 1833 Elizabeth too was soon frighteningly ill with the cholera, seemed briefly a little better, and in a very few days was dead.

After a wait of twenty-three long years they had enjoyed a bare six together. Charles mourned her with passionate grief. He himself scarcely survived the cholera: the shock of Elizabeth's loss was piled on to an extreme physical debility. Older than he as she was, Charles must have faced the possibility that she would die first; but the stark fact infinitely out-topped the imagined likelihood. Shattered, desperate, yet accustomed to carry the woes of others, and unwilling to throw his own grief on the shoulders of another, Charles sensibly kept his first transports of woe to himself, and found an outlet in prayer and in his journal. "Oh God, merciful, inscrutable Being, give me power to bear this. Hitherto I had light and life, but now all is as a dream and I am in darkness, the darkness of death, the loneliness of the desert. I see life and movement and affection around me, but I am as marble."

Once again shock had thrown Charles into a paralysis, the terrible non-feeling he had endured when he was a boy and his first friend had died. At other times he felt too much, was staggered and shaken under the power of his feelings, trembling for his mental balance.

7*

"Oh God, defend me", he prayed, a week after his loss; and two months later—"this is a weakness I wish to throw off but cannot, and grieve with weak unavailing tears. I have just pulled away the bullet that at Busaco went through my head. How little we can judge for ourselves: then I rejoiced at my escape, and now regret it. We know nothing—but we are to act as our consciences dictate, and take what God sends", he told Emily. "When tears are too much checked, comes a terrible feel on the top of my head, which though not real pain distracts me and my lowness then seems past endurance."

To Charles Robertson, the gunner captain who had become a great friend in Bermuda twenty years back and with whom Charles maintained an intermittent correspondence, swinging between rifle calibres and religion, and who stood a little further away from his grief, Charles was better able to talk of Elizabeth ten days after her death. "Twenty-nine years ago I fell in love with her beauty and her powerful mind", and he told of how as a young man of twenty-two he had been bold enough and brash enough to tell her of his love; how she had rebuked him roundly for it, treating him like a spoilt boy; and how, in the end, she had forgiven him. In that suddenly holy light in which the bereaved behold the loved and lost, and which is at once slightly funny and at the same time also perhaps a reflection of the forgiveness of sins, Charles was able to make himself believe that Elizabeth had only befriended him as a help to her young son in the army; that there had not, until he married, been continuous passion between them, and that it was "only by undeviating friendship that I won her heart." Their encounter after Corunna when Elizabeth was staying with mutual friends seems to belie this: she had fallen in a dead faint when she saw him. And all those long visits to Cookham? So proud in other matters, Charles does his own charms less than justice in his anxiety to impress Elizabeth's saintliness upon his friend. It was a rare and pardonable moment of self-deception.

"In forgiving me and granting me her friendship she excited in me a force of love and admiration which never died in my heart," though "as years passed so did the beauty which first attracted my admiration." But his love had stayed, rooted and grounded in him so strongly that he felt unable to marry anyone else. "When she became a widow I was at my ease." It had been the moment of reality, the time for proof. "She was single, she was poor, she was ill. She was near sixty but if I did not mind that whom did it concern?" All his love had "blazed up again". He had not felt one instant's doubt, "and in marriage she answered all my expectation."

"My feelings are numbed and dead. A little time will give me more command of them. Your kind letter is one of the first which has roused me to feeling. Adieu dear friend."

"How selfish is all this despair", he told Louisa; and yet for so much of the time he could not yet rise above it, though his faith in God's goodness and in reunion with Bess was entire. Would Lou come to France with him and the children? "I will not go till the Equinoctial gales have had their fling, not wishing to drown my brats", he added, with a flash of the old fire. He told Louisa that he had offered to Bess to send his two little girls away to school if they were too much for her, "but she, like my mother, would not allow of this, and I will never part with them unless for a time duty should take me where they could not at once go. I daresay they will in time become comforts to me." He was still in his state of feeling nothing. "If they do not I am a thankless being."

He had not been thankful at the arrival of Susan and Emily. But God had a way of turning the unwanted and the unexpected into blessing. They owed him no gratitude, but he hoped they would love him if he did his duty by them, "dear little innocent things". For the moment, like everything else, they had receded into the middle distance, were out of focus. "Ambition, pleasure, all things belonging to this world are departed." The truth was that he had made an idol out of Bess and that her going had turned him into stone. King David had said, Why grieve? and logically why should one? But Charles could not as yet stop himself. If he had not something to plan and to do he thought he should go mad. Even travel would be a kind of activity.

Not for a year was he able to stand outside his grief, and writing to Louisa to console a cousin in like case, could tell her—"Lady Bathurst, good and gentle as she is, will reproach herself with things that she will rake up to her own annoyance: time will soften this, but the pain is very great. Give her my love: I feel for her deeply . . . Certainly I adored my Elizabeth: yet every impatient word ever uttered rose up in bitterness against me and well nigh distracted me . . . though whatever temper I showed was seen by the world, for being alone with her made me so happy I was always in good humour . . .

"God ever gives comfort when he gives affliction; not comfort which attaches one to life, but which renders us able to bear it . . . the conviction that the lost ones are at rest and can defy the world and its troubles; for even if there is no future state death still brings peace. But for those who like me have a full conviction of another life, there is assurance of reunion which supports us and calms the heat that makes one long even for death." Another year passed and he was still writing—"I will not say how Mark Kerr's loss calls up my own, for that is a black sun that never sets. He was away, I was present: there is not much to choose, the result is equally terrible; life is broken to pieces without being lost, and we must patch up the fragments as we can until our own hour comes." Two charming fragments were there to love; what his mother had called "that sort of interest without which we cannot live" had not been denied him.

It is likely that, if we knew enough about them, Charles's activities over the next few years followed some rational plan. But to the ignorant observer, there is, for the first and last time in his life, a kind of uncertainty about Charles's course; a swerving, as of a stricken animal; a jinking, as of a wounded bird in flight. He is in Berkshire; he is in Hampshire looking down from Portsdown Hill on Broomfield where he had been happy with Elizabeth and his daughters; he is at Caen in Normandy, amazed and saddened at seeing poor Beau Brummell hard beset and all but begging his bread; he is in Milford Haven, finishing a book, and ready to dash to Ireland and look at possible farms which John Kennedy is surveying for their joint project. He is arguing with O'Connell; he is electioneering for the radical Roebuck in Bath; his manuscript is lost between publishers, or he loses it himself. Only his affection for his children, only their dire need of him is a sheet anchor: where he goes they go too: in all his searches for employment his thoughts are for them. They, his brothers and sisters, and the never-quenched hope of the role where his greatness can find expression, play their slow part in his recovery, in his escape from the besieging longing for Elizabeth, from the dear-loved chains of the past.

"Cheerfulness returns", he told Charles Robertson four years later; "but the *life* of life never returns." His yearning and constant love for this much older woman never left him. He mourned her until he himself died. But he had become used to having a wife, and was not romantic enough to imagine he could do without one.

*

"I have now formed something of a general plan so that daylight appears," Charles told Emily in mid-September, "I propose going to Paris and teaching my girls French and then taking a farm in the county of Wicklow for the rest of my life. Kennedy and I think we can do that for Ireland which has not yet been done; it requires great exertion and of that we are both capable where great stimulus is, and this will be given to me by the slightest success." Kennedy had been travelling a lot in Europe, and had learned a system of farming which he hoped might make Ireland more productive and prosperous: they hoped to start a school of farming—if the methods proved as good as Kennedy hoped—so that the Irish might in time buy the farms on which they had so long laboured for absentee landlords. "The greatest objection to my plan is that it will remove me from my own family and from the old friends of my beloved Elizabeth . . ."

"My grand object as it was in life is my beloved idolized Bess. While she was here I *loved* life, it was full of enjoyments. Now she is there, I endure it for a while and long to join her." Elizabeth's life had been "one of constant practise of benevolence", and Charles felt that only by doing something so specifically good and unambitious as the work on the Irish farm could he hope to qualify to be with her again. While Kennedy negotiated for the farm he prepared for France. Normandy would be better and healthier for the children than Paris, he decided.

By winter Charles's head was beginning to appear above the sullen seas of grief. He pondered on, trying to make sense of the disaster of Elizabeth's death; of so short a time together after so long and hopeless a wait. "Life is a glorious race between eight hundred million people, all trying to lose. This leads us to religion . . . Fixed principles for moral conduct, yes. Do as you would be done by." He believed in God, in a future life, and in following Christ, but "I do not, as far as my present judgment leads me, believe that Christ was God." No thoughts could bring his wife back; and he took his little daughters to northern France, which was cheap, and would teach them French, and take their minds off the loss of so good and kind a stepmother. They had truly loved gentle Elizabeth, who had believed in reasonableness with children and in listening to them, and not in the continuous arbitrary discipline common to the times.

Solitary, responsible, Charles drew up a scheme for the education of his little Cephalonians. The days lengthened; in the March winds the three of them walked happily together on the shores of Normandy. Religion, French, and sums he taught them himself; the other required subjects were beyond him. Lively, dark-haired, with eyes that sparkled like the seas around their native island, his children entranced him. They were picking up French already—"that lady said What two pretty children", Susan delightedly informed her father. "She is pretty too, isn't she?" Susan had insisted, hopefully directing Charles's gaze to the lady's exceptionally plain Norman countenance. Mornings passed at the book, evenings in increasing laughter. As no medicine could, they healed and restored him, plucked from the sea and thrust at him as they had been.

He read them history, tales, poems. Were they, he wondered, learning enough for the present?

"1) Religion as the foundation; to this I trust for steadiness. [Lady Sarah had been a thought unsteady.]

2) Accounts, to teach the value of money and how to regulate a house.

3) Work, that spare hours may not be lost if rich; and if poor that they may make their own things.

4) Cooking to a certain extent, that they may not be at a loss if a revolution throws them on their own resources; and also to guard against servants' waste.

5) French, that they may not be dumb in a foreign land, which would kill them! These things until they are fourteen, when they shall learn anything to which their tastes incline.

As long as I live my aim will be to make them religious. And as to money, I don't want them to have a shilling more than a hundred a year each, with a house, and that I have saved for them. My hope is that they will not marry brutes or fools, but that is their affair, and the future does not trouble me. He that sent them will take care of them . . . While I live, my desire is to live well [by which he meant, to behave well], and to make those about me happy." Those about him generally were: it was with the outside world that he had his brushes. Another was shortly due.

Suddenly, in 1835, when Kennedy had reported entire failure to find the right farm, and was working on his nephew's, a splendid prospect opened before Charles—the hopeful, pioneering task he had always longed to have. The Australians wanted him, had asked for him, as Governor of their newly-opened territory of South Australia.

"A deputation of Australian colonists arrived . . . reckless of where I lived I accepted; at the children's age the Southern was as good as the Northern Hemisphere", he told Robertson. "I calculated upon coaxing you to go with me; three of my brothers and about a dozen superb fellows besides, all of us taking our families. The excitement this gave me assisted me in the sad struggle I had with grief." But Napierstown upon the Australian Bight was not to be. Charles's old determination to do the thing upon the right terms—or not—tripped him up once more, after months of hopeful negotiation.

At the outset pleased and hopeful beyond measure, for this was the job that both he and his father had wanted all their lives, Charles set out his terms: £3,000 a year to pay himself and a staff of six technicians, a ship of war, two hundred soldiers, and £100,000 to help settlers to establish themselves. This sum was to be "laid out for the security and advantage of the colonists individually . . . in colonizing the immediate interest and comfort of each individual is of the first importance, the expansion of the democratic principle being the only means of preserving the aristocratic one, by making it respected. That the population would be immoral and bad I know, but the greatest rascal would have been satisfied to see Kennedy, Light, and myself, and other good fellows, working hard to forward those very rascals' own wishes and success as colonists. The soldiers also would be ready in case of need, and to them I would give high rewards for ten years' good service, keeping tight discipline. Fifty soldiers would have done as to force, but very small bodies are not easy to keep in discipline; two hundred would be better . . ."

Absorbed by this belated godsend of a constructive occupation, he wrote on. "My plan for schools is all arranged; no other obligation to be imposed on people to educate their children, and the schools should be open for people of all ages. Chinese artizans should be introduced . . . camels for exploring for water places . . . Martello towers and a family of missionaries established at watering places, where exploring parties could halt and provision . . . I design to drill all the boys at school." He was off already, in a well-run faraway world, free of Whigs and Tories who left starving children to stand barefoot at the rainy street corners of the industrial towns; he was under the wide skies of a land of animals and trees and open spaces and hard work, under a hot sun in the company of like-minded friends. (William Light at any rate got there, and left a good name; but for Charles a more complex destiny awaited.)

The negotiations dragged on, the government changed, and all was to be begun again, but Charles had no serious doubts but that he was destined for the Antipodes, and his heart bounded at the prospect. He proposed to himself adult suffrage (still nearly a hundred years away in Britain), equitable taxation, a decimal coinage, and above all encouragement and protection of the aborigines. "Soldiers are necessary on account of both savages and colonists, the latter more troublesome I suspect, as spirits are cheap."

But what about Susan and Emily, unmothered in this far country? What about his own loneliness, his need for feminine society, softness and love; the caresses and the comforts of a wife?

If women knew the real reasons, besides the obvious one, which induce men to marry them, they would probably be exceedingly surprised. Charles's main reason for marrying Frances, daughter of William Philipps of Court Henry, Carmarthenshire, and widow of Captain Richard Alcock, Royal Navy, was his failure to get the governess to come to Australia with him. And, he told Charles Robertson, if he got a bad one to go, he would be lumbered with her for ever, and if he got a good one she would instantly marry, on a continent so starved for women. He had approached the problem of a wife with a certain circumspection.

Fanny Alcock had been brought up by Charles's cousin Lucy Fitzgerald, who had married one of Nelson's band of brothers, Captain Foley. Charles had therefore always known of her, and known her to be kind and suitable. She was a granddaughter of Lord Herbert of Cherbury, but this, as Charles pointed out, would hardly have much message for the kangaroos. He had met her two years earlier, and "I saw she had a good head and no humbug, and this I thought would suit the Kangaroos". Fanny had two sons and a daughter, and enough money to support them, though no more. It seemed a cosy arrangement. He had known and liked Lady Lucy Fitzgerald since he was a small boy, and Tom Foley had been Nelson's leading captain at the Battle of the Nile: anyone brought up by them must fill the most exigeant bill. Fanny's daughter Maria, known as Minnie, was a few years older than Charles's own two: Fanny herself was a few years younger than him. That she was attractive can be assumed from Charles Robertson's comments after they had met at Cheltenham: he had, he told Charles, fallen in love with Fanny. (Charles replied frivolously that he also had fallen in love with Robertson's wife: what about settling near each other and going in for a little wife-swapping?)

Meeting this fifty-three-year-old bridegroom about now, a stranger described him as short and wiry, with a loud strong voice and an alert step. "His aspect was noble and commanding, and when he smiled, of winning sweetness. Wavy locks of iron grey clustering above a broad massive forehead, a nose curved like the eagle's beak, dark eyes gazing with piercing intensity through spectacles that seemed inseparable from his face." He summed him up as "greatness grown weary with waiting".

For the job in South Australia had fallen through. Charles's terms had proved unacceptable; though they had eventually to be bettered in aid of his successor, and even so the administration went bankrupt. Resolutely Charles set himself to write. His book on the Ionian islands and on colonies in general, which did little for the fair fame of Adam and of which he was afterwards ashamed, had not said all he felt on colonies where the inhabitants were in need of care and protection. He wrote another on the principles of colonization—aborigines should be protected, no governor should countenance "the usual Anglo-Saxon process of planting civilization by robbery, oppression, and murder". (This view, in 1835, was very advanced and damning.) In 1836 he is frightening Fanny into fits by nearly dying of inflammation of the lower bowel in a hotel in Rouen, but writing again, polemically as ever—"Republicans are contrary to Nature. God has created us of different sizes, both mentally and physically. Yes, but all the more reason for the large to deal gently and fairly with the small." A dialogue on the Poor Law followed, that hated new system which the well-intentioned Whigs had introduced of late; there was an essay on military law containing an indictment of flogging, a translation of Alfred de Vigny's *Servitude et Grandeur Militaire*. At Caen in his grief he had written a novel called *Harold*, about the Norman Conquest, containing in its narrator a possible self-portrait—"I am a man of advanced age, very ill-looking and much worse-tempered: discontent seems to be my trade in this world. I am fond of walking alone, and then my face becomes marvellously fixed and wizened; on such occasions I look as Sir Hudson Lowe did when he turned Napoleon's coffee sour." When Harold is killed Charles turns into his wife Editha—"the world was now a solitary prison. Death was her only friend, and he refused his aid . . . 'Oh great and good God, in thee do I trust for support in this hour of cruel suffering. Thou tellest me it is not for ever. Oh Harold, my love, look down upon me, guard me, guide me, till death comes . . . Oh come come—if but for one moment come!' " He was no novelist but it must surely have helped Charles to write it.

Settled awhile in a dockyard pub at Pater, near Milford Haven, where Susan and Emily could enjoy the sand and shells and Fanny could enjoy seeing her Welsh relations, Charles diligently revised the book, sent it up in the coach to Louisa in Green Street, where Richard or Henry were to collect it and deliver it in person to Bentley the publisher, so that he couldn't pretend he had never got it. Charles didn't think he was a natural novel-writer, but if the thing sold, he could easily turn out two a year and keep his little girls that way. But back it came. Nothing seemed to take; nowhere did he prosper.

In 1837 Charles Robertson, much more conventional than Charles in both religion and politics, wrote what must have been a long letter to Charles in which he suggested, mildly, that the colonel might do himself better justice with just a trace of accommodation and compromise, might find a job, might get himself where he could really do good. Charles replied with a lengthy credo. "As regards my being employed, I quite agree that my politics ought not to interfere; nor, as far as I am concerned, do they." He had applied to Lord William Bentinck, an old friend and well-disposed, and had been told to wait his turn; and in Charles's view the honest thing was to be patient and do just this.

The other course, seeking to push his claims out of turn, would not only do down a lot of good men senior to him, who needed a job every bit as much as he did: it would also be to do exactly what he continually abused the government for doing—"Those very men whose whole system of government I call infamous because they allow of interest for themselves and their friends, taking the place of justice and merit, because they put Colonel Maberley and my good cousin and great friend Charles Fox into Post Office and Ordinance; and FitzClarence into the Adjutant General's while they leave old officers out.

"Those who love me very naturally magnify my merits, and do not see this in a just light, but as a man of honour I am bound to do what my conscience tells me, viz.—by pushing my claims I should put aside a man who had greater merit and claims than myself." He would, he considered, degrade himself by "asking favours from those

I find fault with, though this does not apply to Lord Hill and Lord Fitzroy, for I believe Lord Hill to be one of the most admirable men in existence, and Lord Fitzroy [Somerset] worthy of being his assistant and in proportion as I admire and respect them I am bound not to press them on the score of employment. When the time comes they will do me justice; if not it is because a vile system puts it out of their power.

"You will say perhaps all this is riding a high horse with a witness. I answer no. We read one great lesson and woe to him who disregards it; the lesson where our Saviour admonished us against ambition, and it signifies little whether the devil tempts us with all the Kingdoms of the world, or with the command of a district as a General officer! The principle remains the same—that one is not to seek worldly advantage by wrong deeds."

Charles was not a Whig or a Tory, both of whom he considered were leagued against the working people. "I see that they oppress them and deprive them of their rights and means of life." Of course neither Lord John Russell nor Peel actually stole, but they used secrecy and dishonesty to keep in power. Lord John was silly, Peel clever but not great; but the sincerity of men like Hill or Wellington one must respect, however mistaken one thought their politics. As to a political career for himself, he thought he would only do mischief as an MP: when William failed them the people of Oldham had offered to take Charles on free of all expenses and he had turned it down.

A note of reproach crept in. Charles was sacrificing money and ambition to what he thought right, "Yet my own family and you and all I care for most, find fault. Now I have told you my motives and you will admit that they are at least disinterested."

As to religion—"I do not think you a fanatic. Sincerity is my test in this. I have no light by which to judge my neighbours and plenty by which to judge myself." He disagreed with Robertson about Churches (having been deeply put off both Protestant and Catholic by a youth spent in Ireland). "From the age of 15 I detested all priests." Only the Protestant church concerned him, but he thought that the Catholic church in Ireland was largely kept alive there by Protestant "infamies and persecutions" and would gradually go with them.

"My creed is easily told. I worship God. I believe in the existence of the devil, and look for salvation by my adherence to the precepts and example of our Saviour Jesus Christ." He was certain that different men could serve God in different ways, exactly as he and Robertson both served the King wearing different coloured coats. "I take my bible, my conscience, and my knowledge that I must die, and I want not the interference of a priest of any creed. All nature tells of God and his goodness. The New Testament teaches me to drink from the pure and original spring, and I want none of the second-hand muddied water." What he wanted to do was God's will, "and I pray for courage and firmness of mind to do it, and every hour I feel my failure". He was quite unfit to judge others, all who were sincere were right and acceptable in the eyes of God, "who gave different lights to different men".

No yielding, no accommodation. For psychiatrists, Charles is almost a copybook case. A bad nurse had neglected and ill-treated him for the first eighteen months of his life, until he had been rescued by the kind and stalwart Susan Frost and his mother, both of whom he adored thereafter. He was accordingly a divided soul, never quite certain whether he was an ambitious soldier or a gentle farmer, the victim of moods and sudden angers. The only trouble about this is that two of his brothers were just the same, only more so; though never subject to anyone but caressing Sarah and excellent Susan Frost. His first year may have made Charles difficult, but may equally have fuelled his astonishing energies. William was certainly wilder and more difficult; but that may have been because the pain he suffered was more violent and continuous. (Nobody, wrote his biographer, who hadn't known William could possibly imagine what he endured, year in year out; not only the physical agony, but the unceasing pressure on the nerves of his spine.)

What is almost certain is that all these children underwent a stringent upbringing as to comforts, after the manner of their day; although to Margaret Craig, who married George, their mother seemed wonderfully indulgent and human with them, un-bossy, a friend. Elizabeth Grant of Rothiemurchus, brought up at roughly the same time, describes how she and her brother and sisters, dressed only in cotton shifts, had to run outside in winter to plunge into a cold bath, after which they were allowed a breakfast consisting only of porridge and a little cold milk. If anyone left any, their father, otherwise apparently an amiable man, was called into play with his horsewhip. Even fifty years later, in far away Russia, the little

Michailovich grand dukes, nephews of the Czar, were tumbled out of their iron beds at six and into a cold tub, to be sustained only by a breakfast of tea and bread and butter. The idea was to toughen children, to prevent them falling into *faiblesse* and luxury. But as Elizabeth Grant says, the likes and dislikes of children were never studied: she herself hated porridge so much that she was sick every day, and undoubtedly, as she says, many healths were ruined. Certainly digestive troubles seem to plague all the Napiers throughout their long lives.

The nursery régime of Susan Frost was, William recounts, Spartan; which means an emphasis on hardihood and on finishing up one's disagreeable food. Her compassion, affection, and charity were great, William thought, as was her common sense, but she was "passionate and vehement in a rough way", and Lachlan Moore, the good horseman who taught the boys to ride and was general man-of-all-work, though he had "a loving heart and sought always to nourish magnanimous feelings", was one who "poured forth his feelings with a fervid eloquence . . . was full of ancient legend, ending always with Glory be to God! however misappropriate". Plenty of love here, and lashings more from Donny and Sarah, from ever-kind Aunt Louisa and from generous, futile Uncle Tom Conolly, gambling away, slowly but surely, one of the greatest fortunes in Ireland and permanently exercised about his health. But what went on all round outside Castletown and Celbridge House also made its mark.

Down Celbridge Street had moved an array of characters calculated to rivet the infant attention in mingled horror and fascination. There was the handsome carpenter, Val Dunne, the local Lochinvar, who had whipped away Nichol's daughter from under the nose of her bridegroom, Lumley the stocking-weaver, and borne her off to marriage in Dublin; there was Nichol the angry father, a gigantic blacksmith who had tried to force his daughter into a hated match. There was old Lock, horse- and dog-mad, nearly always drunk but full of stirring tales; there was the poacher with whom William spent many a night in the moonlit woods before he was discovered; there was Tarrant the Robber and Tim Cooley the Informer and Tim Sullivan the uproarious giant of the Cork Militia, there were the threatening soldiers of another militia.

There was also Molly Dunne, great great grandmother of handsome Val, who would sit at her cottage door sunning herself, "and an awful weird looking woman she was: a Michael Angelo model for the Witch of Endor," wrote William; "large, gaunt, tall, and with high sharp lineaments, leaning on an antique staff, her head bending beneath a cowled Irish cloak of deep blue, her eyes fixed in their huge orbs, and her tongue discoursing of bloody times; she was wondrous for the young and fearful for the aged". Irresistibly drawn, the little Napier boys would stand around her, their crisp hair rising slowly on their scalps, their bright eyes starting from their heads. "The departure of Lord Dangan for the battle of the Boyne was her favourite theme; how he, beautiful and brave, rode forth at the head of his tenantry from Celbridge, nobly furnished with burnished breastplate and waving plumes; and how he was brought back a bloody corse, by the few surviving men of his band." Apart from the Malory and the Froissart, the tales of Greece and Rome, that were their diet at home, the boys had been nursed on the mocking laughter of Castletown's great kitchens, and on the magic eloquence of Ireland; the almost sexual delight in disaster; the eye-witness vividness and fidelity to detail by which events actually unseen are memorized and brought to a wonderful if largely imaginary life. (To have witnessed Lord Dangan in his glory Molly Dunne would have had to be a hundred and fifteen years old or more; and perhaps she was; except that she also claimed close acquaintance with the Maguire massacres forty years earlier, when the Catholics of Ireland killed all the Protestants, and with Cromwell's revenge in 1648, seven years later, when the Protestants laid low an equal number of Catholics.)

This colour-television life might have left the little boys unscathed, had the violence been confined to stories. But when the troubles started, bloodshed was rife all about. Donny's influence alone had twice prevented Celbridge's being burnt to the ground by the infuriated authorities: Donny's opportune arrival in a hayfield had alone saved his five little boys from being battered to death by two angry militiamen whom George, aged eight, had light-heartedly insulted. And there had been a night when Donny and Sarah were in Dublin, and the rebels had attacked Celbridge House in search of arms. While Susan Frost from Suffolk, aided by Lachlan Moore and the children, had held them off for an hour during which every window in the house was broken by musket fire, and the attackers, unable to get in because of the deep stone area, had battered with a ram on the great front door, yelling threats of death all the while, the children had waited and endured. They were rescued in the nick of time by Sergeant Crask, the bailiff from Castletown, to whom Susan Frost, a born general, had managed to send out a message before the siege closed in.

The siege had in fact only lasted an hour, but may have felt to the children like many more, as they crouched on the floor with the threats of death growing ever louder, and the merciless crash of the ram reverberating on the weakening door. Thus twice in childhood they had seen men coming at them with intent to kill them personally, and with every chance of succeeding.

George had been physically the boldest, William the wildest and the most ingenious in time of peril, Richard the cleverest and quickest, Henry the staunch follower; but it was Charles, quiet and small and short-sighted, but full of intense nervous courage, who had had that mysterious physical quality of leadership, now as deeply suspect as physical charm was in the Middle Ages. More searing than any, to him at least, had been the day when the schoolmaster's son had rushed into school eagerly shouting "Tim Cooley's murdered! Tim Cooley's dead!" and they had all poured out to see. They had known many a body brought in to Celbridge dead or dying; but the rebels had murdered Tim Cooley's eighty-year-old mother with him, simply for being her son's mother. The sight of this old woman lying in her blood had kept Charles silent for a week. There were none of his usual jokes; he barely uttered: the memory stayed with him for life.

Altogether, though not two hundred years ago, it was an upbringing far removed from sand-trays in sunny primary schools, from Peter Pan and Kensington Gardens, a hundred light years away from Dr Spock's recommendations. A ceaseless stimulus to derring-do, to feats of blood and glory, injected itself into minds essentially creative. The remarkable thing is that it failed to dement them entirely, that they suffered in health rather than in mind, and then maybe only from an ill-considered diet. Theirs was not, as it would now have been, a child-orientated household. Donny came first with Sarah, and Sarah with Donny; the children came a good second with both. They did not grow up under the relentless pressure of being the primary consideration: they were secondary; and enjoyed all the emotional freedom which that involves.

Nor had the circumstances of adolescence been such as to soothe Charles. The administration of Ireland during the 1780s and 90s—

under the British crown—was of such laziness, greediness and stupidity, and practised so much bribery and chicanery, that it had produced revolution and civil war. The Napiers' father, whom they all adored, had rarely referred to this government in printable terms: for Charles the words administration and corruption seemed synonymous: this feeling he never quite outgrew.

He could lead men to the ends of the earth on hopeless or unlikely causes, but for the ordinary commerce of public life he had neither aptitude nor heart. To Charles every man behind an office desk harboured a black heart. If they would not say Yea or Nay, if they temporized, or perhapsed, or said they must refer the matter back, he tended, sometimes wrongly, to suppose them either fools or knaves or both. If he could have trodden more softly along the corridors of power he might have achieved more of the betterment of the common lot for which his soul longed. With his "fire-flashing glances", his crisp satirical speech, and his earthy downrightness, he probably pricked more balloons in less time than any other operator in the western hemisphere. But the objects thus deflated were the ones who held the reins of power, the ones who could employ or not employ him.

The results were dire. In no circumstances was he ever called into action until the situation was almost past praying for. As a young man in the Peninsular War, newly-made colonel, he had been sent far from the paths of glory to cope with a regiment in open mutiny; so now, with all of northern England seething with discontent the authorities were meditating hauling him out of unemployment to prevent, if he could, an open armed revolution. He was expendable: and a kind of self-preserving instinct warned the administration that, though Charles could be as rude as the devil to the rich, he would never be rude to the poor. He was a cavalier, with all the graces of a cavalier, and all the faults; and unlikely to succeed in a world where most people are, after all, roundheads (which is to categorize both him and them far too sweepingly). At any rate he might now prove to be the cavalier most likely to deal gently with the roundheads of the Chartist movement.

Henry had been very ill at Florence in 1836. He was recovering, deep in a good night's sleep at last, and Caroline, awakening in the small hours in sudden pain and illness in an adjoining room, hoped these would soon pass, and would hardly move for fear that she might waken him. Time passed; Caroline's fear and agony increased, soon she was in a deep pit of illness, aware only that she must make no noise. It was cholera: by morning when Henry awoke she was past saving, by noon she was dead.

Henry's formal journal rarely touches on his wife and children, so that it is difficult to know what his feelings were. It is almost consciously instructive: there are no funny stories such as Charles and William delighted in, of Charley, Augusta, or Richard; and Caroline herself stays shadowy. He did not, like Charles or William, delight in children *per se*: "I should very much like to be cast away on a fertile island, with about a hundred children, and pass my life walking about with them, eating breadfruit and catching turtles" William, despite his own nine children, thought. Wife and family appeared to be to Henry simply "my dearly loved ones", "all that I love most on earth"; they never move nearer into focus than this.

But when his beautiful young Caroline died before she was thirty Henry seemed, thought William, never wholly to recover from her loss. To her, and perhaps to no-one else, Henry had been first, splendid, the finest of all his tribe. "Gentle, affectionate, and one of the most lovely of God's creatures", William had called her. Her sudden loss, and the fact that he might have saved her if he had woken a couple of hours sooner, turned Henry into a ghost. Everything pales, grows misty; it is as if that crisp fair hair lies flat and grey, those blue observant eyes cloud over in abstraction. Nursing others in illness with tireless patience, often devastatingly ill himself, Henry is half a saint and half an eccentric. He passionately loves his children, but tries out odd diets on them; has strange, fixed, and to his brothers, slightly alarming ideas about their health.

His fourth child did die and he was, probably, terrified lest he lose the others. He did not cease his kindness to everybody, his charity to the distressed. Dedicated to his tasks, he moves about the streets of Florence, a gaunt grey man, the handsome lines of whose long broad-shouldered frame and bony facial structure time cannot efface; but anyone who had known him as the agile, laughing, adventurous midshipman of the 1800s with shining hair and flashing eyes, the boy who had teased all the inhabitants of Massachusetts by firing off his guns in a pretended invasion, would have thought this was some other being. Charles and George grieved bitterly at the loss of their wives, soldiered on, and then recovered: Henry, more vulnerable, received the mortal wound.

Sarah's sons had not been lucky. George had married Margaret, sister of his friend William Craig who had died of Alemtejo fever in the aftermath of Talavera, but she shared her brother's lack of "constitution", and after seven years of happiness with George, she too had died, leaving him to bring up, with the aid of Emily, daughters Sarah and Cecilia, and three sons, George Thomas Conolly, John Moore, and William Craig Emilius. George had stayed on in the army, fully employed as colonel of a Guards Regiment; but when this was sent to India, George joined his brothers on half-pay in order to stay on in England and look after his children. He had now five children, one arm, no job, and no wife. The boys were growing up, and George sometimes felt himself not wholly in control; but he looked ahead with hope. Would William, who, with Charles, was seen as the last word in military expertise, have a word with George Thomas? He might take from his clever uncle what he would not take from his father. "He has just joined the 28th, given his ensigncy by Lord Hill, and as it is one of the best regiments in the service, I am delighted.

"Sir Edward Paget has written to me most kindly, saying he is delighted to have a son of mine in his regiment. He is going to take Billy into the Military College next year, and has shown great interest about it; indeed his friendship to me has never altered." So far so good; but "I hope, my dear Bill, you will impress upon George some lessons of military discipline; and do give him what I know is your opinion as well as my own respecting *kindness of manner* and of speaking to the soldiers, and not supposing they have not the same feelings . . . Pray also warn him against idleness and *billiards*, . . . turn his abilities to the good of his country and the honour of the Service. I wish you would also point out to him that the free and easy manner in which young officers of a month's service give their opinion of the military conduct of their superiors, and address them by their surnames as if they had known them all their life, is in the first case very presumptuous, and in the second vulgar to a degree.

"I know you will not mind this trouble, for I am fully persuaded you will be as anxious about his doing credit to the name as I can be myself.

"My boy John is studying hard; he is the cleverest, most ambitious, and most persevering, and will make a proper soldier. God bless you, my dear William."

George Thomas, steering himself between the perils of billiards and surnames, became a full general, as did William Craig Emilius: for John Moore, flower of the flock, a sharper fate was reserved.

Three out of the five brothers had now lost their wives, two from the sweeping swathes cut through European life by the Asiatic cholera. William's Caroline accordingly became a great comfort and stay. "That woman is pure gold", Charles said; she was everyone's "dearest Car" and confidante. Anne Napier, though much admired and liked by all, was a blue-stocking; keen, like Richard, on philosophy and poetry, and of all things, political economy. She even went so far as to publish a book on women's Rights and Duties. Allowances were made; she had no children, having lost her first husband, Captain Thomas Staples, RN, nephew and heir of Tom Conolly of Castletown. Widowed at eighteen, she had devoted herself to a son of exceptional intelligence and promise who died when he was twelve. At this point she had nearly died of grief; and had been rescued, charmed back into life and spirits, and eventually married by Richard Napier, fourth of the brothers, and by a long way the cleverest; but on him, too, blight was descending. Like his mother, he suffered from eye trouble: like her, Richard was going blind. Anne's father, Sir James Stewart, Bart, of Fort Stewart, County Donegal, had wanted her home in his old age; when Richard's sight became too bad for further work as a barrister, they had moved to Ireland to be near him. But after his death, and the Coercion Acts, they had both of them felt that life in Ireland was too unhappy and intolerable under such misrule. Richard, now almost wholly blind, was unlikely to effect much remedy to the Irish situation: the little that could be done to mitigate hardship was being done by Anne's brother and sister-in-law, and they moved to London. They were childless, interested in new movements, and charitable, but hardly basking in fortune's rays.

Emily in 1837, when William IV died and young Victoria became queen, was recovering from a desperate illness in which all the family had rushed to her bedside to say goodbye. Only Louisa Napier, the half-sister, living in Green Street, off Grosvenor Square, remained that *sine qua non* of all large families, a staunch, generous, and competent maiden aunt. Having survived the appalling disaster in her infancy, when yellow fever had carried off her mother, her small sister, and two baby brothers, Louisa seemed to sail thereafter in calmer waters, receiving families when they came to London, distributing presents—Charles's Emily had "skweezed up her neck and opened her mouth wide" with delight, according to her sister Susan, on receiving from Aunt Louisa their two pink satin bonnets with flowers inside—and advice of a gentle kind to this same Susan against being cheeky to her stepmother Fanny. Louisa's only trouble seemed to be, as a half-sister, a tendency to feel a slight sense of neglect when the others came up to London and whizzed about, not calling upon her quite often enough.

The Napiers had been brought up in the usual ethic of their day and kind, with its strong emphasis on one's own duties and other people's rights. From their parents they had learned to enjoy life whenever possible; but they had also learned, by example rather than precept, that when you are thrown on the scrap-heap, as both Donny and Sarah in their time had been, the thing to do is to think hard, rise to your feet, dust yourself down, and try a slightly different line; while in no way abating your principles. Could Charles now achieve this slight but necessary shift?

"One great motive to resignation and patience under misfortune", Henry had written in his serious way, "is the goodness of God and the consequent confidence derived from it. Misfortunes, if rightly understood and used, will surely make us better men." But now, in this sad aftermath of reform, when conditions in England and Ireland so obstinately refused to improve, when the way to accommodate happily to the industrial revolution continued to elude the wisdom of statesmen and the goodwill of the public; where, frustrated, should they turn?

Tomorrow was another day; might afford new chances, new hope, an opportunity to devote abilities, which they could not help knowing were considerable, to the service of a dear country. Such must be their philosophy. Just now it was full stop: as if God haranging Job from the whirlwind were now saying, as He had said to the ocean—"Hitherto shalt thou come but no further; And here shall thy proud waves be stayed."

Donny and Sarah's sons were born too late for the age of chivalry and the swinging broadsword, too early for the age of widespread acceptance of generous ideas. They were not always tactful. "Your prayers will never reach Heaven," William would declare, full in the face of sanctimonious, evangelistic, stovepipe-hatted England, "they are drowned by the cries of the oppressed Irish!" He was whistling down the wind. Nobody yet was willing to listen.

Deeper than Christianity, and older, in their Scots inheritance, was the Napiers' passion for family and devotion to clan; an ambition which sought constantly to glorify and advance a name, a race, a special breed of men, which warred all through life with their higher motives and more spacious ideals. It was this "devil", this intensely purposive force which had sustained them and ensured their survival through those dour and dangerous centuries along the Highland line and the Border, and among the fierce rivalries of the Lothians, which lingered in their bones and in their subconscious long after the need for such cohesion and such strength was past. Were these the proud waves to be stayed? For the moment they pounded, disconsolately, on an unyielding shore. All of the family, now, were in their fifties. It was neap tide, and the flood was full. No progress of the waves, no sound but the long rasping sigh of withdrawal.

CHAPTER XIII

Family Whirlpools

By a powerful effort of will, William had calmed himself after Fanny's death and continued to plough the long field of his History. The complications of having no publisher and therefore of dealing directly with his printers were considerable. But local political meetings continued to draw him like a magnet. Reform had come so far and no further: the task now was to steer it in the right direction, and at the same time to keep a firm military eye on the forces which reform had unleashed, and which showed signs of bolting. The wild stallion of revolution had had a brief run in Europe, begetting goodness knew what progeny before it had again been stabled.

How far should reform go? Charles was not in doubt. Votes for everybody: a living wage for everybody: the doors shut upon "such practices of party government as make the poor wretched, and England weak and diminished in her glory and strength, to give a small number of men enormous fortunes".

"The poor see all this, as the inventing of printing has virtually destroyed the power of chicanery; they will have their rights to the last drop and if not granted in the divine spirit of 'do unto others' and in the spirit too of real wisdom, the poor will rise and take all their rights and *much more.* Now a radical reformer only demands the rights of the poor . . . a radical is the antipodes of a republican . . . My radicalism began, continued, and will end by my belief that it is the only course to *prevent* the destruction of the constitution."

William agreed. Nothing now was wrong with the constitution if it was worked properly, he insisted, "and not as in the case of that most foul and infamous blot on the Whig record", the Irish coercion Bill, which made the constitution look like some appalling bogey bent on bullying and oppression. "Do you recognize in this hideous portrait the broad and honest lineaments of the British Constitution?" he asked a Bath audience in 1835 at a Reform meeting. "We must display the power of the people constitutionally and by degrees; by meetings such as these—by petitions—by resolutions—by endeavours to support the present ministers and to urge the House of Commons to support them." He feared that 200,000 Orangemen and the Tory Lords combined were about to be too strong for Lord Melbourne, and that Ireland would continue to be coerced. From Tory Lords he excepted Wellington: let them never speak against him as a man, only against his politics, "but oppose him in a manner worthy of yourselves and him. Meet him like a frank and true-hearted Englishman; offer him no personal insult; do not attempt to depreciate his great talents and character, but meet him face to face." But they must back Melbourne; oppression was "stalking in all its horrid deformity in Ireland"; and if they did not all watch it, might jump the Irish Sea and start stalking here.

People said that soldiers had nothing to do with politics, but this was a half truth. They had "nothing as a body, everything as individuals . . . if a soldier does not know and love the social happiness springing from equal and just laws, how, in God's name, is he to fight as the soldier of a free nation ought to fight? . . . How many hundreds of these brave, these gallant-hearted men have I seen toiling, struggling against want, fatigue, cold, wounds, all the horrors of war . . . and dying, not with weak lamentations, not with any wailing", but saying "that it was no matter, because they died for the glory of England . . .

"What of England was it that they remembered and loved so dearly in their last moments?" Not the actual earth underfoot, "it was England, free England, the home of their fathers, their own home! That England whose free institutions had nurtured them up in moral dignity and manly pride, and which they knew would protect their children in their just rights after they themselves were gone. This it was which made it a country to them in the burning sense of the word —which made them endure to the last gasp for her safety; and this it is, gentlemen, which always makes free men victorious in the long run over mercenaries and slaves."

The cheers rang; and William could not resist telling Pamela Fitzgerald Campbell (a cousin with whom he had one of those long standing *amitiés amoureuses* that deck the nineteenth century) that it all made him feel much better in health, and that "it is a very grand feeling to make a thousand people shout and toss up their hands and appear like bedlamites." The English must believe in themselves or they wouldn't get anywhere: not to the detriment of other races for sure; but belief was essential, and they had plenty in which to believe. Yet sometimes he had to cool their fierceness. Though inclined to categorize and condemn people himself, he discouraged his audiences from it.

"It is good and conducive to public liberty that large bodies of citizens should meet together to express their sentiments, to hold . . . that that country only is well governed where an injury done to one is considered as an injury to the whole"; but keep it impersonal, he urged. Petty sniping and vituperation were the curse of politics and advanced nothing. Let it never be forgotten that among the Tory party "are to be found many men of pure life, honest intentions, and sincere patriotism—men who would die sooner than pass the bounds of honourable opposition to measures which they disapprove of—I lament their error, but I respect the men".

The William Napiers had moved to Freshford, near Bath, but in the winter of 1836–7 William became so ill again that the doctor ordered a milder climate. His ills were partly of the spirit. There were constant troubles over the History. "His mind frets", Charles reported in April: "he has been pestered by all sorts of attacks. That son of a bitch Sir George Indecipherable shall get a proper drubbing for his dirty malicious lying article in the Quarterly concocted with Croker", Charles furiously told Robertson. William had not improved matters by pacing the garden of an evening in the dewy dusk "in his bedgown, spouting a speech for the Bath meeting". William's daughter Emily was very, very clever, and all his children were good and looked after him devotedly, but "William's imprudence about his health is beyond all calculation".

William and Caroline departed with their two eldest children to Barrèges in the Pyrenees for the warm springs: the hospitable Guy and Pamela Campbell receiving the other five in their house at Drumcondra near Dublin—"it is not common to find such friends," William thought: Guy and Pamela had twelve children of their own. From Barrèges Caroline wrote to Pamela of their "deep and unceasing anxiety and uneasiness". William's misery over Ireland "has I think been hurtful to him, though I cannot be surprised that he should feel it". William counselled Pamela not to be worried about her naughty little boy. "You will get the better of Guy very easily particularly if you appear not to expect any resistance or particular atrocity from him; it is surprising how children set up their bristles against people who tell them they are bad. Some minds are so forward in perception that the judgment is distanced at first, but it will afterwards catch up and all will be right. Of one thing I am quite sure, namely that children should be tamed instead of being broken in. I do not mean tamed down, but tamed to their work, that is coaxed to it."

Charles, too, believed in coaxing children rather than dragooning them, in the current fashion, or tormenting them with guilt. (It was about now that the legendary Fairchild family stole the jam and were taken by their father to see a public hanging in punishment.) Charles was still teaching Susan and Emily their lessons, but often they made him laugh so much that the sessions were slowed down. "Bath is the residence of two brothers [William and George] and that is a great attraction", Charles told Robertson when settling there awhile in 1837. "Peace and war these two chaps and I have been inseparable and here we are with our brats about us, 17 young devils." Occasions for devilment were swelled by Emily's four stepsons, though Henry's brood were too young for love. So many children and stepchildren were certain to become embroiled, and of course soon did.

George's second son, John Moore Napier, fell in love with Charles's stepdaughter, Minnie Alcock; whereupon Charles's wife Fanny had hysterics and demanded that John be forbidden the house. And Edward Bunbury, the second of Emily's stepsons, fell in love with George's daughter Sarah, dewy and delicate and accordingly much mothered by Emily: she first accepted Edward, and then broke it off, to the detriment of family relationships.

Emily backed the rebuffed and wounded Edward, and radiated indignation at his treatment. Louisa backed Sarah, and the sisters for the first time fell out. Both the fathers involved, Henry Bunbury and George Napier, maintained their customary calm and good sense and left it to the young to work it out for themselves. Charles refused to take sides against Em, and kept working hard as peacemaker; though he thought Sarah was right, and Edward Bunbury selfish and inclined to bad temper. William, always more extreme, told Charles he thought Edward Bunbury was impotent, and had teased Sarah into breaking off their engagement in order to get himself out of the scrape—"and now he is playing the devil amongst the women to persuade them he is sorry for his fault. What stuff it all is." (Edward Bunbury, 9th baronet, died unmarried in 1895; but

Emily's step-maternal feelings received their due balm when the third Bunbury son, Henry William St Pierre, a soldier, married George's younger daughter, Cecilia, in 1852. Succeeding where both her grandmother Sarah Napier and her aunt Emily Napier had failed, she gave birth to a Bunbury heir, Henry, tenth baronet; and also to George, William, and a daughter, called, needless to say, Emily.)

At home with Fanny, Charles was firmer: of course he wasn't going to forbid John the house; he was George's boy and Charles liked and admired him for himself as well. Fanny countered with a claim that John was too sudden and impetuous; he had rushed into the house demanding to see Minnie forthwith and had neglected some visiting friends of hers to the point of downright rudeness. —— Fanny's friends; but perhaps Charles thought and looked, rather than said it. More hysterics from Fanny: they were probably her best weapon against this exceedingly strong-willed man, whose chivalry could always be counted upon. Luckily John was posted to South Africa.

The complications of children and love! No sooner did one's own torments begin to ease off than the young settled in to torment one with their like problems. Even the mild and generous George declined to give William's John Moore Napier a job in his Government House at the Cape, since he and George's daughters Sarah and Cecilia were first cousins. George may have thought, but did not say, that they had had enough Lennox first-cousin-marriage disasters in the family already. He would not accept the presence under his roof for months on end of any young man he was not prepared to see his daughters marry, George sensibly concluded. William and Caroline of course understood. And yet, their poor beloved deaf and dumb Johnny! He was clever enough, confident enough, and well-trained for office work—but what was to become of him? He was received into a dreary government office in Dublin, from which, in due course, his father's outspoken political views got him ejected.

Charles concentrated on making peace between his sisters, the passionate and much beloved Em and the sensible, reliable, but easily offended Lou, with a full quota of their father's Scots dignity. What would happen if one of them died, he asked. The survivor would be miserable, and the other one would be greeted after death by an extremely stern father. Resentment was "not an indigenous feeling to hearts like both of yours. Cold hearts or selfish hearts take a quarrel as pleasantly as a glass of gin and feel more comfortable for it, but with you and Em it is deadly pain. You are like my Sue and Em, fiery and affectionate, scolding one another yet never happy asunder." And of course they would be liable to fall out when Em came to London, with too much to do in the time, and got herself into a muddle over times and dates. "She is so nervous and bothered in London that she loses self-possession. Emily has been used to a quiet life and in her old age she comes into the vortex of London and is rolled head over heels by it; whereas you, to whom it is familiar, are at your ease and methodical . . . but Emily has no idea of method and forgets to do half what she has to do, and then you will say sharp things." Charles besought Louisa not to see too much of Em in London, where she would inevitably be rushed and unsatisfactory, and to concentrate on long peaceful visits to Barton where Emily was at ease, and charming and affectionate as ever.

He succeeded, and "my spirits are raised 50 per cent by your reconciliation". As he had refused to take sides he couldn't judge, but was enormously happy that the sisters had cried off their feud. Impatience was a family failing. "Were I on my deathbed I could not say which I love best of George, William, Dick or Hal; but there is a hastiness in our blood which renders us not fit to live together, and a powerful tenderness and affection that makes us ill bear much separation. But if you and Emily depend upon each other in London she will try your temper too much . . . I am sure Emily did not mean to ill use you, if she did there is great merit in forgiving." They were different, and must allow for differences. If he and William were not so totally agreed on politics, war, religion and everything else liable to cause dispute, Charles was sure they would have quarrelled long ago.

Lou's next complaint was about Henry. Only Charles, and George, it seemed, could do no wrong. It was getting on for two years since Charles had written, "I have a letter from poor Henry 3 days before his misfortune—My God how I have felt for his agonies! I trust his mind is too strong to fail"; and now it seemed to Louisa that Henry had not taken enough of a pull after his wife's death. Charles had felt what Henry felt and could not echo the criticism. He was deeply sorry for Hal's continuing grief, "yet the children will in time do more than anyone, poor little things. Who could guard them like Henry?" He had a *point* in living, and that was everything and would in time take effect.

"Yes, I did exert myself", Charles admitted; "but Henry's exertion was made at once, too soon to do good [Henry had come galloping home from Florence], I had a month or two to recover, then the colony roused me. I had many advantages to force me through; he has none. His book would be the best; in time he will go to work. God knows time does little but in me it has produced the wish to set my girls fairly through infancy." Charles had pressed ahead with his own book and he sent it off on May 14th of 1838. William had thought he might get £300 for it, "and that would serve my brats, for I could easily write two a year".

But he had saved up enough, he thought, to keep his daughters happy, and had invested it in a well-recommended company in America. And here Charles took the sensible and discreet Louisa into a matter still painfully near his heart. "I shall now increase their mother's allowance, though her misconduct to me has long since freed me from every claim upon me. I do not mean her marrying again—I find no fault with her for that." (Why again? Had she ever been actually married to Charles?) "I was provoked at her for the moment, and unjustly so because there was no wrong in her so doing, at least not much, though I could prove to you that there was some. However she has always had her allowance and I have secured its continuance by my will; and it is sufficient to support her in a state of respectability independent of her husband's pay as a Greek officer.

"You may as well keep this letter, because if I should die, and also John Kennedy, (who knows Anastasulla's conduct as well as I do)"—the endearing form of her name crept in against Charles's will—"it will be a document in your hands, not to authorize any harsh treatment of her (God forbid), but to speak my feelings that her conduct leaves her no claim upon Susan and Emily but that of a *bad* mother. The claims of a mother must ever remain valid: but she is a bad mother. I am the person to blame in all things; but my conduct from first to last as John Kennedy knows has been kindness, open-ness and truth towards her. Wretched as it made me I resolved to give up my two darlings to her charge, thinking I had no right to separate the infants from their mother, and that my sufferings must be my just punishment. She cast them from her with contempt.

"I made her nurse Susan, and God knows with what trouble, Emily she would not nurse." (There was then no cow's milk on Cephalonia, and few goats: a child's health, and often its life, depended on its mother's willingness to nurse.) "But there are things which even John Kennedy does not know. In short, my dear Lou, she is now Old Pamela to a hair!"

This is the only written description of Anastasia which Charles ever gives: he urged Louisa to seal the letter up for fear of anyone accidentally reading it and upsetting the little girls. It is therefore worth considering the career of Old Pamela. She was the daughter of Madame de Génlis and of the Bourbon Prince Philippe Egalité, and she had married Lord Edward Fitzgerald, the Irish rebel and Charles's first cousin, in the aftermath of Lord Edward's separation from his first love, another first cousin, Lady Georgina Lennox. Beautiful, and wild, and incalculable, Pamela arriving in Ireland had charmed all hearts, including Donny's and Sarah's, in the days just before the Irish rebellion of 1798. After Edward Fitzgerald's death in Dublin Castle, Pamela left Celbridge House where she had been sheltered by Charles's parents and went to Goodwood: Sarah Napier, preparing her brother the Duke of Richmond for Pamela's arrival, had warmly praised her, but added that she was "a character". Not long afterwards Old Pamela had abandoned her three small children, who included young Pamela, now Lady (Guy) Campbell, to the care of their relations, and departed for Hamburg, where she had emigré relatives; and where she soon afterwards married a rich American named Kinnaird. After a year she abandoned him and went to live in and around Toulouse in the south of France. She became, it was said, immensely fat, but retained her beauty and fascination, and her overmastering passion for dancing. She died in late middle age in Paris, in poor circumstances; and the Fitzgerald family were much blamed by Irish patriots for her neglect. But it is difficult to pay great attention to someone who never answers letters, has no fixed address, has in any case married an American after being widowed from your son, and is known to have placed herself under the protection of a well-to-do French duke. She is said to have applied to the Viscontesse de Chabot, a Parisian who was a Fitzgerald by birth and a niece of her first husband, and to have received a dusty answer. The French duke paid for her funeral.

Such was Old Pamela, charming, wild, *insouciante*, a vagrant, the illegitimate child of clever irresponsible parents, the darling wife of a wild young man whose rebelliousness she considerably fostered, the deserting mother of three orphaned children. She was enslaving, and difficult, and doomed; and danced light-heartedly through it all;

careless of who was bruised on her way; and such too was Anastasia, as Charles, in the aftermath of his passion, had become aware.

In spite of his fretting mind, at Freshford William pressed on with his writing and his reforms. He was cheered by a letter from George expressing "unbounded delight" in his Vol. IV, "surpassing even the others, specially that beautiful passage relative to the gallant conduct and death of poor Bianchi, the Italian soldier". This encouragement was as well, as William was engaged in a prolonged battle to have the overseers of the local poorhouse brought to justice for having allowed an old pauper woman and an idiot boy to die of neglect. In such a cause he was prepared to swing the old boy network into action— "Edward Goulburn was in very early life a friend of mine; we were together in the Blues, and he was then a kind-hearted man." The case got nowhere in the local magistrates' court: everything adduced by William was declared to be "no evidence"; and "the only good part", he recorded, "was the feeding of seventeen or eighteen miserable pauper witnesses at the expense of the Government. It was very delightful to see taxes for once well expended."

William continued to stir it; got a new indictment; eventually won through to dismissal of overseers and provision of a better poorhouse. In an anonymous letter the dismissed overseer accused the gentry of the neighbourhood of not having done more for the poor: William, whose charity virtually emptied his pockets, was predictably indignant and said that hardly a day went past without his daughters "entering the poor's dwellings to supply them with food and money; and they have come back hundreds of times faint and ill from the horrible stench and misery they have encountered". Why must such conditions endure? And why must even the most parochial attempt to achieve a square deal for the luckless end in recrimination and anonymous letters? Taking time off to be flippant, William told Caroline that he and some of the children had been to the Zoo and seen the rhinoceros, "very good and gentle, and very like the Duke of York: it puts out its flexible upper lip and takes hold of anything pleasing".

It was now clear that Henry's naval race was run. Long ago Lord Melville had refused to carry out "a twice-made promise of promotion, wherefore", recorded William, "impatient like all his family, of injustice, he reproached that nobleman in a way to have debarred all future employment or advancement". Graham had promoted him, but it had been so far and no further. "Napier was finally laid aside with many other excellent sea officers who having served through the great French war, and being still able and willing to advance their country's greatness, were condemned to pine in hopeless inactivity while their former ships, become the prey of political and family interests, sailed under youths unborn or still at school when the ousted men were heriocally braving battle and tempest", William's brotherly rage recorded.

Henry had now sent in his papers, which Charles thought a pity: while there is life there is hope; and a good battle with a south-west gale off Plymouth in a spanking three-decker was just what Henry needed to restore morale. He was a first-class seaman, as Charles, who had ridden out an American hurricane in his frigate had good cause to know. William, recovering from 'flu, also meditated selling his commission in aid of his children's future: it would fetch £3,200, and his half pay brought in only £171 per annum. His wise friend Bickersteth advised him against it. It would deprive William of the distant hope and challenge of military fame which sustained him in his darkest hours of pain, and give him the courage to keep hold on life. Who knew that he might not in time completely recover? Bickersteth himself had had 'flu and "its full complement of gloomy thoughts and dark forebodings": they would pass.

And William, when well, had still something of the original tiger in him, loping about the countryside with almost his old speed. "There was a spring and grace in his step combined with a power and dignity that I never saw in anyone else", a niece thought. "Be you Major N'pier?" an old Peninsular soldier posted to a newly-made turnpike asked William as he drew near. "I knew it. I was sure of it. I seed you afar off, afore you was in half a mile, and I says to my wife, if my old major be above ground that be he, I should know that walk in a thousand." Twenty-two years separated their encounters.

Though William's illnesses were not "mere weakness to be got over by an exertion, but absolute helplessness, sometimes lasting for six months or more", there were still long spells of enjoyment and activity, of fun with the children, of garden digging, of the putting out of fires in the thatched roofs of the village. The visit of Marshal Soult had been fun: William, appointed official bear-leader, had been embraced by the old Frenchman on both cheeks, and he had asked all the Napier brothers to dinner and called them *mes enfants*, and

William had been besieged by everyone in London entreating for invitations to Soult's ball, to which William was able truthfully to reply that he himself hadn't got one—yet. Soult was asked to speak at Liverpool, and went to the station in his own carriage, but his extremely grand and gilded entourage were all piled into an omnibus: "It would I think be difficult to get so many English dukes and marquises to travel in an omnibus so contentedly", William felt. Soult was lame from a cannon-shot in the hip, and bent with age. "His long grey hair now flows back from his forehead down on to his shoulders, after the mode of Benjamin Franklin, to whom he has a general resemblance; his features are handsomer and less coarse than those of the great American, not such a vigorous compact formation of skull as Franklin, not so much symmetry, but more nobleness of aspect, and a more gracious expression." Soult told a Birmingham audience that he had learnt to esteem the British on the field of battle, for their honesty and candour as well as for their courage. "We fought like men without rancour, without personal anger." Now, meeting them, he found them "equally kind and generous". The applause, needless to say, was deafening. William's answering speech, whose keynote was "profound and lasting peace between France and England", met a milder response.

Life had prospective pleasures as well as past glories. "The railroad coach is an actual lolling sofa; no shaking, less noise than a common carriage, no smell, and the first stage at the rate of sixty miles an hour, ten miles in ten minutes! I got to dinner in exact time." And how delightful to meet Prosper Merimée again—"We are cronies"—and they had been out together to see the Birthday illuminations. They had seen a crowd of boys, running and shouting, and Merimée had cried out "Hah! is that a revolution? Let me see it!" and bounded off, "dancing with joy at an English revolution. He is a very nice, clever, amusing fellow, English in wit and manner, and speaks very well indeed in our language", and William admired his books. "He came up to me very gravely, and taking off his hat, said, 'Monsieur, Sare, is it not the part of a loyal man to go and pay his respects to his king? and here I find you in the midst of a revolutionary crowd, without any distinction! March, for shame, sare! go and put on your orders and your fine clothes, and go to your king, go to your king!' " They had laughed a lot, and Merimée had taken him off to see a new musket invented by a Frenchman called Baron Heurtleloup, "a very marvellous piece of workmanship, it will fire eighty times without new priming, and each time with certainty, whether wet or dry". Life still held delightful people, new and many inventions.

But he wondered deeply why, and for how long, even the simplest pleasures of a full belly and an unleaking roof should be denied to so many of his countrymen. Would they for long endure it, or was revolution still on the way?

Election meetings, the endless vapourings at a political dinner during Roebuck's campaign in Bath at Christmas 1837, had made Charles also wonder this. The new Poor Law had utterly failed to alleviate the misery he saw spreading around him: were the liberal-minded, with their speeches, their ignorance of what was practicable, their cloudy detachment from human nature as it now was, making still more of a bog of the country than even the old order had allowed? Could no-one within the present set-up come to terms with these monsters of steel, these roaring machines which had changed the pattern of centuries? The "prodigious energy" and the "whirring wheels" of Wolverhampton iron-works had given William "tumultuous feelings"; and it was all very marvellous and stirring until you moved on to the cotton-mills further north and saw the children working them. But the misery of unemployment and poverty, even of downright starvation, that seemed the inevitable results of these glowing and wonderful monsters, and the helplessness of democratic government to relieve it, were turning Charles savage; he had moments of fierce frustration, of impatience with the entire scheme of things, with the infinite slowness with which even the most modest reforms were carried out. "Ever since the Bath Dinner," he wrote half-mockingly, but only half-mockingly, to William, "and from what I see daily, my thoughts are strangely turned to a good tough despotic government, *sufficiently bloody*, as the best of all possible forms of ruling."

William had been ill, but had got out of bed to come to Bath. Charles and William Napier "dominated the meeting" one witness reported—did anyone else get a word in?—"which carried resolutions in favour of universal suffrage and shorter Parliaments". "We must display the power of the people continually, by degrees, by meetings such as these", William told them: we must "insist on government by just principles, for the benefit of the people".

But where did it all get anybody? Settling down to his translation of de Vigny and Blaize's *Lights and Shades of Military Life* from the

French, Charles felt mounting impatience at popular misery, at his own uselessness. The *Liverpool Standard* had firmly slammed William down for his Bath speech, asserting that he was a coward, a hypocrite, a traitor, and an old decrepit wretch scarce able to crawl; and warned him he would be disappointed if he tried to fight an election—"as his brother the Pirate was at Portsmouth".

This referred to their first cousin, Admiral Sir Charles Napier, Black Charlie: contesting Portsmouth as an independent, he had asked the soldier Charles to support him. Charles felt doubtful. As an independent, Black Charlie would not want to affront Tories, Whigs, or Radicals; and Charles felt certain of affronting someone. "I am dead Wellingtonian", he told William. "He thought reform bad and opposed it; now being law, if he has to execute it he will act honestly to his country." And this really was the key and pith of being governed by gentlemen.

How far, Charles wondered, had party politics got them? Like Labour in the 1960s, the Whigs, at last in office, had come up against the harsh facts of life and badly disappointed. What had they actually done for the starving townspeople of Britain? The prosperous merchants, under all those vulgar hats that Wellington had complained of in the reformed Commons, had proved as jealous of their private interests as any feudal landlord of them all. "Your politics are nearly mine", Charles told William. "A Tory well chastised and taught that he is like other people, is well enough; but Whigs have all the Tory faults and their own besides. A Tory is a bold open bandit who avows his trade and takes all chances, doing at times handsome and generous things. The Whig is a sneaking pickpocket, pretending to elegance and honesty while he commits every dirty trick recorded in the Newgate Calendar—so long as it is safe."

A private duty that he must soon perform nagged often at Charles's conscience. The time was coming to take his children to Greece and introduce them to the mother they had known in infancy and now barely remembered. In his much-loved Cephalonia, or on the mainland, a meeting must and should be effected, though it seemed likely to bring them, as well as himself, nothing but pain. For them it would also bring the misery and stress of divided loyalties, the bitter necessity of laying the blame somewhere. A letter in August of 1838 obviated the need for this dire project. Anastasia had died.

Charles's relief was real. No need now to expose Susan and Emily to the emotional strains of divided parents; no need now, in the midst of their vulnerable adolescence, even to tell them about their mother. There would be time for all that when they were grown women, preferably with husbands of their own. Yet he was beset by melancholy and lowness, by guilt and grief. Anastasia dead seemed again the melting beauty who had beguiled and torn him apart. How much had their love been the cause of her roving life and early death? "My dear Lou, it makes a man feel deeply how endless are the evils of a small deviation from the rules of right. Had I never fallen in love with my beloved Bess I should have married early and avoided the trouble which befell. Yet in youth we neither foresee nor avoid ills, in this life the devil lays his snares and we fall into them. God has spared me the bitterness of seeing my girls suffer, but he has at the same time deeply impressed me with a sense of my own misconduct." He was arranging a pension for Anastasia's father, and for her old grandmother; and it was at least a relief to feel that he had always behaved to her with kindness and affection.

And a breath of searching sadness blew on Charles's heart among the dark hills of Wales, as he remembered the sparkling seas of Cephalonia, the brilliance of light, and the wayward daughter of the island, in whose arms he had renewed a passionate youth.

CHAPTER XIV

A Troubled Ocean

Charles's hope of a job seemed to be forever in retreat. He had stuck to his principles and pulled no strings, patiently waiting his turn; but it was a real jolt when in March of 1838 he learned of the appointment of Sir Leonard Greenwell, his junior in rank, to command a district in Ireland. This sparked off a letter to Lord Fitzroy Somerset, in which for the first time he discoursed of ill-treatment. "I shall not affront them", he assured Louisa, but he would not let this pass in silence, though "I think you will be satisfied I did not write a violent letter . . . I am always afraid of making myself of more value than I am, but still 42 years and 5 wounds and never having avoided a single duty or been reprimanded, and 14 years in the colonies make me think it hard to be passed over." Yet nothing would make him think ill of Somerset and Hill.

Charles felt he could surely be made use of somewhere in Ireland; and they stored their furniture in Bath late in the summer, "being resolved to give Ireland a year's trial before we fix". In April he had written sadly to Lou, "My answer from Lord Fitzroy is come. They say in a civil way that I have no claims and they cannot employ me. I give up all expectation, indeed I never had much, of being employed." A note of bitterness crept in, and he quoted Old Pamela. "As Lady Edward Fitzgerald used to say, they want a man to be their valet and if he resists this they will cast him off. It is *their* service, not public service, they look to. However it don't much signify, and I shall not worry myself about it.

"Life is a wet day affair to all, and lucky are they who have their daily bread, the shelter of a house, and a home. I feel ashamed to grieve when I look on my dear girls and know how many see their Susans and Emilys perish before their eyes for want of food and raiment; and parents whom starvation, without any fault of their own, has cast into the damned Bastilles of the New Poor Law, torn their infants from them and sent them to perish in another Bastille far away where they can neither know the treatment they receive from strangers nor if they be sick or well. Lord Stanhope has had proof sent to him that numbers of infants have thus been killed—I did not send it to him but I know who did."

Howitt said, in 1838, he thanked God that "the poor have their objects of admiration and attraction, their domestic affections and their family ties, a thousand simple and substantial pleasures".* These, their sole wealth, were now threatened. The old feudal regime, whatever its shortcomings, had at least never dragged families apart as the New Poor Law did. "When I think of these woes and tortures inflicted on the poor I do think how fortunate I am in being rich, and that God demands that I should labour to save others rather than complain of my lot: yet sickness and worries do often make me discontented. I think you are much more philosophical", Charles told Louisa. "Your present lowness is from illness, which no-one can resist. Lord Fitzroy's letter is very civil, and not so hopeless as at first I considered it."

In June he rejoiced over George's appointment: he felt sure that his brother would be the best governor the Cape had ever had. Thank God his son John was recovering from a bad illness; though George was "too fully impressed with religion not to know that we live with such losses hanging over us all the time." Bentley had refused his novel, and he thought Lord Fitzroy was about to refuse him the governorship of Jersey, in which case they would be off to Ireland directly.

In the midst of mounting political tension William's speeches went on. He continued to urge his radical audiences to cool their passions and to moderate their immediate demands. Addressing the Working Men's Association in Bath in September of 1838, William told them that he was with them as regarded the ballot, universal suffrage, and short parliaments. "But if there is any secret or avowed intention to use words which have been addressed to you at your last meeting, '*to pull down all priestly and kingly institutions and to establish a republic on their ruins, to bring America hither*,' then I will oppose it myself, and join with those who oppose it."

America! they must surely be daft. Mr Bartlett, the speaker who had uttered these felonious words, maintained that countries without

* William Howitt, *Rural Life of England* (1838)

king or aristocracy "produced better morals, more justice . . . Is Mr Bartlett serious? Has he ever read a line of history? Has Dutch conduct* in the East Indies been wise, disinterested, and humane? Have their massacres at Amboyna, their conduct at the Cape of Good Hope, and in Java, and Surinam, and Demarara been the result of republican virtues and probity? What has been their treatment of their slaves?

"Has America never waged war with the Algierines, the English, the Red Indians? Will Mr Bartlett characterize her conduct towards that unfortunate race as a result of republican virtue and honesty? Was it honest and moral to war against the Seminoles and deprive them of their country? to entrap their chief by an infamous breach of faith? Is the superior morality of America to be traced in the keenness and rapacity of her commercial dealings; or in her treatment of black slaves, more than two million in number; or in her laws to prevent the spread of education amongst these unhappy beings lest they should learn to assert their natural rights?" The hapless Mr Bartlett must have squirmed in his seat.

"Tar and feathering, lynch law, are they just, decent, virtuous, humane? Are the savage duels of the Americans, their frequent assassinations, proofs of superior morality?" What of their murders in State Assemblies during debate, their burning of the Catholic establishment at Boston, and of the houses of the Anti-Slavery Society in Philadelphia? "And their respect for public faith and international rights is proved, I suppose, by the seizure of Texas, an immense country belonging to the Mexicans?"

"Bring America hither indeed! Bring the savage slave-driver with his whip into England to teach Englishmen what freedom is! No! let us still be Englishmen in heart and thought and deed; let us still be the people who have, who can, and who will, I trust always, lead mankind in glory—the glory of arts, the glory of arms, and the still higher glory of establishing the true principles of freedom and good government. Let us seek for our springs of action in our honesty of purpose, in our own upright hearts, in our clear heads, and ask no American slave-driver to teach us what is due to humanity.

"But though I thus proclaim my firm adherence to the abstract form of kings, lords, and commons, do I advocate their irresponsibility with respect to the people?" Were they omnipotent, irresponsible? Far from it, each was responsible, controlled and restricted by

* Holland was then a republic

each other—the Commons by the people at large. But how? "Why, by universal suffrage, by short parliaments, by ballot, by a legitimate constitutional power residing in the nation, to be freely and frequently exercised—namely the power of dismissing bad representatives and choosing better.

"I know it has been said, and it is true, that the people may be deceived, that they may and often will choose bad men, that they will be taken by the flashy, factious demagogue, oftener than by the modest and wise patriot; yes, I know they are not infallible—who, or what on earth is? But still, if they possess the power of constitutionally changing their law-givers, without tumult, without bloodshed, without breaking up the bonds of society—if they possess and exercise that power freely and frequently—it will be impossible that the bulk of the nation can ever be long or grievously oppressed . . .

"I call upon you in the name of God, whose aid we invoke in our struggle, . . . to achieve your end by the power of reason, by the power of union, by the power of perseverance—not by violent means . . . Do no injustice to others, and beware of letting hot-headed, vain, and silly men, or secret traitors to your cause . . . instigate you to attempt to alter the form of the ancient English constitution. Your rights will be entirely secured by universal suffrage. Go further, attempt a Republic, and your cause will perish, and with it will perish a multitude of yourselves . . . Working men, I have done. I wish you all just and reasonable success."

The pacific effect of all this was slightly marred by an incident in the next speech, when the speaker, calling Wellington a knave, told by William to retract, and refusing to do so, was confronted by a furious William leaping across the platform, striking the speaker a round blow, and having to be restrained by force from following it up. His blood was still too hot to allow him to sit mumchance and hear Wellington abused: perhaps he would not have made a very convenable MP.

Charles, still in Wales, did not see the blow but read the speech—"I think it is the most argumentative and powerful one he ever made, in balance between the two factions, one wanting to refuse the people their just rights and the other wanting to overturn the constitution and establish a republic. He was surrounded by these last, and yet bearded them in their very den, for a democratic meeting is such, and required a man like him to do it; but he not only attacked republicanism, he also defended the Duke of Wellington, a still bolder deed."

He thought William's speech magnificent. "There is no man in Europe to be compared to him is my opinion, he not only surpasses but absolutely towers above the miserable fiddle-faddle politicians of the day. There is no man that can equal Podge," Charles continued in passionate approval, "no man rivals him in historical writing, he could not take such views of war and politics without an extraordinary genius, and with half the (nasty) world against his opinions and a host of writers against him, and all failing in every assault. I do think him one of the greatest men that ever lived" Charles assured Louisa, "but being poor he can do nothing in England, riches being a necessary of public life in this country. However his history will leave his name high enough, but even that is on a subject in which only a limited number can estimate his genius."

And when it came, this June, Charles's KCB was marred for him by William's being still without one—"my feelings are uncomfortable at getting what I think he deserves much more than I do, it deducts from the gratification I should otherwise feel at the honour. At the same time I do feel proud of this and wish my father had lived to see two of his sons knights of the Bath and the third more distinguished than either and who will be one also. I do not deny my satisfaction." But William and Black Charlie, "the two most distinguished of our family are omitted—it does vex me. Fanny is very funny about being my lady and so are the brats . . . I hope they won't make this a put off—I would rather have Jersey."

And the absurd thing was that everyone seemed to think that a KCB involved cash: Charles's begging letters had reached epidemic proportions, and often they were terribly moving. Charity did not invariably work well with the recipients; if William Stone was behaving so badly in Louisa's service it showed little feeling, when Charles had supported the family for twenty-five years and still gave the mother a pension.

"My object is to have few wants," Charles firmly told Louisa this summer, "but our passions disturb our philosophy. The having given up Australia often torments me. I do not think I was wrong, but I should have passed life more pleasantly with a great occupation.

"I suspect Emily heard I am such a horrible temper and so violent and impracticable and disobedient from the Holland House people, for Adam's father, it is said, rules that old noodle Lord Holland. I see Sir Fred is to be Commander in Chief in Ireland—let rascality flourish! The ministers are displeased at my politics, they prefer hypocrites who will not say what they think, and who would betray them tomorrow." Late in the year he was refused the governorship of Jersey. "Nothing will make me abuse Lord Hill, or Lord Fitzroy; if they are unjust it will be from some cause they cannot control. But I am low."

They were in Dublin, and the state of Ireland was not such as to raise anyone's spirits. Charles sought a job, and Fanny sought a house, but all they actually acquired was a persistent cough for Emily which distracted her father with worry. He would give up any job, any hope of any job, to take her to Switzerland for the winter, he told Charles Robertson. Meanwhile he took the girls to Kingston, where the air was said to be the best in Ireland, and left them with the governess in lodgings, and Emily was cured. The doctor had sworn that it wasn't her lungs, "and he was right", Charles triumphed. His relief and delight started him off writing again. He always feared that his little Greeks wouldn't stand up to the British climate.

They were growing up fast, Susan now fifteen and Emily fourteen, and growing into all the difficulties that such an age involves. "I am very glad you wrote to Susan as you did," Charles told Louisa, who had taken her niece to task about being attentive to Fanny, "for she has been most impertinent and made Emily so too." They had a new governess, kind and gentle but "unfortunately not over-encumbered with wits". Charles's quick little Cephalonians made rings round her, and he had had to punish Susan for downright rudeness to her stepmother, and a few days earlier Emily had told Miss Rossiter, the new governess, that Fanny was *not* her Mamma and she did not care *what* she ordered; she and Susan only cared for Papa. "So your advice came as pat as if you had been present at my lecture. I wish you from time to time to press upon them love and respect for Fanny."

Love, unhappily, is not easy to press; and Fanny was perhaps a thought ungenial to her husband's bright-eyed and maybe indulged children. Emily's cough may well have been psychological. 'Young' Pamela (Lady Campbell) had had the children for a party at Drumcondra "and Emily coughed three times on arrival and never since!" Over the three days the worrying cough vanished under the aegis of the enchanting Pamela. Charles found that he liked the

Leinsters, his Fitzgerald cousins, as much as ever: they were good, kind, sensible, and had asked him and Fanny and Minnie for a visit at Carton, "but not the monkeys, which annoys me rather". But he was going to take Sue and Emily to Celbridge as soon as he had the chance. "I have got a delightful horse for twenty pounds!" Ireland for ever!

Long ago Aunt Louisa Conolly at Castletown had known what Ireland most needed, and she had founded her school in Celbridge, where Protestant and Catholic children learnt the three R's together, and were taught handicrafts and sang songs and played games and grew up without thinking the other sect were bogeys; while the priest came in to teach religion to his flock and the parson came in to teach it to his. The experiment had worked well; but then Tom Conolly had died and Castletown had been inherited by his niece, married to Thomas Pakenham, who had been so infatuated with his own ideas of good and evil that he had broken the school up with an injudicious zeal. Why should his wife's aunt by marriage, Lady Louisa Lennox by birth, very little educated except by contact with the intelligent, and not even an Irishwoman, be supposed to know best? Thomas Pakenham, who took the name of Conolly, had insisted that all the children should have the Bible read to them daily, and the Roman Catholic priest had immediately ordered his flock out of the school, and the whole experiment had ended in increased bitterness. As it might have done anyway. Or it might have caught on, and spread over Ireland, and many good and innocent people who now are dead or maimed might be alive and well. To George Napier, who had been Louisa's executor and who knew how deeply his aunt's heart had been in the school, and who knew also that she had sacrificed half her jointure so that Castletown might go to Thomas Pakenham free of debt, the new owner's insistence on having his way with the school had seemed a wilful and ungracious act.

Domestic life no longer enjoyed the smoothness and total understanding that had been Charles's with Elizabeth; but slowly his spirits recovered under the influence of warm-hearted old friends. He was working on *Lights and Shades of Military Life*, a translation from Blaize that a publisher had commissioned. Would Lou ask Lord Mark Kerr if he still had that original letter of James Wolfe's saying that he had been at the Battle of Culloden and that the superiority of the bayonet over the broadsword and targe was there evident? Did

Mark Kerr ever publish this letter, "and if I have occasion, will he allow me to quote it? as there is a controversy about the bayonet. Give him my love and tell him to read my notes (*Naval and Military Gazette* of November 17th) and see the difference between a radical and a republican." The republican brush was one with which Charles hated to be tarred.

Lou would be glad to know that Harriet Clancarty was well, and kind, and still exactly like herself—"But alas, seeing her brought back all the happy past." In a great wave of memory Charles had returned in feeling to his warm and shining childhood (all sorrows fled away) with Donny, Sarah and Aunt, at glittering Castletown with its candles and its dancings and its blazing fires, or in the laughter of home, the crowding reassurance of his parents in their lively prime. "How can they who disbelieve a future state bear these losses that are the lot of all?"

John Kennedy, refusing several good jobs, had now taken employment on his nephew's estate at Loch Ash in County Tyrone, where he was trying out methods of farming that he had learnt after long study on the Continent, and making an outstanding success of them. On his own little estate of only £150 a year, John Kennedy had settled thirty-five Irish families who, Charles reported to Robertson, "had been six years ago all paupers, begging, robbing, and idling, and who now, from land previously waste, arc thriving". Inspired, Charles published a book called *An Address to Irish Absentees on the state of Ireland*; it cost him £40 to get it into print, but he thought it might do good. Kennedy himself published another, called *Instruct, Employ, Don't Hang Them*; a title taken from Arthur Young. This last was not a success: Charles thought bitterly that its title had dished it—"Captain Kennedy might have known that there is something so revolting to society in the idea of *not hanging Irishmen* that such an injunction was imprudent." Yet O'Connell, however good his intentions, was doing harm—"His words", Charles thought, "have great effect here in making one people hate the other, for he tries to father everything on the English, no matter what their politics are."

The government decided that John Kennedy's well worked-out agricultural plans for Ireland were too visionary: none was adopted. The Irish famine came a few years later. This, whatever horrors may be laid at its door, precipitated another John Kennedy to his destiny across the Atlantic.

In England William was still imploring Irish reform, at meeting after meeting, with all the eloquence at his command. He was whistling down the wind. Influential Tories owned land there, as did also influential Whigs; and the Orangemen of the North remembered 1641 and the Maguire massacres when an estimated ten thousand English Protestants had died at Irish Catholic hands; just as the Irish remembered Cromwell and the savage cruelties he inflicted in revenge. All this was two hundred years ago: could no-one in Ireland forget, or put a bit of heart into the Lord's Prayer, which all alike repeated daily?

Over Christmas of 1838 Charles was in bed for seven weeks with shingles breaking out round the site of an old wound; but continued his amicable arguments with Charles Robertson about rifles and morality. Non-resistance? For men who were seeing their children swept into Poor Law Houses? Not on your life. "Where non-resistance is the rule tyranny becomes also the rule. If resistance to unjust power be culpable, we have no right to arm ourselves against an invading army of savages. If the King of England deprives me of my just liberty or of my children, he does as much wrong as the general of an invading army. Should the right of self-defence be abolished and the good abandon themselves to the bad? God had given men reason as a protection against such advice." And reason to recognize unjust and implacable power when we saw it. "I am not likely to be employed as a governor anywhere", he mourned. "I should like to go to the Ionian islands more than anything."

But this was of all things least probable. By 1839 the Napiers were all in the doldrums; but on no-one's craft were the sails flapping more idly than on Charles's. Where, for them, were Trollope's "elastic springs of delicious and beneficent labour"? Charles's race seemed to be run; he was just another crotchety unemployable retired colonel; not only a praiser of times past, but adding radical notions to his general crisp eccentricity. He was fifty-six, and known to authority as "an impractical man who quarrelled with everyone". As William said, he would always be so if resistance to oppression could be called quarrelsome. But what, mourned the authorities, could you do with a fellow, however able, who went on and on about lost causes, about effective military help for Greece, about Ireland being fairly governed, about starving women and children being fed; who made difficulties over every sort of half-baked, half-organized project, and stirred up problems over Poor Law and child labour instead of letting sleeping dogs lie?

The new year found him restless, when there was so much to be done. All his hard efforts, all his great ideas and his careful plans had dissolved into nothing, were foam on a fretful sea. Politics, writing, the army, Ireland—nothing fitted, nowhere was he wanted. "You and I and George are like worms chopped by the spade", he told William. "We twist about, heads and tails separated, not knowing where to look for each other."

The wild and lovely Anastasia was dead, and Elizabeth, the glory of his soul, was dead. His wife Fanny was in general a good helpmeet and he was grateful and affectionate to her, but not much more. He was as it were stripped for action: but no action was forthcoming. Faith still burned; hope still glimmered; charity, except towards the powers that be, continued to flow. But sometimes he felt a deathly sense of disorientation in a world that would not let him help to cure its ills.

Growing older, William's children had required better schooling; and William himself, getting stiffer in the back and less able for the saddle, to be nearer reference libraries. He and Caroline left the West Country and settled into a house at Streatham which Charles had not thought a good buy—"William's house holds together by force of habit alone." Political agitation was mounting: William told Roebuck in 1840 that such proposals for forcible action were voiced to him, that if they had come by letter, "I should have been guilty of misprision of treason if I had concealed it." He continued angry with the Whig leaders—"men who had so deserted their promises and avowed principles, and turned so maliciously against those whom they had before excited, were not fit to have power, and it was the duty of all honest men to aid in tumbling them from their high places." Arson, machine-breaking, and other civil troubles continued.

"Without good order and law," Wellington told William in August of 1839, "there can be no liberty or even satisfaction in life. England cannot be the country which has produced such men as you are, if such evils as we have witnessed lately are suffered to continue." It was a moment of extreme windiness above, of radical agitation below. Could civil war be averted?

William's political persuasions and his lively and bitter pen would be needed more than ever. England was rolling into the hungry forties, still in the dream that Laisser Faire would solve all. The misery, grime, and squalor of the Midlands and North appalled all who came fresh to them: Charles and William were both on the boil. Visiting a factory in 1838, William found "the noise of the machinery was deafening, the heat intolerable, the smells disgusting, and the haggard faces and distorted forms of the women and children employed were heart-sickening. Misery of mind and body, pain and fear and hopelessness were in every countenance: it is a hellish system. And yet one gentleman who was with me, having a wife and half a dozen children of his own about him, on my remarking the diseased looks of the factory children, told me that tables had been made out that proved these squalid creatures to be more healthy than any other class of working people."

Soon the pen of William would be free to lash, for by 1840 he was finishing Volume VI, the last of his long History. It had taken him twenty-three years to write. He was at Hemel Hempstead, in a house that Henry had taken, and again he had been very ill, "I feel my life ebbing away", he told Caroline, "and I want to be as much with you and my dear children while I am in this world as I can"; but he couldn't get well enough to come home. Henry had done everything, nursed him day and night. "When I told you he had made himself a slave to me I meant it literally." A few days later William was up and writing the last pages—"without you I could never have written it at all", he told Caroline—but feeling no elation of spirit in having at last concluded; only a kind of flatness, like a woman after a long exhausting labour, too spent even to take an interest in the child.

The voices of Henry's children came up to him from the garden, Charley and Augusta, young Richard Henry, always called Bam, and the baby born shortly before Henry's Caroline had died, and soon to follow her. William distracted his ears from their cheerful sound: this was the final draft, the final paragraph. "Fortune", he wrote, "however always asserts her supremacy in war, and often from a slight mistake such disastrous consequences flow, that in every age and every nation the uncertainty of arms has been proverbial." The flukes of fortune! He had known them himself, after the war as well as during it; the buying of the 43rd's regimental command over his head by a man who had the cash if not the ability, the good chance of his literary start, the ill chance of Henrietta's death, Johnny's disability, the long-drawn-out pain of Fanny's illness and loss, the failure of his first volume, the pain of his wounds, misery over his country; and through it all the strong tower of Caroline's love and the peace of being with her, the hours of happiness with his children.

Napoleon had chanced his luck, William concluded, in marching on Madrid in 1808, leaving his flank exposed: from that all else had flowed: to that his eventual extinction could be traced. (Others, with more information at their command than William had, have judged differently.) Yet what had victory done for England, though it had left her "the most triumphant nation of the world"? It had also left her "with an enormous debt, a dissatisfied people, gaining peace without tranquillity, greatness without intrinsic strength, the present time uneasy, the future dark and threatening". What would life be like for his children, the eldest born to him in the last desperate years of the Peninsular War when he had wept at the dying of so many friends? The railways were now here; the world, as Charles had pointed out, would be five times smaller now that one could travel at sixty miles an hour instead of the coach's twelve. Where would these iron chariots carry his country?

"Yet she rejoices in the glory of her arms! And it is a stirring sound", William was obliged to admit. War was at once vain and necessary, terrible in its effects, splendid in the qualities it called up in men. "War is the condition of this world. From men to the smallest insect all are at strife, and the glory of arms, which cannot be obtained without the exercise of honour, fortitude, courage, obedience, modesty, and temperance, excites the brave man's patriotism and is a chastening correction for the rich man's pride. It is yet", he warned, "no security for power." The splendour of his intelligence, until power corrupted it, the might of his arms, had not saved the French Emperor. "Napoleon, the most wonderful commander, the most sagacious politician, the most profound statesman, lost by arms, Poland, Germany, Italy, Portugal, Spain and France."

William was too honest, too conscious of Allied shortcomings, to claim with pious effrontery that God had been on their side. Taking ink for a final sentence, he put it in a less moralizing way. His black hair was fast going grey, but sprang thick and turbulent as ever; people still remembered him as the handsomest man they had ever seen, thick-necked but wiry, tall, beak-nosed, rather like Sir Stamford Raffles. The song of birds in the garden, the sounds of the spring day died out of his ears; he thought again of Napoleon, dead long since on that high bleak island in the South Atlantic where William felt he should never have been sent to waste out his life in boredom; of his lightning moves, his guile and strategy and quickness of perception; of the way the French cavalry had so willingly died in hundreds for him in that last great battle in the Low Countries which in some strange fey manner he had almost acquiesced in losing. "Fortune, that name for the unknown combinations of infinite power, was wanting to him", William concluded firmly, "and without her aid the designs of men are as bubbles on a troubled ocean."

But fortune, "that name for the unknown combinations of infinite power", now suddenly blew a fair breeze upon the Napiers; and as if acknowledging their essential unity, it blew on the brothers almost together. William's finished History became an international success, was translated in the end into French, German, Spanish, Italian, and, surprisingly, Persian; and he was presently made KCB and Governor of Guernsey; a nice quiet billet where his bullet-ridden back would not hamper him. Caroline had an easier life, and all the daughters had prettier dresses. William's native confidence returned, the courage of his convictions deepened in him. Henry, remembering how greatly *his* Caroline had wanted him to finish it, pressed on with his History of Florence from the earliest times, sneezing his way gallantly through the Florentine archives to its completion; no mean effort for one whose formal education had ended when he went to sea at the age of fourteen. George was made a general and a KCB, and sent out to govern the Cape Colony: a widower for twenty years, he married an old friend with whom he became very happy, a widowed Mrs Williams-Freeman, to help him cherish his daughters Sarah and Cecilia in a far country, and to run Government House. In January of 1839 the much loved Charles, *primus inter pares* among the whole brotherhood, received similar promotion; and—"I feel like a bull turned out after being kept in a dark stable"—was appointed to the Northern Command of England.

Part IV

Thunder in the North

"Those who had more money in their pockets kept him at arm's length, and cared not whether he lived or died." Manchester cotton-spinner, quoted by Mrs Gaskell, *Mary Barton*

CHAPTER XV

The Dark Satanic Mills

"Hast tha seen thy child clemmed to death?" asked a cotton-weaver of Mrs Gaskell, wife of a Unitarian minister in Manchester in the late 1830s, when she tried to console him for hard times with talk of coming reforms. Appalled by the stark reality of this question, she listened to his grief, and in time came on to hearing his politics.

Them as is strong in any of God's gifts is meant to help the weak, the cotton-weaver insisted.

Was he an Owenite? Was he for equality and community of goods?

Na; he was no fool. If all were equal tonight, some would get the start by rising an hour earlier tomorrow.

What of his faith?

He would have gone after the Bible rules if he'd seen folk credit it. They all spoke up for it and did clean contrary; he had come to think it a sham put on poor folks. It was not long he tried to live Gospelwise when everyone else said Stand up for tha rights or tha'lt never get them. The slow starvation of wife and child had spoken loudest of all.

Listening, sympathizing, recording, Mrs Gaskell, who was herself still quivering from the loss of her own four-year-old boy by scarlet fever, wrote her book *Mary Barton* to ram home the plight of the cotton towns. In this preview *Uncle Tom's Cabin* of industry she hoped to force people to understand the bitter and dangerous division which Industrial Revolution had wrought between man and man.

It puts a sting into starvation itself, the cotton-weaver told her, that those who had more money in their pockets kept him at arm's length, and cared not whether he was sorry or glad; whether he lived or died. No heap of gold should part him and his brother so far asunder. For he was a loving man before he grew mad seeing such as he was slighted, as if Christ himself had not been poor.

Thus wrote Mrs Gaskell, sweetening and clarifying utterance no doubt with a dash of Uncle Tom sentimentality, in her effort to speak through literature to the hearts of her fellow-countrymen, and being smartly rapped over the knuckles for her pains. The *Edinburgh Review*, in ringing Lady-Catherine-de-Burgh tones, asked her if she had taken sufficient account of the improvidence of the artisan; friends accused her of starting a class war; and the *Manchester Guardian*, in a particularly snide passage (February 28th, 1849), complained of "Mrs Gaskell's morbid sensibilities to the conditions of the operatives", in accordance with "the fashion set in of late among the gentry and landed aristocracy".

Accused at once of snobbery and revolutionism, Mrs Gaskell continued unshaken. What she had described in her book—the slow remorseless starvation that took first the children and then the aged and the weak, the futile search of skilled men for work, the miserable dwellings with men and women sleeping on dank stone floors while the sewage seeped upwards for lack of drainage, was all "as real as my own life". This *was* the Industrial North.

In the early months of 1839 the government suddenly became aware that it was confronted with an incipient revolution. The Chartists had hopefully marched to London with their ten points and been refused a hearing: in bitterness of soul they tramped back, feeling that even the Queen did not care that their children were starving. They wanted no charity; their demand was for justice. Soon they ceased to mutter and began to gather and arm. The Corn Laws were unrepealed, food was expensive; many of the cotton mills stood idle while the American cotton-growers hung on for a good price, and the Continental market for the finished goods continued sluggish. Relief was spasmodic and scant, and at the mercy of mayor or magistrate, who could be efficient and helpful but were more often slothful, agitated, inclined to moralize, or in a tizzy about what their wives might say. Into this whirlpool of injustice and discontent arrived Charles, appointed to the Northern Command and taking over at Nottingham in April of 1839. Perhaps the Horse Guards felt he was expendable; perhaps, to take a kinder view, that he was the only man for the job. He would, they knew, use no violence unless *in extremis*, and more important still, would provoke none. "Once more in harness. But I am too old", he told Robertson. "I don't much like the work going on at Nottingham, but *pikes* must be put down—it is madness. I hate the idea of this work." And particularly as it looked as if things had already arrived at a pitch when he would have to use force—"May God forgive me if I am wrong." He asked leave in March to go directly to Nottingham "because things look very ugly in that quarter", he told William, "and I want to get the reins in hand and not assume command in the middle of an insurrection". He was still desperately worried about Emily's cough, in case it should turn to the ever-dreaded consumption—"My God, how good for nothing a soldier is with a wife and children!"

Arrival cheered him, as did the presence of a nephew, one of his own inimitable, reliable, saving breed. "Billy is a capital ADC, so steady, so like old George." The situation was grim, but he felt more able for it. "We are in a sad state with not half enough soldiers and I fear we shall have an outbreak." He had hated separation from his family, but Em was much better when he left. "Is it not terrible to see the poor starving and arming with desperate resolve to overthrow everything?" The magistrates seemed apathetic and blind: he hoped to rouse them.

The Liberal Government had an awkwardly small majority; and in any case no wish to be repressive. Lord John Russell, Home Secretary, was essentially pacific, and in theory all for liberty; but he had a kind of Woburn-based obliviousness to the realities of life. The struggles over the Reform Bill had made him a popular leader, and his wife praised his "calm and hopeful spirit"; but of the petition of the desperate men who marched to London that harsh spring of 1839 he wrote with dreamy detachment, "There are at this time, as I am afraid there will be at most times, men . . . whose means are exceedingly scanty." There is of course scantiness and scantiness; yet Mrs Gaskell did not exaggerate. "Deep and ravaging distress prevails", the *Manchester Times* was to record; "the picture which the manufacturing districts now present is absolutely frightful. Hungry and half-clothed men are stalking through the streets begging for bread."

Because they might lead to arson, the government forbade torchlight processions in the winter of 1838–1839, but otherwise the Chartists were left very much to themselves, and *The Times* of February 12th thought it "excessive indulgence". Things hotted up in April: much drilling and arming went on in working class districts; and the government issued a proclamation against such activities, telling the magistrates and Lords Lieutenant to form and arm militias in the counties affected, and to call up special constables, also armed. The results, needless to say, were spasmodic and muddled. Threatening utterances came from the other side. "Every man", declared the Chartist William Benbow, "and every boy of twelve years of age, should have a stiletto a cubit long, to run into the guts of any who should attempt to oppose them." But Charles thought trouble was quite as likely to come through a nervous provocation by authority, and that the tenseness was due to exaggerated middle class alarm.

"Chartists are thick about Halifax, towards Leigh and Bolton", he told Robertson on April 24th. "All this comes of bad governments and a long course of misrule. Now we approach the fight and all questions as to cause drop: the whole work must be to hold our own" and maintain the social order, "but I have to deal with men whose fears are their councillors. All look to the military, no manly exertion among themselves, every magistrate calling for soldier guards." "The Chartists are bent on plunder and conflagration", he told Louisa on May 2nd. "However bad they may be, they have much to complain of. Such wild works as they would carry on must be stopped by force or our throats would all be cut; but I yet hope we may avoid it. I think it will be confined to Lancashire. God Almighty's hand rules us all and in that we must confide. That the people of England have been and are ill-treated and ill-governed is my fixed opinion, but were government to be put right with pikes at the will of a small part of the community, against the opinion of the great mass, we should be worse than ever and little better than the French revolutionists.

"I always foresaw what I fear is now coming upon us, and all this arises from the madness of Commerce and Manufactories; in short the worship of Mammon, which renders the minds of men base, their bodies feeble, and their morals bad. I have heard that the excessive improvidence of the people here exceeds belief, if this is so it is one of the consequences of manufactories, which I repeat debase man, woman, and child . . ." He seized on comfort—"Billy is as fine a lad as ever I saw and works like a horse."

Delighted though Charles was to be back in command, he was not cheered by his task. "Civil war was to him a sound of horror," William recalled, "but remembering that his father in 1798 with like commiseration for the wronged multitude and like contempt for the government of the day, had, though only a private person, stept between contending parties and staved off many terrible inflictions, he hoped to do the same." Charles had every feeling of sympathy for the distress, but none for "the folly of riotous assemblies assuming to represent the whole people of England, and a right to change laws by violence". The trouble was brought on, he considered, by the Corn Laws and the Poor Law—"Poor people! In their distress is the great danger."

At Nottingham he found "Funk is the order of the day, and there is some excuse for the people seem ferocious enough. The magistrates are divided into Whigs, Tories, and personal enmities, and every mother's son of them prepared to go to any length for his sect and creed." In the midst of all these municipal nerves and cross-currents it had been a comic relief when the Duke of Portland looked in on his way to Newmarket. "The old cock showed no fear." Urban miseries were outside Portland's province; like the Duc de Grammont in France, he would go on hunting and racing up till ten minutes before the guillotine.

Charles thought that the people might well rise, and that if they did there would be horrible bloodshed. "Poor men, they go wrongly to work," he thought of the Chartists, "they are giving vigour to the worst Toryism and the prospect is gloomy." The thought of firing on his own countrymen made him feel ill: he must defeat the rising before it began, and without killing or wounding. "This is dreadful work, would to God I had gone to Australia. At this moment," he told William, "the best hand-loom weaver can only earn five shillings a week, the price of food being such that this will not give him bread without firing, clothes, or lodging: hence a good workman in full wages must starve! And with this fact our rulers are called statesmen." The reason was clear to Charles: greed held the country in its grip. "Mammon has supplanted God: our rulers have worshipped the evil one, and evil are the results." Coming down to more immediately practical matters, he urged his two seconds-in-command to write to him freely, with any ideas or suggestions; "I am not such a vain fool as to think a general has more brains than his neighbour because his head is under the dreadful plume they have stuck in his hat! No! Write just as you think."

At evening, sitting in his cheap and comfortless lodging, he steeled himself: might he "so act that when death comes we can meet him with intrepid and undoubting hearts". Somehow, he must reconcile loyalty and honesty to his superiors, the freely elected government of his country, with mercy and justice for the poor. "God send me to go through this work as a gentleman should."

As May went on the rumours of the intended rising thickened about his ears. "Next week will be a ticklish one", he told Louisa on the 17th. "I believe and hope we shall get over it quietly. They say half a million men are to meet close to the town on Saturday next, but I am sure they will be quiet and orderly: I am not the least afraid. Both Government and Horse Guards support me well *as yet*." Fanny had behaved admirably and he loved her for it. This was no fun for her; a house in Nottingham was unobtainable and all they could find to live in were lodgings over a baker's shop in 25 Wheeler Gate, with stone-floored sitting-rooms behind; but he got no complaints and much comfort in having his family, though less in leaving them in Nottingham while he came north. If the indications of trouble grew stronger, Lou might find his whole party arriving in Green Street one morning. "There being no troops in town, my lodging may be plundered. This is between you and me and Dick. Matters look queer this last 48 hours. Mrs Koe would take Fanny and the monkeys you could stow away." He was more frightened by Emily's recurrent cough than by all the Chartists in the district.

With such low wages "no wonder they are Chartists! I had Oastler's pike in my hand yesterday, it had been given him by the Chartists.

"I must go to work." Lou's letter to Susan hadn't been at all too strong, he assured her: Susan had been so rude to Miss Rossiter that there had been a row; Emily, out riding with Charles, had told him that Susan didn't know what made her do it; something came over her with a rush. But it couldn't be allowed—Susan needed to be made sensible of her faults.

It would not be a bad thing if the magistrates were made sensible of theirs too. Why could they not defend themselves, barricade their houses and arm themselves and their servants, instead of incessantly demanding detachments of troops from him and then making no attempt to billet them safely? His troops must be kept mobile but together, not open to easy destruction in scattered small groups arrayed against thousands.

"Would I had been saved this work, produced by Tory injustice and Whig imbecility. The doctrine of slowly reforming when men are starving is of all silly things the most silly: famishing men cannot wait. And", he reiterated to William, "that the people of England have been, and are, ill-treated and ill-governed is my fixed opinion."

By May 1st he had felt his command better in hand: at first all had been darkness. "I groped about like a mole." Things were no less threatening; all that had improved was his power to contain the threat. On the 6th he thought that "within 36 hours a horrid slaughter may perhaps be the precursor of a bloody insurrection." His sympathies were with the men he might soon have to kill—"the unhappy Chartists, so sadly deluded." They went about singing:

By pride and sword your freedom strive to gain
Or make one bloody Moscow of old England's plain.

A nice piece of advice, Charles thought: he hated to see honest men deluded into thinking that massacres would solve their problems.

But could men be prevented from fighting "whose minds have been making up for it these many months? I fear not, but will try. God assist me to act justly." The magistrates, when not in a fuss about possible damage to their houses, appeared apathetic, and the country gentlemen on the whole uninterested, as though what went on in the towns was occurring in Timbuctoo. Manchester was in confusion: the mayor and the borough-reeve involved in a private fight with each other which wiped all other thoughts from their minds. There was something to be said for calling out the yeomanry, if they didn't get too carried away with themselves and precipitate a crisis by an excess of zeal. "It would strengthen the weak and faint hearted, give a high tone to public feeling, and daunt the republican portions of the community by one of those decided public expressions of loyalty which tells the world that, whatever diversity of opinion there may be as to what is good for the country, whenever the safety of the throne is endangered, all unite to crush the disloyal."

The threatening roar continued. In all, Charles had under five thousand troops; and the Chartists were said to have a quarter of a million men under arms. This he did not believe, but "a fourth of this number would destroy the country . . . This morning I hear the Chartists have told off thirty men to fall on each soldier. But I have also heard of a society among the labourers for assisting each other when out of work, where a fine is inflicted on any man who speaks about Chartism." And three days later he believed "the people are tired of the physical-force party, and if magistrates and armed associations would but give them courage they would reject the violent Chartists".

"People are misled, not bad in the mass", he announced firmly at this crisis. If the Chartists marched on London he thought to make a stand at Nottingham; but his great object was to persuade them not to. They were as capable of reason as the next man.

He did not think the great assembly would have hostile intentions, but "so many fiery spirits and bad men will be there that it is impossible to say what will take place", he told Lord Fitzroy. "If not interfered with the anger will probably evaporate in harangues and seditious language." He had entreated the borough-reeve not to interfere on Kersall Moor, but had, of course, no power to prevent him. "There is a widely spread spirit of mischief, and it must be opposed by a widely spread spirit of loyalty and self-defence. The regular forces cannot be everywhere . . . I am endeavouring to spirit the civil power here to more activity, for I find a lamentable desire to bring the soldiers and people at once in contact, as if no civil power existed." He expressed approbation of Sir Thomas White's yeomanry and their soldier-like conduct, "but I hope they will not be too ardent but keep cool and patient, remembering the innocence of most of the people they might find themselves charging."

On May 19th he had demands for troops from Bradford, Dewsbury, Barnsley, Huddersfield, Ashton-under-Lyne, Bury, Preston, and Congleton, and had barely troops enough to send a small detachment to three of these places. Lord Wharncliffe, standing out amongst the local magistrates, had come from Barnsley to tell Charles he would be responsible for that district with his yeomanry.

The day of the meeting approached, with wild rumours as to the numbers who would gather, ranging from a million to a quarter of a million in accordance with the nervous system of the reporter. Manchester's mayor and corporation continued besottedly at odds with its borough-reeve and constables. All south Manchester was quiet; but its north-eastern districts were in a seethe. Once again Charles besought the borough-reeve to allow the people their immemorial legal right to meet in peace.

He had taken pains to get a secret introduction to the Chartist leaders through Bingham, "a gentleman intimate with the Chartists if not one himself, and begged him to show them how impossible it would be to feed and move three hundred thousand men [in their projected march on London] and that armed, starving, and interspersed with villains, they must commit horrid excesses". He told Bingham that if armed crowds really did move on London, as their leaders were urging them to do, he would have to attack them; to which Bingham replied that peace had put the army out of practice and they would not be able to use their artillery.

"He was soon convinced that was nonsense, and reported my observations to the leaders. I offered him no abuse, said many Chartists who acted on principle were to be honoured, others to be pitied as acting from ignorance, and certain bitterly to repent when they saw the terrible mischief that would ensue. This I believe had a good effect." Possibly a still better effect came from Charles's secret meeting, through Bingham, with the Chartist leaders themselves. He emphasized that there was nothing unlawful in their gathering, that they were right to lay their grievances before Parliament, "and I will take care that neither soldier or policeman shall be within sight to disturb you. But meet peaceably, for if there is the least disturbance I shall be amongst you and do my duty. Now go and do yours."

"The Government", he urged the authorities, "should be prepared to consider the Charter in parliament and cultivate the good will of the people, or take measures for disarming them; there is no wisdom in letting complaints be rejected and pikes made." He was not troubled by fear of being cut in pieces by a Yorkshire mob, but horror at what he might have to do if some chance sparked off violence hung over him like a great dark cloud. Conciliating with one hand, he showed strength with the other, arranging for a reinforcing regiment to arrive in separate halves to make it look like two, making great play with the arrival of one or two more guns and with practice firings, moving cavalry about the countryside to give the impression that there were more troopers than there were. A surprising bit of luck affected him: the arrival of troops from Ireland who happened to be Highlanders. Oh the racial memories inspired in the men of northern England by that terrible kilt! "How small accidents affect men's minds and decide events . . . the 79th being in kilts terrified the Chartists more than a brigade of other troops."

Dressed in plain clothes Charles went to the great Chartist meeting on Kersall Moor, where he found "twenty-five thousand very innocent people, of whom ten thousand were women and children. The remainder might have been Chartists, expressing orderly legal political opinions pretty much like my own.

"If there were five thousand rascals wanting bloodshed and pillage it would be the outside. Fifty dragoons would have routed all that came to fight. Yet I know there were armed men among them who would quickly have got up a row if the imposing force in the barracks had not spread an alarm more powerful than their exhortations. Many a man will join a row that will not begin one, and many would begin one when he sees no force arrayed against him, who would never attempt it if he sees there must be a fight . . .

"Colonel Wemyss addressed a few of the people in high Tory oratory, and argued with a drunken old pensioner, fiercely radical and devilish sharp; in ten minutes an eighth of the whole crowd collected round Wemyss and cheered him! These certainly were not Chartists! . . . Mr. B. says the supposed increase of force decided the Chartists not to attack: thus the kilt, which was no force at all, and the division of the 10th, which was weakness, contributed largely to our security."

Charles was right in thinking that his sensible measures had averted trouble, and "the evil inevitably attending even a disciplined army". By "stirring the magistracy of Manchester to protect the locality", writes a recent authority, "by making a display of troops to overawe the district, sending personal messages to Chartist leaders tactfully warning them of the impossibility of success . . . he laboured unstintingly to prevent bloodshed . . . That the Whitsuntide crisis passed peacefully in Manchester and elsewhere is largely to the personal credit of Napier. Of the Home Office little more can be said than that it allowed the sagacious general to have his way."* As so often, the army, which was (then as now) steadily despised, traduced, and belittled throughout the years of peace, in the event was the only body with enough intelligence and coolness to save England from the bloody event.

But what a near miss! Charles gasped at the narrowness of the escape—"Good God what work! To send grape-shot from four guns into a helpless mass of fellow-citizens; sweeping the streets with fire and charging with cavalry, destroying poor people whose only crime is that they have been ill-governed and reduced to such straits that they seek redress by arms, ignorant that of all ways that is the most certain to increase the evils they complain of." No-one, not Lord John Russell and the entire Cabinet rolled into one felt more relief than Charles did—he whom his enemies so constantly accused of

* F. C. Mathers, *Chartist Studies*, ed. Asa Briggs

bloodthirstiness. "A bird escaped from a cage must have the sort of feeling I have now."

It was yet to be seen if the government would learn its lesson and use its breathing space either in granting reform or in reorganizing its civil and military law-and-order forces on a better basis.

CHAPTER XVI

Hell is Hung with Manchester Cottons

"We are all at hammer and tongs again", Charles commented gloomily, as the summer wore on. "God knows how it will all end." Nottingham had finally cured Emily's cough, and that was the one ray of light. "Everyone is very kind, I am killed with dinners here and know not how to avoid them. I am very uncomfortable in this lodging but make up my mind to it. I wish to get to Chester, clear of manufactories—My God what scenes of misery and vice and improvidence and cruelty and sickness they are. Heaven defend us from all which encourages them. If the Chartists only destroy our manufactories that alone ought to ensure their reward in this world and the next. A clergyman here told me that the greatest disgrace to a girl here is to pass the age of ten and not have a paramour! These factories are the hotbeds of ill health, wretchedness and rascality."

Family life didn't stand still, for all that; and sometimes Charles seemed to write one letter of sympathy after another. He had barely done consoling Henry for the loss of Caroline before he was writing from Carlisle about the death of Henry's youngest child. "His only comfort is that which David had", Charles told Emily. " 'He cannot come to me, but I shall go to him', and with this we must bear our losses." Henry had watched Caroline die; no grief could be more terrible than that. "Yet this blow is dreadful to a warm mind . . . We are lent to each other, not given. Henry has a firm and religious mind. He knows he can and must bear this; but there is no pain like it. May God cheer him in his bitter grief." And then William's youngest was desperately ill—"My God what suffering William and Caroline go through, of body and mind"—and Charles Robertson's child was thought by him to be dying, and again Charles poured forth affection, sympathy, faith—could anything be any good?

It must at least strengthen, cheer a little, in any case make those in agony feel that they were not alone. One must not long for death:

the powerful feeling of self-preservation implanted in everybody implied the rule of not jumping the gun in this matter. From time to time Robertson urged on him the comforts of organized religion and the sacrament of communion; but Charles's youth amidst the sectarian horrors of Ireland had forever disenchanted him with priests and parsons. "We both think precisely the same only our way of expression is different", he assured Robertson. "That is to say a belief in God and in our Redeemer Christ. That good works are the fruit of faith and the only measure of our sincerity that we can give to God or man. Adherence to the orders of Christ is our first duty and only hope of salvation, and although we do wrong yet an honest and hearty endeavour to do right, and God's mercy, will save us; and that he alone, not we ourselves, can do this.

"There is so much cant, and it sets so many against the truth." Priests, for this reason, were out. Yet for Charles, his friend Robertson, retired Artillery major, was priest. "To you I may avow my utter humility before God because you will believe it."

The Edward-Sarah row grumbled on. "Emily is very angry at me because I do *not* pity Edward Bunbury, but I do not pity him none the less. I only hope Sarah's health will not be hurt nor her prospects." He couldn't change his opinion of Edward, though Bunbury himself had acted with great prudence and calm and he was sure had prevented mischief from Emily's lack of judgment. Charles was not going to weigh in unless George, away in South Africa, asked him to. "I sincerely trust that Sarah may never marry Edward whatever his conduct was, is, or may be in future, and I imagine George will think so too." Charles only wished he had a proper place to ask her to stay in. "I am afraid she will suffer bitterly."

Fanny too was creating over John Napier's insistence that he loved Minnie Alcock and that Minnie loved him. John wouldn't do for her daughter, Fanny insisted: Charles must be firm with his nephew. In Charles's view it was Minnie who should be firm, if she felt that way: she was twenty-three, capable of taking her own decisions. John was fine: he admired him, heart and mind. They must settle their own affairs. More violent hysterics from Fanny followed this dictum.

Perhaps the stone-flagged lodgings of Nottingham did little to soothe the feelings of the new Lady Napier. Not even a life in Portsmouth lodgings with the late Captain Alcock, Royal Navy, not even the chill winds of Sheerness, the rains sweeping down St Aubyn Street, Devonport, can have prepared Fanny for the unpredictable life she led with Charles.

Charles's thoughts dwelt in love upon his brothers, upon his own family and its comparative absence of fuss and fallings out. By autumn the threat to Charles's sight had lessened, but "my poor Richard, I fear his eyes are in more danger than mine, and he has no child's voice to hear. I wish he had a pursuit, there is no happiness but in a pursuit; a house, a garden, animals. He is all honour and goodness." And his thoughts turned, as so often, to his father, Donny, in "a holy reverence for his goodness and talent and character, the feeling that we shall soon meet again". If he himself died in these troubles Charles trusted that his children's enjoyment of life would not be spoiled for long, and believed that it would not; he hoped to get away "with least pain to my wife". "How small others appear when I think of him", Charles mused on the anniversary of his father's death in October; "he cared little for those things which ordinary men seek so eagerly, he was too great, too majestic."

A visit from Henry, still grief-bound, made him feel sorry Henry was out of the Navy, "for his abilities are great and his mind active, but is losing its activity from living alone". Henry should not shut himself up to write his History. "Contact with the world can alone keep up self-confidence. He forms ideal pictures of perfection, and because he does not fill the framework holds himself cheap. Were he to work in the world he would find his own level, which is far above most men: he would thus be taught his real powers. Man ought to live an active life", Charles concluded firmly, being quite incapable of leading any other sort himself. "Christ and Socrates lived amongst men, a recluse is useless." And perhaps there was the unwritten thought that Henry should take a deep breath and marry again as George and he had done: the perfect person could never come again; but there were a great many good fish in the sea. Henry for his part thought that Charles was doing far too much; always up at five or soon after, and rarely in bed until one or two in the morning: "His purse too is pretty well pulled by these visits of inspection."

Whatever civil outrage the army might be called on to act or to face, Charles rejoiced at being back with them. The pace of change, the lack of technical development, was such that he could be out of touch with the army for a quarter of a century and come back to find it just as he had left it. "Just returned from a review on Kersall Moor", he told Robertson in mid-June. "I had 3 regts. of infantry, one of cavalry and 2 field guns. I had not commanded since I left the 102nd in Bermuda 26 years ago but it is so ground into me that I was—*entre nous*—more at my ease than 2 of my young commanders if not three." Before this he had been writing since five in the morning with no time to read over—certainly army paper-work had increased, and his official letters cost him £10 a day in postage (for which of course he had no allowance) and they left him no time for private correspondence.

He dearly hoped not to have to take his soldiers into action, but, by the end of July at Nottingham, "I fear these poor people will be led into a contest with the troops." The magistrates were really *very* odd, at Loughborough they had sent urgent messages for troops as "life and property were in danger", but when Charles's troop of dragoons arrived the young officer in charge found that confusion reigned, and though no law was being broken the magistrates had all run away, leaving the town in charge of three aged men acting as constables. These tottering Dogberrys had been much surprised by the dragoons' arrival.

"Cries for troops reach me from all directions and I cannot furnish them, yet imagine if any town to which I refuse troops is burned, and, if I do give them, Nottingham is burned in their absence and my guns taken? This is no sinecure, my dear friend", Robertson was told. Charles's eyes were again so bad that he could hardly open them, and the dread of his mother's blindness was in his mind. But "it is not what happens to us but how we bear it that signifies". "All quiet now", he reported in a moment's lull early in August. "I do not imagine we shall be so for long. The causes of discontent remain."

The causes of pleasure remained also, one great one being the soldiers, in whose company he delighted. Had he lived too long among women, with governess disputes, and stepmother disputes, and too many kerfuffles and what he called fiddle-faddle concerns? Naughty Susan was in trouble again, between her stepmother and Miss Rossiter; Charles decided it was just her age—fifteen—and that she would grow out of it. Since he was in Yorkshire it was a pity he did not advertise for a governess. He might have got one of the Brontës, and that would have been a fruitful encounter for all concerned.

His journal, his mother, Emily, Lou, and William, receive the sad side of Charles: reading the journal and his letters one would never know that he was widely reported to be exceedingly good company, much loved by his staff, full of jokes, spirits, and funny stories. He deplored the muddle of army management, six heads instead of one at the top—"God help the English army among so many cooks"—(only God and Florence Nightingale were to help it in the Crimea in fourteen years' time), and there was far too much fiddle-faddle and paper work and reading "drivelling correspondence". But how splendid officers and men still were! The chestnut troop of Horse Artillery, beautiful as ever, how celebrated it had been under Sir Hew Ross all through the Peninsular, when at the desperate action on the Coa river they had fought a French battery across the river and "beaten Johnny Crapaud out of the field". The death of Sir Alexander Dickson later in the year saddened Charles, as did this event's slight repercussion—"Surely the leader of that terrible artillery which thundered through those great battles cannot die and be forgotten like an ordinary man? I hope England will not let him pass away unnoticed. England had before beaten France, but when was France what she was when Wellington overthrew her armies?" "The men who fought in Spain drop fast", he mourned to Sir Hew Ross, who had been one of them: yet there was consolation—"The immortality of fame which Wellington has cast over us like a mantle of light will endure."

More and more he wanted to live once again, and for longer, among them. Many of the young men filled him with hope—Colonel Cairncross behaving so calmly in the riots at Bolton-le-Moors; the humane and cool conduct of Captain Bush, who had refused to fire on the crowds when all the civilians were crying out *Slaughter*! "The soldiers are all staunch to the Queen, no disloyal feelings, no hesitation about them, all resolute and ready, nay even eager for a fight, but averse to fire on unarmed people. The troops are all that their country could wish; humane, obedient, bold."

At Lancaster there was Surgeon Orr, the military vet who had looked after Charles's horse Blanco on his voyage home, and appreciated him to the point at which he had asked the captain of the ship to say a prayer over him when he died and was buried at sea. The ship's captain had been horrified: "Yet I am sure Blanco has a soul as good as most masters of merchant ships." Blanco had shared the starvation and the battles of the Peninsular, brave in war, playful in peace—"How I did love him! Noble excellent animal, you were good and brave and faithful as ever charger was." At York were the cavalry, unchanged since the day they learnt their lesson at Bannockburn, and about to learn a worse one at Balaclava in their half-a-league-onward at the Russian battery: "They are excellent as to non-commissioned officers and privates; but their officers really know little beyond fox-hunting, horse-dealing, dancing and shooting; they are however a very fine set of young men, extremely clever and zealous also when put to their work perforce. Caring nothing for their profession and thinking it a bore, they know nothing of it. They are nevertheless the makings of the finest cavalry in the world," he exulted to William, "being full of spirit and talent, and ready for anything but the dull routine of duty. Few of them mean to stay in the army and they will not study. I could indeed make anything of them in a camp, but it is vain to try in a district embracing nearly the half of England. Two things are certain: they will do their work with spirit when brought to the mark; and the devil himself can't make them read."

Continually the young reassured him, made him feel that England's greatness was not done, as his contemporaries so frequently insisted. What about Lieutenant Huband of the 8th Hussars, caught in a horribly tricky situation at Bradford but acting with "full intelligence and energy"? Stupidities of course still went on: the promotion of Colonel X, "not a bad man, only one with a hundred horse-power temper and the judgement and ability of an old's maid's tea-kettle" over splendid Campbell of the 98th. But Major Hope Grant of the 9th Lancers, as live and intelligent as they come, provoked from Charles the exclamation that there were no officers on earth so fine as English gentlemen.

"What is glory, why do we love it?" he asked himself. "Why love those who fought by our side in those dread contests in Spain? Aye, love even those who fought against us. What a fond bond of union is throat-cutting. Verily we love it and devilish queer animals we are therefore. The fact is men in the field are generally healthy, strong, and full of spirits, life is enjoyed and dangers past are bonds of union . . ."

In July in the middle of all this he had been summoned to an investiture; and after the miseries and squalor of the northern manufacturing towns the Court seemed to Charles needlessly lavish and trifling; and the evidence of time's relentless hand on old friends was saddening—"worn, meagre, grey-haired, stooping old men", who had been so tigerish, so laughing, so bright-haired in Spain. "There was our pretty young Queen, receiving our homage, and our old shrivelled bodies and grey heads were bowed before her throne, intimating our resolution to stand by it as we had stood when it was less amiably filled. I wonder what she thought of us old soldiers? We must have appeared to her like wild beasts, I dare say she looked on us as she looks at the animals in the Zoological Gardens. Lord Hill is old, and has lost his teeth; poor Sir John Jones looks like a ghost; and Sir Alexander Dickson is evidently breaking." And he thought how once these men had directed the British thunders of war.

Thunders of another kind were rolling from the Horse Guards. It was nothing to do with Sir Charles if the people of northern England were starving; and would he please confine himself to his job? Even Lord Fitzroy Somerset seemed to think it was " 'only a passing discontent', and he is so clever a fellow, and so good a fellow, that to own the truth he almost staggered me". "Did the government not realize that the example of one rising might be followed thoughout England; for the agitation is so general no-one can tell the effect of a single shot; all depended upon avoiding collision. I met the magistrates every week and impressed on them the necessity of not attacking the people, of letting them meet and speak also, as they have a perfect right to do. That if any orator excited them to overt acts of treason, burning, murder, he should be arrested *after* the crowd had dispersed, that if any went armed we could seize them as being armed. Otherwise to let the people alone. This line we pursued."

Urging the government "to meet the evil with making concessions on the one hand, and organize a strong constabulary on the other, (what sort of a law must it be that has to be upheld by soldiers at every turn?)", he was told by his superiors, "I suggest you avoid all remarks having allusion to political questions . . . it is better that you should confine yourselves to what is strictly your province as military men." "They are fearful of looking facts in the face or of involving themselves in difficulty", he told William: it was not a bad description of Lord Melbourne's ministry.

Manchester in particular was badly in need of an independent police force; the present men were wholly under the cotton-manufacturers' thumb. Undiscouraged by his snub, Charles told the Under-Secretary of State that concessions must be made to people's feelings, or "of a sanguinary collision there is great danger finally, though not now". He urged once again that the soldiers should be kept in strong detachments; he had found forty-two troopers quartered in twenty-six billets in Halifax, "small detachments could be cut off and butchered, the soldiers would lose confidence. The rebels' defeat finally would be certain, but much blood would be shed which need not be shed. No man can measure the limits of the present danger", he insisted, in a vain attempt to stir the administration up into doing something, "but the troops form a strong barrier round the throne". Don't, he urged, in mild terms, muck about with them.

The warm weather of June and a revival of trade had brought a lull; Charles set off round his diocese. "Lancaster delighted me . . . Westmoreland and its lakes were delightful . . . those gems of bright waters in their rude mountain setting, bursting on one's sight in fresh changing forms with all their lights and shadows, exhilarate the spirits and give a calmness and happiness to the aching mind which seems like the peace of Heaven . . . I could live on the banks of one of those lakes and feel happy . . ." How far from the grimy miserable manufacturing towns, with their tight-fistedness and hardness and greed for brass—"Nothing happens to mankind that is irksome but what he himself has chosen." He went on to "Merry Carlisle, the old castle spoiled by foolish people; far-famed York and its cathedral. How many hypocrites have entered there to preach and blaspheme and oppress the poor . . . What a magnificent pile! I would like to live near it, to go in and pray and be calm if but for an hour. I see wrong and dare not put it right; and that is called command."

In July a cotton mill near Manchester was burned; but everyone from Lord John Russell downward insisted that the storm was blown over. "You and I", Charles told William, "know the remedy, but were we to tell them, the only question in their minds would be whether Bedlam or Newgate was the place for us. They mistake palliatives and expedients for remedies. At times I am tempted to give it up, because the real state of the country is known to me without the power of doing real good. We are resolved to sacrifice everything to the *cotton lords* . . . we neither remove real evils nor prepare for their effects. What does our present distress arise from in Lancashire? The cotton lords work as little raw cotton as possible because they want to compel the Yankees to lower its price; they know Jonathan wants money and must sell . . . meanwhile, they starve thousands of wretches." Added to this, the soldiers, upon whom all depended, were ill-lodged and ill-fed. The Under-Secretary, in reply to Charles's last, had come up with the suggestion that they should send down Lord Strafford to advise him.

"That Byng is a good fellow, said a soldier of the Guards in my hearing in 1803. He is, said another, whats of him, the most part is boots and cocked hat—he was very young. He shall not be my dry-nurse, better or worse. I am ready to give up but while here no privy councillor over me—thats as flat as a pancake." No, repeat No, political commissars.

By July 26th, "the pot boils every way". Rumours of war from Carlisle, merry no longer, from Newcastle, from all parts of Lancashire. Demands for troops from the county magistrates—"a miserable set generally: they insult the people, are hated, and in every alarm grow frightened. As matters stand I am for a strong police, but the people should have universal suffrage—it is their right . . . Good government consists in having good laws well obeyed. England has abundance of bad laws, but is every man to arm against every law he thinks bad? No! Bad laws must be reformed by the concentrated reason of the nation acting on the legislature, not by the pikes of individuals acting on the bodies of the executive."

On July 30th came "Alarms! Trumpets! Magistrates in a fuss. Troops! Troops! Troops! North, South, East, West, Lord how they make me swear. The people are not ready for a fight though: there may be bloodshed and burnings, but no fighting. I have indeed nineteen regiments, but also half England to garrison and defend . . . Oh, the old state carriage, how it shakes and jolts in the deep ruts of folly and quagmires of knavery. We shall upset it at last and God help the passengers." But at the meetings every night in the market-place there was "good sense talked by the speakers. My advice to the magistrates is not to interfere unless the peace be broken—why should they? When men assemble to express their political opinions it is unjust as well as foolish to disperse them."

But by August 6th the long hot summer was hotting up again. "The plot thickens. Meetings increase and are so violent and arms so abound that I know not what to think." At nearby Welbeck the Duke of Portland, now with his ear close to the ground, told Charles he had no doubt of the intended rising. "Poor people, they will suffer", Charles exclaimed with passion. "They have set all England against them and their physical force and they talk of their hundreds of thousands of men. Who is to move them when I am dancing round them with cavalry and pelting them with cannon-shot? And when in desperation and despair they broke to fly, how would they bear five regiments of cavalry careering through them? Poor men! Poor men! how little they know of physical force."

Ominous hush continued, and still nothing happened; though on August 11th "the silly magistrates of Mansfield are in labour and a troop of dragoons has gone off to deliver them of their fears". Three days later they demanded that the yeomanry should be called out, but Charles refused—"If the Chartists want a fight they can be indulged without yeomen, who are over zealous." July had seen a terrible row in Birmingham (outside Charles's area) caused by the violence of the authorities. Why had they sent London police there? There should be, thought Charles, a full enquiry instead of an increase in panic, more prosecutions, and savage sentences.

In the midst of all this Charles was threatened by his doctor with blindness. "My God what an awful thought, it makes my blood run cold. Yet . . . all that a brave man can do is to look his trials in the face without flinching and thank God they are no worse." But if the suffocating feeling in his nose came on too? "I will repine not even at the loss of sight if spared that horror of horrors. I will not think of it." The sacred month of no work, proclaimed by the Chartists, had failed to come off; and an unnatural calm had fallen. Some ring-leaders were seized, and the Home Office was convinced that the whole thing was over, but "the haggard faces of the poor suffice to tell any observant man that all is yet alive; a stern look of discontent, of hatred to all who are rich, a total absence of merry faces among the manufacturing poor: a sallow tinge and dirty skins tell of suffering and brooding . . . Yet often have I talked with scowling-visaged fellows till the ruffian went from their faces, making them smile and at ease; their looks of sad and deep thought are not natural, poor fellows.

"I was mad not to go out as Governor of Australia. I could have founded a great kingdom, and by this time my whole plan would have been in operation—a systematic education, universal suffrage, vote by secret ballot, annual parliaments, abolition of primogeniture as regards land." All this was almost exactly what the Chartists were demanding; and everything else they asked—pay for members of Parliament and no property qualification—has since become an accepted part of life. Nothing had been settled, Charles told Portland in September, because a few ringleaders had been caught and punished.

"Men are restless and discontented with poverty in manufacturing places", he wrote in his journal. "They have all its suffering and have not the principal pleasures which make men content under it—health, enjoyment of country scenes, country air, interest in the seasons and in nature . . . The countryman worships God, the manufacturer worships gold, which alone can relieve him and his sickly family from the misery they endure." What was there in the towns for them but cards, the gin palace, revolution? Who succoured them, cared for them, bothered about them? Not, a hundred times not, the owners of the cotton mills, or the Poor Law overseers, all of whom were uncontrolled despots and corrupted by their power. (He hoped, incidentally that he himself wouldn't get corrupted by his own power, not that he had very much.) Smoke blackened the air of Manchester, starving men trudged its streets. "Hell may be paved with good intentions but it is assuredly hung with Manchester cottons.

"Our prosperity has not a foundation on sense or honesty", he mourned over England. "The riches of a country do not altogether consist of money but in just government and a happy people."

The gloom was not without its rays of light, mostly contributed by a few intelligent people. Parson Hamilton of Sheepshead displayed "a just course between the effervescence of an alarmist and the stagnation of those who will see no danger," and Mr Thompson of Bradford kept a clear head and refused to be bullied by a mob. Charles was stirring up the mayor of Nottingham, Rowarth, to take measures to relieve starvation—"The streets of this town are horrible. The poor starving people go about by twenties and forties, begging, but without the least insolence; and yet some rich villains, and some foolish women, choose to say they try to extort charity. It is a lie, an infernal lie, nothing can exceed the good behaviour of these poor people, except it be their cruel sufferings."

But Mayor Rowarth was excellent; together they put out an appeal and raised £4,000, an action instantly condemned by the Poor Law authorities as likely to encourage idleness. Then there were the banking Wrights—"one family here that would save a city from God's wrath; a better fellow than Wright never rolled in riches". And Rowarth "joins me in all my opinions as to the thrice accursed new poor law, its bastilles and its guardians. Lying title! They guard nothing; not even their own carcasses, for they so outrage misery that if a civil war comes they will be immediately sacrificed." He had seen them turn away a starving old man, telling him to come back two days later; and in midwinter a woman with two tiny children and another imminent, saying "Good or bad, tell me what to do?" had had the door shut in her face. "They give outdoor relief everywhere in the manufacturing districts," it was true, "but they still separate parents and children which the people will not bear and they are right."

The revolution took a peculiarly English course, which perhaps prevented it from being a revolution. At the height of the August crisis most of the magistrates disappeared for the grouse-shooting, thus preventing anyone from being actually sentenced; and in November when Dr Taylor was preaching revolution Sunday after Sunday to his Yorkshire congregation—"I have seen revolution in Greece and France and shall see one in England in three weeks"—the borough magistrates declared he was outside their jurisdiction, and the local magistrate had moved to another part of the country where the hunting was better, so that no arrest could be made. Most English of all were Charles's experiences just when feeling ran highest in late July: a small peaceful procession assembling itself in Nottingham Market Square caused the mayor such concern that he besought Charles to appear with some dragoons while he read out the Riot Act. As soon as it had finished assembling itself, the procession moved off. There was something so indescribably funny about the mayor in his chain solemnly continuing to read the Riot Act to an empty space, with a few surprised women looking out of their doors, that Charles started to get the giggles. But the mayor's blood was up; he found another harmless crowd and told it to disperse, and when it declined to do any such thing, he told Charles to charge it with his dragoons. But Charles by this time had lost all control of his facial muscles and was laughing fit to bust, the dragoons all started laughing too, the crowd delightedly joined in, and the whole incipient Peterloo collapsed in a gale of mirth.

But how much longer would this saving good humour prevail over the tightened belts of the men, over the pale women making do with so little, the children drooping with hunger in their sodden houses?

"I found this distinguished officer lodged with his wife and daughters in the upper stories of a butcher's shop", Captain Hope Grant reported of Charles, about now. "He was a noble fellow; he had nothing but his pay and did not choose to get into debt." Another young officer, complaining of his quarters, was given short shrift by Charles—"Never put into a list of real grievances things which are imaginary. I have been living for nine months in a lodging with stone floors, and my wife and daughters bear them very well. Soldiers must not be delicate; my own room is seven feet by ten and is stone-floored." In the spring he noted in a letter to William that his well-recommended American stocks were dwindling away to nothing. And he was finding the job very expensive, endless journeys and no allowances. His American stocks were so low that his £300 a year of private means was dwindled almost to £0 a year. Necessary travelling round his command cost him another £100, he found—from Nottingham to Chester, to Manchester, through Lancashire to Carlisle, across to Newcastle-upon-Tyne and South through Yorkshire and the Tees and Humber towns and so back to Nottingham. He had spent £50 out of his own pocket in making a survey of the district's barracks, and shocking the most of them were too. He "found those of Rochdale, Todmorden, Blackburn, Bolton-le-Moor and Wigan infamous. Strange that when all depends upon the troops, the government makes them uncomfortable and discontented both as to quarters and food—they complain of having too little to eat, and this in the middle of disaffection and when every effort is being made to corrupt them."

The darkness of early winter was not lit by intelligence from on high. The pettiness of party politics in the face of so much misery deeply riled Charles. Even in this crisis the authorities couldn't seem able to unite behind the one great rock of stability and strength, the monarchy. The Tories were sulking because they thought the Whigs, via Lord Melbourne, had put the young Victoria permanently in their pockets. At what he had hoped would be a non-party dinner in Yorkshire—"the ordinaries"—the loud acclamations at the first toast, Church and State, alerted him to its being a Tory gathering, though Lord Scarborough, the Whig Lord Lieutenant, was presiding. "The next toast was the Queen. Glasses were filled, but not a sound of applause followed: her Majesty's health was drunk in significant silence. No man cried God bless her, except myself." His chance came when his own health was called, "with long flattering speeches". Charles rose to his feet and proceeded to let his audience have it. "In my reply I laid emphasis on the devotion of the army to the *Queen*."

In November some of the younger members even of this loyal institution let him down. A Mr Proby had "used opprobrious language about the Queen" at a public dinner; and not a soul had protested, Charles heard, though a lot of young cavalrymen had been present. "Allow their sovereign to be reviled in their presence—What! Officers sitting quietly to hear a young Queen abused! What should she have done to merit this?" Charles stormed; but the officers of the 20th asserted firmly that they had been at the other end of the table and hadn't heard a word Proby said.

If the Tories went on like this they would find themselves landed in a republic; and what, after all, was republicanism? "Let us suppose the whole people wanted and could force a republic. What would result? A desperate struggle between the manufacturing and landed interests, ending in a civil war, to be decided finally by a military chief who would not be fool enough to wear a hat when a crown was in his hand."

The army was loyal to the crown, and not to Whigs, Tories or Radicals, and this was all that held the country together at times like these. "Yet an army is no joke and the soldiers well know that the game is in their hands. [At Hull the soldiers and the crowd had once joined together to thrash the police.] A private of the 81st put a letter in the Bradford paper plainly saying so, yet professing the greatest loyalty, which I am convinced the soldiers feel. There is but one thing that controls a standing army, viz., the will of a sturdy and united loyal nation. Let that be removed and the soldier is master: he may use his power well or ill, but he is master." Yet the army was stinted of bare necessities. "The devil was sick, the devil a monk would be", Charles had written furiously to Sir Hew Ross on August 28th: "Just so with the magistrates all over the north. When the Chartists put them in a funk, Oh barracks! yes, as many as you please. When they get soldiers and the Chartists are quiet, really we can't afford barracks, they are too costly. I do not understand how gentlemen, having due regard for promises, can retrograde in this fashion . . . Show them this letter. At Mansfield and Loughborough they have performed their promises like gentlemen; but your cocks of the north are moss-troopers and want Belted Will among them again." Only York's cavalry barracks were good. "What mad economy", he wrote next spring, "to have bad barracks for troops:

health, spirits, discipline, everything suffers, even their loyalty." The 96th in good barracks, were all healthy: the 79th were pallid, with bad chests and numbers in hospital; they were lodged in an airless mill. "This is one of the ways in which poor factory children are destroyed."

It was a long cold winter; and no less politically hot than the summer —"I am tired of folly above and below." The Duke of Wellington told William that his political object was to heal the dissensions of the time, in which cause he was prepared to forgive Whig iniquities; a piece of news which delighted his brother—"Yet he is an oak", Charles thought. Could he bend to the mood of the times? No good old Portland telling him that the trouble could be stopped by arresting O'Connor, "one of many leaders and amongst the more moderate. Dr. Taylor is the most violent, and wishes, nothing more, to see O'Connor out of the way. Taylor frequently exhorts the multitude to the use of arms. The Chartists keep their arms, we may suppose they intend to use them." Bradford still seethed, and at Newport in Wales, which was outside Charles's command, this November brought an outbreak in which nine Chartists were killed. "Everywhere agitation: alas, with good cause. Want and misery, all that man can suffer they suffer." "If the government means to defend the throne it must make preparation by giving the people their rights, being ready also to resist outrage and defend social order by having a strong police in every large town" (making dead sure it was *not* paid and run by the local factory bosses to assist them in grinding down their employees).

He was warned against assassination. But if the Chartists shot him from behind a hedge, so what, as far as their cause went? "The magistrates have in reserve 164 other major generals, all anxious to be employed", and if those were all scuppered, "it would only be a godsend to the colonels." He thought a mixed force best. "If the Chartists take proper means of fighting in a town, we know cavalry can do little better than get out with all possible speed", he told Sir Hew Ross. He had gone on and on at the government about abuses, about relief, about proper barracks, concentration of troops, but "I am shackled by, *Will be fully considered*—there is not such a pair of manacles in Newgate as that sentence." In December he had "certain intelligence that many sales of gunpowder have been made to countrymen this week. Poor fellows! No wonder. But the whole quantity sold would not furnish more than 8000 cartridges. Poor wretches, they surely will not provoke with such a miserable provision . . . I am rather uneasy about Bradford, but the hussars have been re-inforced by infantry from Hull . . . Fireballs and caltrops are being prepared here [Nottingham] and at Sheffield for an outbreak—pretty Christmas gambols!"

Yet the government seemed convinced that the whole business was over and that they need trouble themselves no further; because Lord John Russell had acted sensibly in managing to imprison or transport some of the more dangerous ringleaders without provoking an outbreak. "A few miserable violent fools and some resolute knaves have been put down, or rather checked by the array of force exhibited against their mad acts: but the Chartist spirit is not broken, it has only been made cautious and therefore perhaps stronger."

CHAPTER XVII

A Passage to India

January of 1840 brought no noticeable improvement. Trouble at Sheffield; "feeble, badly arranged, and base", Charles thought it; no lives were lost, but "one poor dissenting preacher badly wounded, shot by the insurgents"; then there was a fire at Barnsley barracks, "attack baffled by the good sense and presence of mind of Lieutenant Yates of the 1st Dragoons"; and next Peter Bussey, "the great moderate leader of the Chartists, fleeing for his life from Bradford where the extremists threatened to murder him because he would not join in a town-burning project". On January 16th came the anniversary of Corunna—"Oh that I should have outlived that day to be at war with my own countrymen!" Charles groaned. "Better be dead than live to see a civil war. But, I repeat it, Chartism cannot be stopped, God forbid that it should; what we want is to stop the letting loose a large body of armed cut-throats upon the public. My wish is to prevent an outbreak, not to provoke one." The police were getting steadily better, and he rejoiced at their sense and coolness.

The Chartists thought, he was told, that in a march on London they could live on the rich: would they never realize that there weren't enough rich to go round, and that if there were, they would form the majority and thus be unassailable? All that the dispossessed could do by *force* was to torment the majority and make life wretched for all—never could they win. "Misery is running riot through the greatest part of this district", he told William; and he thought that the good sense and good heart of Mayor Rowarth had alone prevented Nottingham from being burnt to the ground. The cruelties and separations enforced by the new Poor Law were really inflaming men. "The hatred to this law is not confined to Chartists nor to the poor, it creates Chartists, it makes them sanguinary: they mean to spare no-one who has a good coat if they once get to work: in short it is all hell, or likely to be so in England."

And he wished that Lord Westminster, instead of sending him a haunch of venison, would eat one with him and be told what a state his people in the Isle of Man were in over their new shilling, worth less to them than their old one of fourteen pence. Could anyone so rich as a Grosvenor ever understand the poor and how intensely twopence mattered to them? Yet men like Mayor Rowarth really redeemed a city; he was worth a host, so zealous, temperate, and active, and Lord Normanby was a staunch fellow.

Charles was a great one for anniversaries, and the old revolution of two hundred years back tinged his mind with its lurid colours. "This day," he recorded on January 30th of 1840, "my great great great grandfather Charles the First, was be-nobbed; and well he deserved it: he was as jesuitical hypocritical a rascal as ever wore a crown; a bad king and a bad soldier. He died with pluck, God rest his soul." And Charles, indirectly called after him through his mother's well-loved nephew, Charles James Fox, hoped to do the same, should the need arise, as he thought in these dark January days that it very well might.

Touring Lancashire in the spring, with rheumatism brought on by riding his many night patrols, he felt very ill. His eyes streamed, and "I must swear at rheumatism, in the face of all the saints terrestrial and celestial." At Burnley was a handsome landlady and her three pretty maids—"such beauties, my eyes have been much better since I looked at them"—but at Manchester hundreds of letters awaited him, and influenza, both of which made him feel iller. "I know not what ails me, but I have a fearful depression not to be shaken off. Yet I must work, my pay from the public goes on and so must I: better die honest than live a rogue. My pay comes out of these poor men's pockets and not to work is to cheat them." At Halifax he felt so bad that after working all day he went to bed with opium—then prescribed as freely as aspirin now is—"called by doctors morphine, but opium is opium", Charles admitted candidly.

In April he was back in Nottingham, still with a sore throat and cold, "but I daresay I got over the influenza better than by coddling", he told Louisa. "I am delighted at William's immortal work being finished"; though he feared that William had been really ill. He wrote to William urging him to start writing again as soon as he felt able for it, and offering to pay for the publication of anything William felt he couldn't afford himself.

William answered thankfully, but doubted if he would write

anything else—"I am getting constantly weaker and have continual pain and the prospect of more." He was longing to write about China but did not think it would make any impression "on a public which seems to have decided beforehand that we have a right to beat and ill-use the Chinese and that it will not be more difficult to do so than if they were South Sea Islanders. The expedition to Cabul also is looked upon as great and beneficial." William thought we were in a fair way to risk all we had in the east—"We have quarrelled with Persia, we have disputes to settle with Nepaul and Burma, and we have made war upon China, a nation of nearly four hundred millions of people fifteen thousand miles off, and this on the supposition that they are fools", which there was no earthly reason to suppose they were. He thought the Cabul expedition very ill-conceived—"It has opened India to Russia's ambitions. What you say about an Irishman commanding an Irish regiment is quite true: they are always bad"; one minute ferociously insisting on their dignity and the next joining in to foment trouble.

Ill or not, in the election William supported the candidature of the radical Roebuck at Bath with no less verve than of yore. On the hustings William's attacks on the shortcomings of the Whig ministers were greeted by roarings and hootings from the Whigs, but "at least 5,000 people called on me to go on", William reported rather wildly. " 'That is fake', one of the Whigs called out; I told him I had proof of its truth. 'That is falsehood also,' " and the man in question had sprung on to the platform; "so I knocked him over and went on with my speech." Roebuck got in, all the same. "Duncan behaved very well, he seems an honest fellow and much more than a Whig song writer."

The Chartists had not been appeased by the departure of the moderate Peter Bussy. "They now want to burn towns, with all the sick, and infants, and aged! All this has been provoked, but sane men cannot join in such bloody work . . . I had positive information of an intended general attempt to fire all our barrack. Our officers were either worn out by constant threats, or over-anxious, and were harassing our men, who on the other hand, were, though perfectly loyal, making long strides in liberal opinions; I however never say this," Charles told William, "because you can have no idea of the touchiness I have to deal with in some quarters."

Charles's return to Nottingham was greeted by the news that "a poor and extravagant government will do none of the things I have proposed for the soldier: my report will be thrown away." In April the Chartists were on the boil again, this time at Newcastle. "Will there be an insurrection? My position will be personally very awkward. I am not afraid of myself, but a great deal of my masters." Yet at Chester in May there was "all the world and his wife racing. The scene is beautiful, the old walls overlook the course, the old river Dee glides on his course . . . Those who go to the course have some fun, but those who hang over the Row-balconies all day like old clothes, see nothing, hear nothing." Quiet or not, "Chartism goes on silently, but we shall have a quiet summer for trade is reviving a little, and the people are patient beyond conception; they are a fine race and it is a sin to govern them so ill. Some great convulsion is approaching the world . . ."

It was a convulsion that he both longed for and dreaded. Some change must and should come. "When a press is in full activity bamboozling must die a natural death", he hoped. "Truth is on the march, sadly shackled indeed still by ancient follies, but the press will set her free, and the next hundred years will produce more change in the condition of man than the last thousand", he accurately predicted. "What separation will there be when we travel fifty miles an hour? Will not a thousand motives produce union of interest between countries now divided by distance, is not nationality wearing away, provincialism almost ceased?" Yet an instinct warned him that technology, like patriotism, is not enough.

The new and overwhelming greed appalled him: again and again over these years he exclaims, "We are in the grip of the devil." England was obsessed by the worship of Mammon and by the fierce anger such worship aroused. The mill-owners who would not pay their workmen enough even for food enraged Charles himself above measure—"God forgive me, but sometimes they tempt me to wish they and their mills were burned together." A visit to Nantwich had brought to mind happier days for England, "when there were no cotton manufactories with their long chimneys; when men worked in the fields and were robust, and fit for war and happy in peace; when they thought of nature when they laboured, and breathed pure air among her works. Now they breathe smoke, wheeze cotton fuzz, and only think of gin at the palace." One could be happy with little in the country, Charles thought, inclined as he was to judge by his own minimum wants. But towns seemed to him "all misery, poverty, uncertainty of wages, and grasping greed".

Life in those shoddy little back-to-back houses was inconceivably dull. For the ex-countrymen who filled them there was to be no more of the fun of field and stream, of May-day rites and village-green games, of Easter gambols at seed-time and the bucolic joys of harvest-home. Rowlandson's picture of this last, though doubtless its innocence and happiness is as much exaggerated as was the squalor and degradation he elsewhere paints, still conveys a warm co-operative simplicity—the welcoming farmer at the entry of his hospitable barn, the parson with his violin leading the harvest home, the dancing peasants and lovers, the heavy wains, the little boys with cherub limbs bearing their sheaves of corn. Sentimentalized, but basically real. In the towns there was as yet no choice between gin and the evangelical minister: all pleasures of the flesh save those arising out of greed were frowned upon.

Silently over the last fifty years, a revolution more total and profound than any dreamed or willed by individuals had been at its subtle work; engineered by no group, planned by no band of hopeful dreamers met together in an attic. Feared and hated by many besides the poet Blake and the soldier Charles, like a thief in the night it had stolen up and taken over under its own momentum—industrial revolution, like a whirlpool sucking men away from the land and into the factories, away from growing things and into the making of all things by machine. Infinitely increasing the comfort, ease, and pleasures of life, broadening horizons, changing the very nature of human existence, it would leave them with an inexplicable sense of confinement and unease.

Men would be filled with the fullness of life, and left mysteriously empty. Enormously increased and enriched, the human race would come to feel indefinably poor. Upon rich and poor alike this revolution would in time lavish gifts beyond the dreams of pampered Bourbon princes; health, wealth, education, mobility; comforts and conveniences none had ever dreamed of having; and leave in existence an enormous number of objects they would soon never dream of being without. There was an inevitablity about it all, as of a self-propelled and powerful steam-roller. It would make straight a path in the wilderness of poverty and ill-health, and roll the terrain so flat that nothing henceforth would grow there. It was bounty from heaven, wearing the chains of hell.

Like Mrs Gaskell's cotton-operative, Charles was no believer in equality, which he thought must always be a sentimental sham. Justice, mercy, fairness—yes; but he had no wish to see the infinite variety of humanity racked and chopped on any bed of Procrustes. He believed that most people, "where a man's toil gives sufficient clothes, food, and lodging for himself and his family, with a cottage and garden to interest him, will not envy rich men. They feel they have enjoyments, some, nay most, beyond the power of riches to give, and many which riches take away." If they felt differently they could rise by "time, frugality, and honesty"; for if they got there through greed and envy it would breed them no content.

In the old world, where most of the population lived by the land, strangers might be deceived but participants were not: all the yes-my-lording and very-good-my-lording did no more than mask a close knowledge between man and man, and a felt equality in value as a soul, whatever the grades in importance or the differences in treatment. They were together, against famine and bitter frost or parching weather. When it came to getting in the hay or the corn, all but the grandest worked and ate side by side. Pompous, arbitrary, hunting-mad, and frequently drunk the squire might be, but he was, perforce, *concerned*; and more likely to be the doing-good-by-stealth-where-it-was-most-needed Matthew Bramble, than the vain indifferent Sir Walter Elliot. Nobody starved at his gates as they starved in the towns; it would be too bad for his image; and the story of what happened to Dives had been lammed into him since infancy.

But now both Charles and the cotton-weaver knew that some fatal rift had opened between man and man; that an argumentative and uneven but happy marriage was going on the rocks. Divorce was become certain, though the decree might not be made absolute for many years. In those small communities of the village in which most Britons lived, everybody had had a part and a lot in life, an identity, a standing, and a pride in that standing, whatever it might be. All were valuable to each other—cobbler, stocking-weaver, ploughboy, wheelwright, smith—and all were valued. But now, in the great industrial towns, individual value was no more. Disraeli's two nations would here confirm their being, an estrangement that came from lack of communication between bitter workmen and remote boss and was underlined by brutal foremen; the evil seeds of repression and envy; life as competition, as a rat-race without starter, judge or stewards, and the smartest alecs for winners. Here socialism was born of bitter need, the class-war here was cradled, and jealousy exalted into a religion. This was where the hating had to start.

To recover, the British people would need all their redoubtable qualities, all the bounty of their good-humour and their salty native wit, all their imperviousness to publicists self-righteously and incessantly belittling their country and selling it short (for reasons obscurely seen by them as good), forever chiselling at that basic belief in themselves that countries need as much as human beings. British roots were deep; they would survive; but parching times were nigh. Corn Laws would in due course be repealed, easing their hunger but driving ever more of them from the land; conditions would be improved by the Factory Acts brought in by Lord Shaftesbury, one of those interfering landed aristocrats so deeply deplored by the *Manchester Guardian*; the Chartist movement as such would peter out in a grand march from Kennington to Parliament in 1848, to which not enough people came and those that did were too discouraged by the heavy rain to protest at their dispersal (though a nervous Home Office had urged Queen Victoria and Prince Albert to go away, and they had departed protestingly to Cowes). Yet the gulf was set.

"The English are a quiet people" was Wellington's comment on this last event; which was true enough. But they did not feel the less. Neither the misery of the forties, nor the callousness that did so little to relieve it, would ever be forgotten; though Charles, who did so much to save England, and William, who was now once again steadily refusing requests to put himself at the head of a rebel army, soon would be. Both had done their share to make certain that at least the gulf had not flowed red with blood.

In June a rather un-quiet young man took a shot at the young Queen—very low of him, as she was expecting a baby. "The attempt to kill the Queen is quite horrible", Charles wrote to Louisa on the 15th, "and I fear the young vagabond will escape as she will never sign his death warrant. She seems to have shown good courage and Albert behaved well too." Edward Oxford, the young man in question, was found to be mad and not therefore executed; he was sent to an asylum; but his miserable dwelling was found stuffed with revolutionary literature, which, like sadistic and violent films, is harmless to the sane, but lethal to those whose mental balance is in question. Charles, not yet having heard that Oxford was insane, thought that the law had better take its course, "because the system of assassination is increasing", but most of it, he thought, came from the misery caused by bad government; not that that excused it.

"I shall be very glad when they give me a regiment, but I hope not to be melancholy till then", he told Louisa. Yes, Emily and Susan looked pale, but were well; he thought their pallor was natural and inherited from their mother. It was such a relief to him to be able to write and talk endlessly to Lou and to Mary Kennedy about them, knowing that they both also doted on his children. He was trying not to spoil them and give them too great an idea of themselves; which would be bad for them, and bad for him, and altogether impious; but they came out with such funny remarks and such shrewd ones that at times it astonished him. Emily had celebrated her birthday by being very nearly killed by her frightened horse, which she had sat with wonderful skill and calm. When Lady Bathurst died next winter he felt very sorry for all her world whom her death would leave so badly bereft; she was the last of all that Lennox generation and he was sad to see her go. Lou and he and all of them were now the older generation and would probably all be gone in another twelve years: he was right about himself and Henry. But the young would take on, and he was starting Susan off with an allowance on her sixteenth birthday, though Fanny had thought it far too young.

But if he never got another job what would the allowance be paid with? Fanny had her own money; but as head of his family Charles felt his financial responsibilities keenly. Who would now finance William's next book? Or Henry's great History of Florence, if it were ever completed? All his small inheritance, all his careful savings, were now sunk without trace in America. His Scottish inheritance had proved a pipe-dream: an old friend and distant cousin of his father's had left him an estate that would have solved all problems; but closer cousins of the dead man had contested the will, and Charles's lawyers had told him that as an expatriate Scot and a more distant cousin he would not have a chance in a Scottish court and had better not even try. Susan and Emily, his adored natural children, would receive no pension. The crux of his life was at hand; and how would he meet it?

They had moved to Chester, lodgings again, and a bit decrepit, but better than Wheelergate, for all that Charles I was said to have lodged there. Charles Napier had been quite unable to return hospitality there, so on leaving Nottingham he had given what he hoped was a banquet to all his kind friends, in the George, with an enormous salmon at each end of of the table and plenty of other things in the middle. "Splendid", he gathered, "is the correct cant word; everything now is splendid, or interesting, or lovely. Ten were pre-engaged for dinner, but we sat down twenty-two. The salmon was *lovely*, the turbot *most interesting*, the champagne *splendid*; it was an agreeable dinner to me because all those kind people were good enough to be pleased.

"Thank God we have had no row in Nottingham, and not a drop of blood has been spilled. The gentlemen here are so good as to give me credit for this", but Charles thought it was more because of the general benevolence and generosity of the Nottingham gentry. "They do much. But it will not do, the rich manufacturers are too hard a set"; he feared their ideas would win against good men like Rowarth and Wright. "As a principle, my belief is that Chartism becomes more general. I may be wrong, and my abilities are too small to give much weight to my opinion, nor do I ever talk politics; but while going about the district and listening to others I see, or think I see, great distress, great party violence, and a want of confidence in the present government even amongst its own party. Hence arises a very general idea that a great change is at hand: some fear it, some wish it, as they are influenced by imagined personal interest." *Chartism is at a discount* was the great cry; but the colliers at Newcastle were in action again, and at Colne the Chartists had thrashed the new police, and the troops, both horse and foot, had had to come from Burnley to their rescue.

He shared Louisa's and Em's concern for Henry's continuing illness and for the grief that obstinately declined to decrease. "He mopes not only himself but his children—his health is the worst part. Poor fellow his trials have been terrible, and enough to drive him mad"; but at least he was coming up to Chester to stay and Charles hoped to cheer him.

Locked in a dream of Caroline, Henry was unaware of their worries. Taking to ink rather than the bottle, he was happy with his poetry, and would write:

Oh Florence, Florence, how thy name recalls
Departed hours of happiness and rest!

Those antique gates! Those solemn cypress groves
Wave o'er the form that I no more may see—

he was back in the sunny cemetery, blue with the irises of a Tuscan spring (and never mind whether gates can be said to wave or not),

Where all my dream of life lies cold in clay.

When Henry is describing the portrait of a woman the qualities he celebrates with the most obvious delight are "un-mixed softness and innocence": was it with these that seventeen-year-old Caroline had bewitched his heart? Beautiful and good, but dumb? She was, we know, attention-riveting, a head-turner; perhaps a bit of an Irene Forsyte, without living long enough to develop that heroine's obsessive image of herself as a mother.

There was a feeling, Henry knew, that his best course was to marry again: in a drugged, enchanted, manner he rebutted it:

I cannot change! She never changed to me,
Nor ever erred, by vanity misled.
Better than all the moving world I see
I loved her living, and I love her dead.
I would not change, I would not part from her

he insisted. Those who suggested it could not possibly know what Caroline had been to him.

Through many a wayward irritable hour
She meekly bore my fretfulness of will,
And kept, with sunny smile, the softening power
To change, and calm, and draw me closer still.

Incurably romantic, Henry put the thought of a new love from him and braced himself to loneliness.

But why lament? She's far beyond the skies
And dwells in peace and Harmony divine

Where Henry sincerely hoped she was not forgetting him, and

That the pure spirit's memory ever dwells
On those impassioned souls it leaves behind.

Consoled and refreshed by getting the poem off his chest, Henry was soon out dipping into the uncharted seas of the Florentine archives.

That Henry could have recovered is later made clear by the engaging Miss Edgeworth, over from Ireland early in 1841. She had first met Richard, she told her stepmother, writing to her from Croydon —"one whom you know and like—Mr. Napier—who was very agreeable and appeared so charmingly well-bred among the Americans and Croydoners that 'it made his sense with double charms abound' and would have made even actual nonsense please by sound". And from Henry she had equally been able to strike sparks. She had met Captain Napier at another dinner, she reported home from Forest Lodge, in Kent.

"He is very conversible and clever and full of humor when he forgets himself in conversation as he did last night. He has been to all parts of the world I believe—Navy Captain—loves Ireland and the Irish and even Irish tone and brogue when he met them far away in one of the Virgin Islands on the coast of America. 'One moonlight night I was walking home late' said Captain Napier, 'and I met a party of poor Irishmen to whom my heart warmed when they begged a trifle from my honor and told their stories—all lies, very likely, I knew—but still—I could not help you know giving him a trifle. The fellow into whose hand I put it thought it was a penny I believe, but as he walked away he looked at it—started—and I heard him exclaim as he held out his hand to his companions, See here—by Jasus! it's a dollar then!

" 'By Jasus! all unanimously joined and rush they ran back again all together but one got before the rest and throwing himself at my feet clasping my knees looked up and by the pale moonlight I saw the eager look—Your Honor! Would there be any one in all the Virgin Islands ever did ye an ill turn (the rascal!) you'd wish to be revenged of? Tell me! Tell me this minute! You've only to spake the word and with all the pleasure in life we'll bate him dead for ye! We'll *do* him for you now and God bless you forever. Ye have only to say the word.'

"Captain Napier was sure they would with all the pleasure in life as they swore, have that instant done his bidding, if he had bid them murder any man in the country, or they would have set fire to any house he had pointed to—Paddy forever! This *gratitude of revenge* is characteristically Irish *entirely*, and whether a virtue or a vice or a mixture—the materials for both or for either—who shall decide?" Miss Edgeworth asked. In the same letter she reported that "Governor Napier—Governor at the Cape—(our Mr. Napier's brother, one of his many wonderful brothers whose names meet me everywhere) advised Moffat, (who had translated the Bible into Zulu) to have it printed in London" where they were more likely to get it right.

Delightful, plain, clever Miss Maria Edgeworth, and sorrowful, handsome, humorous, clever Captain Henry Napier, whom she could so clearly charm out of his griefs—why was no-one there to foster their friendship, to give them just a little push? Maria had written *The Parents' Assistant*, and no parent could have been more in need of assistance than Henry, with his Charley, Augusta, and Bam, "really like children of poetry", his sister Emily assured Charles this winter, "especially Charley". All were pleasing, and good, and Augusta was delightful and full of spirits. "God grant poor Hal may not lose any more of them!" Here was a fine field to furrow, if Miss Edgeworth had a heart for it.

Like Henry, Charles too could be a prey to occasional nostalgia. The anniversary of the Coa action, when George had been so desperately ill the night before, and William badly wounded defending the bridgehead while the guns rolled over the river, and when all of them had been amazed and thankful to find themselves and each other still alive, sent Charles's thoughts back to Celbridge. How much happiness and home life he had missed: how much of the short spans of his two youngest sisters, both dead before they were twenty-two! "My charming, my beautiful, my gentle sister Caroline, for whom I still grieve, my equally dear sister Cecilia, my mother, Susan Frost." (He had called his eldest daughter after Susan Frost, faithful nurse for twenty-six years to them all.) "To have them was enough of happiness. They are all gone and I never lived long with any of them. Always we were separated, and for what?" A haze of autumn sadness hung over life and thought, over what seemed the long waste of his military life.

Next day he was himself again, riding out on his cherished mare, Reiza, and thinking, "One loves horses from one's heart." There was nothing like them, with their fire and obedience, their dogged endeavour and great-heartedness, their wickedness, their intelligence, their contrariness, their occasional stupidities. "I long to live in their company like an Arab", he decided. "I am an Arab. I hate a home and wish to go about with my women and my horses and my tent." His thoughts returned with joy to his daughters. He had taken much too expensive a house near Chester for next March, and he thought of walking about with them in the spring sunshine of Cheshire. "My two merry little affectionate girls; I fear they are idols but cannot help it: the godly tell us we must have no idols. Perhaps they are right, but for all that fathers and mothers will have them, and I have no idea of being singular in that respect." His determination not to spoil them was weakening.

George's Sarah was staying with them; it was clear that her broken engagement had shattered her—she looked terribly delicate She stayed some while and began to look better, to the joy of her uncle's heart. "One of the most delightful young women I ever met with, and one of the most sensible and noble-minded, but so delicate and so interesting that I tremble for her. She has hitherto gone through much, may she now have that tranquillity which her extreme frailty demands is my prayer." Recovered under Charles's aegis, Sarah departed to stay with her impetuous brother John near Bath, where she presently met and married an army doctor called Thomas Clarke, and, alas, lived but a short while longer. Her encounter with the Bunbury family had been a more bruising one than her grandmother's: she had none of Sarah's or of George's robustness and much of the delicacy of her short-lived mother, George's adored Margaret Craig.

September brought riots in the Isle of Man with the usual demand for troops, and Charles sat down to read all the reports over again before deciding whether to comply. "To protect life and property—the old song." William roused Charles with talk of a Russian threat to India. "You are right," Charles wrote back, "Circassia and the Caspian appear the places to meet Russia and cut her line to India. If Russia sends an army to Bokhara it will be difficult for us to make war there." No such inhibitions applied to the eastern Mediterranean, from which threatening sounds emerged. French designs on Egypt menaced the usual delicate balance of power in this tricky area. Mohammed Ali of Egypt had rebelled against his Turkish suzerain and the French were backing him. The presence of his first cousin

Black Charlie "and some strong ships" reassured Charles. "War appears imminent. I may yet command an army. Yet I am without any wish for war; it is the worst thing that could happen to England." In the winter Acre was taken, Black Charlie personally confronted Mohammed Ali, and the peril passed.

Charles's mind swung back again to the haunting local miseries. He had written to the Home Secretary beseeching immediate measures of relief—"The people of Lancashire are in a dreadful state of starvation." No reply from Thomas Babington Macaulay. "What they propose to do Heaven knows, but the starving goes on . . . the people propose to have starving processions here, which in a town like Manchester is no joke, they also say they will take bread when they see it. Then come the soldiers on the stage and the convulsions of famine are quieted by the bayonet", and Charles's anger and bitterness increased. At Colne, Benbow had advised the Chartists to kill Mr Bolton, but, instead, they had killed the constable who was trying to protect magistrate Bolton. "Pity Mr. Bolton was not smitten instead of poor constable Halstead. This Bolton treated the soldiers like dogs until I put that to rights." "September 1st. Untoward day for partridges. Were Mr. Secretary Macaulay one I would turn sportsman."

On his birthday he turned from anger to look back in joy. "This day fifty-eight years old, and a wayward life of adventure has been mine. A good romance it would make, full of accidents by flood and field, stories of love and war and shipwreck, and escapes of all kinds. I dare swear that what is left may be the most eventful of the whole", he accurately predicted.

A second summer had dragged on. "Still the poor starve that 5 per cent esquire may become 10 per cent esquire. Now to my treadmill, to that labour that bears no fruit." Spring had brought a brief refreshment at Windermere—"the mountains hanging over the still water and the wild look of the place are enchanting"—but in towns the hungry processions went on: haggard, gaunt men, with lined pallid faces and limbs they could barely drag along. Charles was out with twelve dragoons one winter night when "a mob of 2000 followed us with abuse so violent as to make me fear they would end with stones, a large heap being at hand. I told the magistrate and the dragoons to ride on while I spoke, and I rode back alone. To my surprise all fled, pushing each other down in their haste." Such things gave him a terrible feeling. "The quiet which force, acting on wretchedness, produces is hell to me. Against a Chartist with a pike in hand and bent to fight, I can stand with a bold front; but against pale faces and humble conduct there is no fighting!" All he could do was "what as an honourable man seems right, just and humane to all, in hope that what is good for the people may follow. So far as falls within my limited sphere all shall be done to assist the poor, for they are ill-used and suffering."

It was extraordinary how many people expressed the same stupid opinions and demanded "*Vigorous measures*—that is to say hanging a dozen men called agitators; men who differ in opinion from the men who demand their death". As if one could hang for opinion! He heard that the poor Chartists were in league with the French, but if they thought they would get any financial help from there they had another think coming. One thing must be said for the Whigs, they had resisted the pressure on them to start hanging: even good and charming men like Colonel Wemyss were in favour of it when the police got thrashed at Lancaster in August. "God send that our rulers may not take up this idea."

As cold and winter deepened, the misery of the poor increased. And what, Charles demanded, was the Church doing about it all? "I quite agree with Bishop Kaye, who seems to be a very clever and a very good man, that unless we pray, education is a very idle affair, but bishop, we must be fed before we are content. God gave the poor brains to understand their own case. Your eloquence then is vain to produce content without food . . . The bishops must talk more wisely if they expect the present generation to listen to them: for if they preach forbearance and patience under heavy burdens such as this they will only concoct scorn and hatred for themselves." Could one take bishops seriously when they were so rich in the midst of such starvation?

Thanking God on Christmas Day of 1840 that he and his family were all well, Charles wondered, "Does the Deity enter into such matters? Who knows? The Bishop of Chester of course. I wish he would tell me, but I suppose he won't unless in church and in an orthodox manner. It is too cold a day for that, and there is no assurance that my belief would follow. Such things require undivided attention and I should be thinking of his ten thousand a year." And a few days later it was "a fearful day, the cold is terrible. God help the poor people in their terrible suffering: well may they exclaim, we want justice, not charity." All the same, as Henry noticed, he was forever emptying his lean pockets on their behalf. Doubtless the bishops gave too; but they had seats in the House of Lords; why did they not raise a dust there?

More effective were men like the poet Coleridge. "If we are a Christian nation we must learn to act nationally as well as individually as Christians . . . Our manufacturers must consent to regulations; our gentry must concern themselves in the education of their national clients and dependents—must regard their estates as offices of trust with duties to be performed in the sight of God and their country. Let us become a better people and the reform of all public grievances will follow of itself." Such voices in time would win a hearing. But not yet.

Cold rain, hungry faces, the season of goodwill. "I am sure we shall have a rough winter", Charles had felt in November. "The Chartists are colloguing together with much more caution and arrangement than last year." The increasingly dark nights made meetings and secret drillings easier, yet Charles could hardly believe they were at it in the low, wet meadows in midwinter. "Whether they meditate using force or not I cannot say. I rather think not, but they are in great distress", and he knew that the making and collecting of arms still went on. At the other end of the world the British were pushing on for more trade: would that help Lancashire?

"We seem to go on well in China, but John Chinaman is a cunning knave; and it cannot be believed that 300 million of the most self-sufficient proud people in the world will take a kick from Admiral Elliot and be brought to their bearings by the capture of a little island like Chusan." Should he pursue his destiny in China? "I asked Lord Fitzroy to send me out there, but was refused." Charles held no brief for the East India Company and its determination to cash in on the passion of the Chinese to smoke the more powerful form of opium grown in India, in preference to their own; but he was a soldier and not a policeman: anything would be better than this miserable work of containing the desperation of hunger without the power to relieve it.

On December 27th he had heard the happy Christmas news that he would not be allowed his travelling expenses, "though I have now posted 5250 miles in this district, and lived above 100 days in hotels with my ADC and servant". But at least the government were considering his plan to spend the necessary £50,000 on proper barracks. On the last day of the year worse realities racked him. "The people are starving and the government do nothing. Confound these men who call themselves statesmen . . . What will the coming year produce? Fate settles these matters luckily, for if God left all to us what wild work we should make!"

In the spring of 1841 he rejoiced that two years of this dread command were over. "No it is not command, it is slavery under noodles. Lord Hill has not his own way and he is no noodle, he is a glorious soldier, but a little too good for the Whigs and Tories he has to deal with. I shall have my way about barracks yet if I am patient. It is very disagreeable to be daubed with government slime, and at times it inclines me to cut the painter. Yet how give up my profession?"

How indeed? How live, if he cut the painter himself? And if he did resign, that would not help the misery of the north; the government might put someone worse in his place. (This in the end happened: four generals were appointed to do the work he had been doing, and probably got their travelling expenses as well as the £1,000 a year he had had; he was unlucky about money. They were unable to prevent the bloodshed that followed Charles's departure, and the consequent punishments, the hangings, and the transportation of some fifteen hundred men.)

He still hankered after Australia. Sitting in his chill lodgings, after a night patrol through the drizzling streets full of hungry men adrift on a tide of discontent flowing ever towards violence, he would dream of transference from this bitter place where he could do little good into a sunny continent where he could do plenty. News had come from South Australia that all was as Charles had foretold—"all ruined. This I am sorry for; it is by the folly of the people I quarrelled with." The substitute government had in truth run itself into debt to the tune of £100,000, which was exactly the sum Charles had asked for to establish the colonists and finance the colony—"I asked for it as a loan only." Colonel Ganlon was being blamed by everybody; he might have made mistakes, but his task had been made impossible for lack of capital. In the end the government had allowed his successor in the Australian post far more money than had been refused to Charles. Why was he here, in this hateful place? He prayed that his health would stick it. His old wounds plagued him in the damp and cold of wintry Manchester. "Am I on your road of pain?" he asked William. "If so I am done."

Yes, he would be charmed to go to the Ionian islands, Malta,

Gibraltar, or Bermuda; any one of them would be most acceptable, he told Robertson. He just wanted a quiet billet where he had not to enforce injustice. "But my dear friend I am very careless about money-hunting." What he dearly needed was something to do. "It is health to me—I am too old to hunt or shoot or even dig in the garden. But like an old pack horse, I can go well enough in harness." "I wish they would send me to Corfu or Malta or Gibraltar", he moaned to Louisa, as the sad new year rolled in. Ambition was dead in him and he did not care where they sent him—"Content is the thing." All the same, the Horse Guards needed reorganization. "Lord Cardigan is mad", he added, "and I hope will be turned out." This hope was vain, and Lord Cardigan now all set for the Charge of the Light Brigade fourteen years later.

A better state of trade might keep people quiet, but "that Chartism is spreading is certain, and I think a revolution approaches. The very quiet of the Chartists, and the good sense with which they are now regulating all their society for united action is to me a proof that their movement will be a mighty one, and shake the whole kingdom." In a strange way, as William truly said, his head was made for war and for action, though his heart longed for peace. He needed another kind of struggle than this, where heart and head could alike be engaged: if civil war really broke out, might he be far from hence.

"Gladly shall I get away from this district, for how to deal with violence produced by starvation, by folly, by villainy, and even by a wish to do right, is a hard matter: hard I mean to deal with it conscientiously, for act as you will it must be with some injustice: honest men on both sides furnish rascals with pretexts, and then blindly follow those rascals as leaders. A man is easily reconciled to act against misled people if he has an honest plan of his own; but if he is only a servant of greater knaves than those he opposes, and feels he is giving strength to injustice, he loses the right stimulus to action." He feared that if the Tories came in "violent measures or what they call *vigorous measures* would be taken: that I could not bear, and rejoice to have escaped the trial. I may wrong the Tories: Peel is a clever man . . . The duke will do no good I fear. First, because he won't try; next because he would be overwhelmed with reproaches, and because his ancient feelings are so strong. He is like a gnarled oak; there is not a bit of bend in him . . .

"Every element of a ferocious civil war is boiling in this district, and if asked what class of men appear most just and most anxious to avoid it, I should say the officers; but of all classes the worst are the magistrates. The Tory magistrates are bold, violent, irritating and uncompromising; the Whig magistrates sneaking and base, always ready to call for troops and yet truckling to the mob; at least", Charles added with his besetting honesty, "this is the tinge on my mind in my intercourse with them, though I cannot bring any body of facts to bear me out. As to the Chartist leaders they are not trustworthy; they are demagogues for evil, not for good; they would all fall under the mischief they have provoked, and are now provoking."

At the beginning of the job there had been at least the hope that the government would come to understand and relieve the situation: such hope was now dead. Where the Whigs had conspicuously failed, the Tories were most unlikely to succeed. For far too long they had both gone on being exclusively concerned with their image as Whigs and Tories.

The Tories who presently came into power were in fact rather better than the Whigs; tougher, but more clear-headed. Peel and Graham told Lord Talbot and Arbuthnot (one of the generals who succeeded Charles) to arbitrate between masters and men and secure redress of legitimate grievances: "You will faithfully represent the Government by marking a kind sympathy with the feelings and just claims of the workmen." "I strongly suspect", Peel said, "that the profits in many of the collieries would enable the receivers of them to deal with much more liberality towards their workmen than they do at present", and as soon as the trouble died down he appointed a commissioner to investigate mining abuses in the Midland coalfields.

But the Whig Lord John Russell continued "calmly and hopefully" convinced that practically all was for the best in the best of all possible worlds, and did his utmost in 1848 to prevent the Prince Consort from presiding at a meeting of Lord Ashley's Society for Improving the Conditions of the Working Classes. Whig Lord Howick feared that nothing could be done to allay discontent "without entire subversion of the existing constitution"; Whig Macaulay thought that "universal suffrage would be fatal to all purposes for which government exists, and utterly incompatible with civilization". With these views Lord John in the main concurred; and it is hardly surprising that his grandson Bertrand suffered from a considerable reaction.

*

Work in the district went on, though Charles gave himself little credit for what he did, and received less from the government he served. Later authorities have thought differently: "Napier's radical sympathies and soldierly firmness prevented revolution", writes Elizabeth Longford; and other writers have held that to no soldier in time of peace does his country owe a greater debt than Britain owed to Charles. But in the cheerless spring of 1841 he set his sights happily on the house in the country near Chester, to which they were to move in April after two years of cramped town lodgings. Calverly Hall near Tarporley, belonging to the Davenports, would be a fine refuge between bouts of work in the sad and stricken towns. Clear air, fine views, a roomy garden—he would have all the family to stay, and restore them as well as himself and his own. Richard and Anne had moved across from Ireland and taken a house in London, from which they would surely need a change; Henry must come with his children (though he was already saying the journey would be too expensive); the building up of George's Sarah could go on better here in this "calm retreat from worries". He still felt very uneasy about this beautiful niece, especially with her father in Africa. "All is done to cherish her that can be done. She is clear-sighted and decided in her character, but yields to those she loves, from gentleness not from changing her opinion. I hope Emily's confidence in her life being safe is well-founded." Her youngest brother Billy had sent Charles an amusing account from the Cape of a full-dress Kaffir Ball given by his father George "with all the guests in full undress".

And Louisa of course must often come, he told her on St Patrick's Day, "(which will end in hundreds of Irish soldiers being court-martialled for drunkenness, but I am paid for the job so no grumbles)". She must be at Calverly as soon as it was warm, and if she was still feeling ruffled about anything, let it blow away as all ruffled feelings between brothers and sisters should. Charles loved her dearly, he told her, and knew that she loved him even though he had refused to take sides in her breeze with Em. "I mean the girls to be much in the open air and but little at lessons." He was teaching them geography, his final subject. He had taught them French, English grammar, arithmetic, and English history; now they could go on "as far in each as their natural bent chooses. After geography I wash my hands of all but advice." Calverly was expensive, but his long-suffering family deserved it, and the chasing round the garden and the riding over the hills. He looked forward to a benevolent year as an ageing but cheerful paterfamilias.

In this same month the painter was suddenly cut for Charles. "I have at last gotten into a good house", he told Robertson on the 25th, "and had not been in it three days before I had a hint that if I like to go to India as Major General on the Staff next autumn I may do so." He was weighing it all up; would Robertson, who lived at Cheltenham, surrounded by "old India birds", find out a thing or two for him? "Can I take my family overland to Bombay? Four women is an awful charge and unless they can travel in some sort of carriage from Alexandria to Suez, I do not see how it can be done. Fanny is so *terribly afraid* of a sea voyage that I am puzzled what to do.

"The pay is £5,000 a year. Can I *save* in India upon that pay? For if not, I see no good in expatriating myself at 59 years old.

"Will India injure my daughters' healths? They would be 16 and fifteen . . . if you would find out these things for me you would greatly oblige me as the step is a serious one."

For a month Charles deliberated, telling William, Richard and Henry to find out all they could in London. He knew nothing of India and had never wanted to go there, having a low opinion of the general goings on of the East India Company that still ruled it, gleaned from the talk of his father's younger sister, who had spent much of her life there, married to a soldier. "This has been very kind in Lord Hill", he told Lou; "both in the thing and in the way he did it, but I have great doubts about accepting." Would she tell Em and no-one else; the brothers already knew.

"For myself I delight in the idea of it but my girls are my object. If I go for 5 years I am certain from all I hear of saving £10,000 at least if I live." The doctors had assured Charles that they were old enough to benefit from the Indian climate. "If they had been 3 or 4 years younger it would not do at all. They will marry and I do not like that at all as it would fix them in India. The separation would be hateful to me; but what is important is that I think life in India bad and dangerous for a woman." By June 16th he had made up his mind and written to Lord Hill and accepted. "I am now easy. While I had to think and think and think I was worried. Now I am not. Whether I am to go in autumn or next year I know not", and he had been told it was still a secret.

Had there been a wave of gratitude at the Horse Guards? Was it thought that the old boy had averted what might have been a nasty dust-up in the north, still had his wits about him and was active enough? In India the Afghan business was not going too well, might be prolonged, might even be disastrous; could Charles pull this Whig chestnut out of the fire? Why not give him a chance and send him to India? At least it would stop him coming up for ever with these awkward political questions. It is thought that Wellington, as Minister without Portfolio, was the precipitating agent.

Susan and Emily were wild for India, Charles told Louisa; which was as well, as they were the reason for his going there. He was a bit uneasy that war with America might intervene. His £8,000 in the Yankee funds was lost anyway, but "I do trust they won't drive us into a war." Obviously McLeod, over whom the dispute arose, was but a Canadian no-good; "but if McLeod is hanged it may be the death warrant of many a good man on both sides. I must say I think the statement made by the American lawyers who are McLeod's counsel is very discreditable to their nation and satisfies me more than ever that republics are bad. However we are in a ticklish state here just now." He thought India would benefit Fanny's daughter as well as his own; but felt low at leaving his brothers and sisters. He would be back in London in six years' time, 1847, "and then I shall run to earth like an old fox. Whether I shall find you all in peace or in civil war I know not: my doubts are unpleasant on that point."

All the same his spirits rose steadily, in spite of rheumatism that made it next to impossible to ride or even to put his hand in his pocket to take out his money. "The climate in Bombay is the best in India", William assured him, "and the money comes in fast and it will be advantageous to the health and probably to the happiness of your girls but it is a long way off and I feel low about it, ten thousand miles gives little hope of our meeting again; but the best rule is to accept whatever seems good without referring to difficulties and dangers that may never happen"; and he sent Charles a cure for rheumatism that consisted mainly of brandy first thing in the morning and never mind what the doctors say.

"Secret!" William continued. "I don't wonder at the Whigs being afraid of and hating me. I have discovered that they had actually a secret convention in London for a rising in 1832 and had got the poor devils of Chartists to organize themselves as officers and non-commissioned officers in districts of London for the rise. Their folly and wickedness is incredible." He hoped Roebuck was really going to institute reforms now he was in the House. "Something must be done effectual soon by some party or the country will go to pieces." The popular leaders Vincent McDowel and Glannon were too ignorant and conceited to be able to do anything. He fully felt for Charles in his inability to find a good home for his two horses Gog and Magog, "but I have always observed that in our family luck and ill luck have always been chequered, and we have upon the whole done well in serious matters. I am therefore always rather superstitious about small reverses as clearing away the balance and I hope you will find it so."

How would Charles's luck hold in India? Once, long ago, when he and Elizabeth were together in France, she had woken up from a nightmare, crying with terror. She had seen Charles fighting for his life, under a relentless sun, outnumbered hugely by savage enemies. She had heard the shouting, the thunder of the guns, the wild cries of rage and pain. What she had not seen, nor lived to see, was the outcome. *Peccavi—I have Sind.* But Charles was old, rheumatic, an unlikely candidate for immortality amongst the foothills of the Hindu Kush. His mind was on matters other than glory or war.

And yet exhilaration haunted him; even away in Carlisle, beset by business, mourning the death of another dear friend, Considine, plagued by the ever-recurrent expense of such tours—which involved post horses, an ADC, and a servant—"a general officer is known everywhere, and it is impossible to resist the tyranny of innkeepers who think me as rich as my neighbour Lord Westminster"—they would always put him in the Apollo—"a man cannot travel half over England fighting over sixpences." Robertson's thought-to-be doomed daughter had recovered, and Charles poured out his joy, though he had no time to write adequately; but "to love you from my heart and to rejoice at the prospect of your dear child's recovery is all I can do and this I do to the brim".

Louisa, feeling low at his going, he turned to tease; as once so long ago he had turned to tease Louisa Conolly from the Potomac river in the 1812 American War—"Tell Aunt that out of regard for her I don't bayonet many children"—and his old familiar vein broke out anew. He told Louisa he was to be sent to a camp called Sukkur on the banks of the Indus where there was no large town and might be hostilities, so that he must leave the family meanwhile in Bombay. He was going, he told her, to shake the pagoda tree till it tumbled riches into the laps of Susan and Emily; he was going to ravage the land, sparing neither age nor sex; he was going to come back and live on blue pills at Cheltenham, going all holy and evangelical after his excesses, and talking in a high moral tone of the virtues of faith, while Susan and Emily founded schools for evangelical children and the general odour of sanctity spread for miles around, "and we shall all be as rich and rascally and evangelical as Mr. Close could wish. To turn from joking, I am sadly vexed at what you and Emily tell me of Henry, but what can one do?" Change alone could help him.

Charles's own change filled him with joy, but it was mingled with apprehension. So much hung on his own life. Susan and Emily's happiness was now totally dependent on its continuance. His brothers, he knew, would care for them; but George was in Africa, Richard nearly blind, Henry an invalid, and William a very uncertain life whose loss would leave his own wife, six surviving daughters and deaf and dumb son with a minimum on which to live. Louisa's money kept her, but did no more: Emily's money was all Bunbury's. For six years Charles must stay alive.

"My spirits were very low until my mind was fixed for India, when they rose", he told George; and to a friend who had wished that Charles would at long last find scope for his abilities, he answered, "Many thanks for your kind wishes; I am very rational, my wishes are only to barter a great lack of sovereigns in this country for a lac of rupees in that. I am too old for glory now. If I was as active a man as when I smashed that [indecipherable], I might do some good. If a man cannot catch glory when his knees are supple he had better not try when they grow stiff! All I want is to catch all the rupees for my girls: and then die like a gentleman. I suppose if I survive six years I shall do this."

It was a monumental gamble. If he died too soon, his family would barely have enough money to pay their fares home. Amidst the falling leaves of autumn 1841, feeling to the full the approach of his sixtieth birthday, his stiff knees, the autumn of his own physical being, Charles made his preparations. By October the 8th they were at Boulogne after a passage so boisterous that it made them all but too late to cross the harbour bar "victoriously but with a blow that shook us much and might have wrecked us: however here we are all safe and sick as the devil." By the 16th they were at Maçon—"The girls bear travelling like heroes and eat, drink, and sleep and draw, which last they do wonderfully quickly and correctly."

"I am very anxious", he told Robertson. They must catch the ship at Marseilles or he would lose the £600 he had paid in advance for their passages; and he condemned the French roads for their lack of either science or common sense, as Henry had done eleven years before. They had been at Chalons the previous day and he hoped to get to Marseilles with a few days in hand. "The post boys' jackboots are the chief things to be observed because ever before one, and there is no scenery to draw off attention", he grumbled worriedly. The ship was bound for Syra in the Greek archipelago, and the voyage should be delightful, but his wife had been so ill on the crossing that the outlook was grim—"I am sadly afraid for Fanny who suffered cruelly." He hoped, optimistically, that such seas would be unlikely further south.

The ship bore him past the remembered coasts of Greece, warm still in the lingering sunshine: what would now happen to the Greeks? "They are now free and roguish, living on their character of past times, cultivating their literature and proud of what they once were, yet giving no indication of again becoming great." Were they still "sick with slavery" and incapable of great achievement? "Otho seems to think that injustice and cruelty is the way to enlighten a clever high-spirited people, after ages of misery and darkness. The Greeks are a proud people, and Otho by treating them well would save his adopted country and himself from much suffering." The high stony islands and promontories floated past in the last of light as Charles was borne from them to his toughest assignment yet. His thoughts lingered with the Greek people he had liked so greatly; but his family turn of mind, his habitual royalism, asserted itself. "They seem inclined to throw Otho overboard; to tie his hands with a constitution would be more sensible; killing kings is a bad habit which unsettles all government."

Ill, anxious, resilient, undefeated, holding in his innermost heart what barely acknowledged dreams, hopes, imaginings, he had made his careful selections of all that must last them for six years, his cautious preparations with what little money was left. Now they were launched. The dark seas of Greece foamed behind him, her long mountains faded into night. Ahead lay Egypt, the cross-country journey to Suez, the fabled shores of India.

He had tried to insure his life, but his many old war-wounds had meant that no company would even consider him. The passage to Bombay for his wife and family cost him the last six hundred pounds he had in the world.

Rockingham and Great Easton, 1968–72

Short Bibliography

MANUSCRIPT SOURCES

NAPIER PAPERS: Duke Humphrey's Library at the Bodleian, Oxford

NAPIER PAPERS: British Museum

ELLENBOROUGH PAPERS: Public Record Office

Various family letters from many different sources

Unpublished journals of Captain Henry Napier, Royal Navy

PRINTED SOURCES

BRIGGS, ASA, ed.—*Chartist Studies*

BRYANT, SIR ARTHUR—*The Great Duke*

The Age of Elegance

BYRON, LORD—*Letters*, ed. John Murray

COBBAN, ALFRED—*History of Modern France*

COBBETT, WILLIAM—*Rural Rides*

COLERIDGE, SAMUEL—*Letters*, ed. E. H. Coleridge, 1895

EDGEWORTH, MARIA—*Letters*

FINLAY, GEORGE—*History of the Greek Revolution*

GORDON, THOMAS—*History of the Greek Revolution*

GREVILLE—*The Greville Memoirs*, 1817–1860

HAMMOND AND HAMMOND—*Village Labourer*

HOWITT, WILLIAM—*Rural Life in England*

LONGFORD, ELIZABETH—*Victoria R.I.*

Wellington—Pillar of State

MARCHAND, LESLIE—*Byron*

MOORE, D. L.—*The Late Lord Byron*

MOORE, THOMAS—*The Memoirs of Lord Edward Fitzgerald*, ed. MacDermott

NAPIER, GENERAL SIR CHARLES—*War in Greece*

Harold

NAPIER, GENERAL SIR WILLIAM—*War in the Peninsula*
Life and Opinions of Sir Charles Napier
Life and Letters, ed. A. Bruce
NICOLSON, SIR HAROLD—*Byron, the Last Journey*
ORIGO, IRIS—*The Last Attachment*
POOL, BERNARD—ed. *The Croker Papers*
ST CLAIR, WILLIAM—*That Greece Might Still Be Free*
TREVELYAN, G. M.—*English Social History*—Vol. IV
England in the Nineteenth Century

Index

בברכה מאת

יד חיים ויצמן

רחובות · ישראל

For Anne, Dick and the children — a Merry Christmas!

WITH THE COMPLIMENTS OF

YAD CHAIM WEIZMANN

REHOVOT · ISRAEL

Meyer W. Weisgal
& Julian L. Meltzer